Customer Communications in Marketin
2001–2002

The Chartered Institute of Marketing/Butterworth-Heinemann Marketing Series is the most comprehensive, widely used and important collection of books in marketing and sales currently available worldwide.

As the CIM's official publisher, Butterworth-Heinemann develops, produces and publishes the complete series in association with the CIM. We aim to provide definitive marketing books for students and practitioners that promote excellence in marketing education and practice.

The series titles are written by CIM senior examiners and leading marketing educators for professionals, students and those studying the CIM's Certificate, Advanced Certificate and Postgraduate Diploma courses. Now firmly established, these titles provide practical study support to CIM and other marketing students and to practitioners at all levels.

 The Chartered
Institute of Marketing

Formed in 1911, the Chartered Institute of Marketing is now the largest professional marketing management body in the world with over 60,000 members located worldwide. Its primary objectives are focused on the development of awareness and understanding of marketing throughout UK industry and commerce and in the raising of standards of professionalism in the education, training and practice of this key business discipline.

Customer Communications in Marketing

2001–2002

Gill Wood

Published on behalf of
The Chartered Institute of Marketing

BUTTERWORTH
HEINEMANN

OXFORD AUCKLAND BOSTON JOHANNESBURG MELBOURNE NEW DELHI

Butterworth-Heinemann
Linacre House, Jordan Hill, Oxford OX2 8DP
225 Wildwood Avenue, Woburn, MA 01801-2041
A division of Reed Educational and Professional Publishing Ltd

   A member of the Reed Elsevier plc group

First published 2001

British Library Cataloguing in Publication Data
A catalogue record for this book is available from the British Library

ISBN 0 7506 5303 5

For information on all Butterworth-Heinemann
publications visit our website at www.bh.com

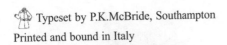 Typeset by P.K.McBride, Southampton
Printed and bound in Italy

FOR EVERY TITLE THAT WE PUBLISH, BUTTERWORTH-HEINEMANN
WILL PAY FOR BTCV TO PLANT AND CARE FOR A TREE.

Contents

A message from the author

The primary objective of this book is to help you pass your CIM Certificate Customer Communications module. The coursebook has been designed to give you an overview of the Customer Communications syllabus and contains lots of activities to help you put your reading into practice and to enable you to apply your knowledge in the examination (or in continuous assessment assignments).

You are probably at a stage in your life when you are busier than ever and this is where using a coursebook tailored to your needs, will help you save time. However, just reading the book will not be enough and you should be prepared to read around this module, to work through the activities contained in the book and to take some time out to consider how you can relate your learning to your own work or personal situation.

On a personal note, I would like to thank all those who contributed to the book and those who gave permission to use material, in particular, Lexis-Nexis. I would also like to thank Colin without whose help and support the book would not have been completed. Finally, I would like to dedicate this book to Alexander who has so often missed out because of it.

Good luck in your studies and in your career.

Gill Wood

Senior Examiner for Customer Communications

An introduction from the academic development advisor

Over the past few years there have been a series of syllabus changes initiated by the Chartered Institute of Marketing to ensure that their qualifications continue to be relevant and of significant consequence in the world of marketing, both within industry and academia. As a result I and Butterworth Heinemann have rigorously revised and updated the Coursebook series to make sure that every title is the best possible study aid and accurately reflects the latest CIM syllabus.

The revisions to the series this year include both restructuring and the inclusion of many new mini cases and examples. There are a number of new and accomplished authors in the series commissioned both for their CIM course teaching and examining experience, and their wide general knowledge of the latest marketing thinking.

We are certain that you will find the new-look books highly beneficial study toolS as you prepare for the CIM examinations. They will guide you in a structured and logical way through the detail of the syllabus, providing you with the required underpinning knowledge, understanding and application of theory.

The editorial team and authors wish you every success as you embark upon your studies.

Karen Beamish

Academic Development Advisor

How to use these coursebooks

Everyone who has contributed to this series has been careful to structure the books with the exams in mind. Each unit, therefore, covers an essential part of the syllabus. You need to work through the complete coursebook systematically to ensure that you have covered everything you need to know.

This coursebook is divided into units each containing a selection of the following standard elements:

- **Objectives** tell you what part of the syllabus you will be covering and what you will be expected to know, having read the unit.
- **Study guides** tell you how long the unit is and how long its activities take to do.

- **Questions** are designed to give you practice – they will be similar to those you get in the exam.
- **Answers** (at the end of the book) give you a suggest format for answering exam questions. *Remember* there is no such thing as a model answer – you should use these examples only as guidelines.
- **Activities** give you a chance to put what you have learned into practice.
- **Debriefings** (at the end of the book) shed light on the methodologies involved in the activities.
- **Exam hints** are tips from the senior examiner or examiner which are designed to help you avoid common mistakes made by previous candidates.
- **Study tips** give you guidance on improving your knowledge base.
- **Insights** encourage you to contextualize your academic knowledge by reference to real-life experience.
- **Definitions** may be used for words you must know to pass the exam.
- **Summaries** cover what you should have picked up from reading the unit.

While you will find that each section of the syllabus has been covered within this text, you might find that the order of some of the topics has been changed. This is because it sometimes makes more sense to put certain topics together when you are studying, even though they might appear in different sections of the syllabus itself. If you are following the reading and other activities, your coverage of the syllabus will be just fine, but don't forget to follow up with trade press reading!

Unit 1
The importance of the customer

Objectives

In this unit you will:

- Look at the different types of customers that you and your organization deal with.
- Examine the various ways you and your organization communicate with customers.

By the end of the unit you should be able to:

- Understand the importance of effective customer communications in marketing.
- Identify the internal and external customers in a given situation.
- Be aware of what is meant by the terms *stakeholder* and *decision making unit*.
- Appreciate how communication methods and messages alter depending on the context and the customer.

Study guide

This unit provides an overview of the relationship between people and organizations and their customers. It covers indicative content area 2.1.1 of the syllabus. Some of the unit is revisited in Units 7, 8 and 9 where there is further information about the various communication formats.

The unit links to the Marketing Fundamentals syllabus indicative content 1.1. The topics covered in this unit also link with content in the Marketing Fundamentals workbook in Unit 1.

The key point to be made here is that, although 'customers' are dealt with on each syllabus, from this module's perspective you are dealing with customers purely from the perspective of how you communicate with them and the impact on service delivery but not from a broad marketing perspective as with the Marketing Fundamentals syllabus.

You should take one hour to read the unit and a further hour to complete its activities. You are advised to spend some extra time drafting an answer to the examination question you are referred to at the end. You will find the questions at the end of the book. Compare your answer with the specimen answers, which can also be found at the end of the book.

Study tip

After reading this unit you could develop your understanding of this area by selecting two different organizations that you are familiar with. Compare and contrast the organizations in terms of size, objectives, industry sector (or whether public or private sector) and the type of customers they have to communicate with. Then consider the various ways that these organizations communicate with their internal and external customers and consider how their communications could be improved.

Why are customers important?

As very few people live or work in isolation, communication with others is a fundamental part of most people's lives. Most jobs can be achieved only through communication, whether that involves giving/receiving instructions, sharing ideas with colleagues or giving information to external customers or suppliers. Away from work, the ability to communicate can affect the quality of personal relationships. In addition to this, communication is integral to marketing, involving as it does, communication initiatives that range from persuasive sales calls and presentations to clients, to the production of simple brochures and leaflets and the creation of sophisticated packaging, logos and advertising.

Communication is, therefore, a core skill that marketing professionals need to use daily. Consequently, the module Customer Communications in Marketing that this text book relates to, forms the bedrock of the CIM qualification and the foundation to the other subjects you will study.

The Customer Communications in Marketing syllabus was introduced as part of Syllabus 2000 and replaced the Business Communications syllabus. Its development is in response to feedback received from employers, tutors and students. It takes account of the changes taking place in the world of marketing and seeks to test candidates' communication skills in a variety of marketing situations. Thus the focus of the syllabus, and of this book, is on business communications from a marketing perspective. Much of the original Business Communications syllabus content, such as the communication process, oral communication, written communication and the interpretation and presentation of statistical information, continue to be featured.

However, the changes made to the syllabus reflect the impact of technological innovation on communications and the increasing emphasis being placed on how organizations communicate with customers. The syllabus has also been extended, not only to include the role of marketing research in determining appropriate customer communications but also to consider the wide range of promotional activities used by organizations in communicating with customers.

So it is important for marketers to develop their understanding of who they communicate with, why they communicate with them and how communication can be improved. If you define a customer as 'a person one has dealings with', then clearly everyone, irrespective of job role, organization or industry sector, is affected by the issues arising from this subject.

> **Definition**
>
> **Customer communication** in business is the process by which information is transferred between one individual or group and another, both within and outside the organization. The communication can take place verbally or non-verbally and may be transmitted through a variety of communication methods, such as reports, presentations, letters, advertising or in meetings.

Why do people communicate in business?

The main reasons for people to communicate in business organizations, internally and externally, are:

- To *build relationships* internally and externally with individuals and groups.
- To give *specific instructions* to others on a range of business matters, procedural and strategic.
- To *disseminate information* on a range of corporate matters such as the mission statement, policy issues or, in the case of the external market, on price changes or new promotional initiatives.
- To *share ideas and values* on general organizational issues, possibly to maintain or subtly change the corporate culture, and on work-specific issues or procedural tasks.
- To *negotiate* matters of policy such as a joint venture or merger.
- To *discuss* or negotiate on personal or professional matters such as remuneration and other higher- and lower-level hygiene factors.
- To *motivate, interest and stimulate* employees for commitment and loyalty to the firm.
- To create an awareness of the organization, its products or services and *persuade* the external market, for example to make a purchase decision or to request further information.
- To receive feedback in order to monitor whether the communication was understood and the reaction of the recipient to the message.

If you consider who you communicate with, why and how you may be surprised at just how many people you actually communicate with, how many are inside your organization and how many are outside of it. You should also consider the people and organizations from whom you receive information.

If, for instance, you are working in the marketing department of a firm that makes and sells garden furniture and you have responsibility for the organization's marketing communications, then in an average working day you may communicate with a large number of people in a variety of ways . . .

You may receive information by post from potential suppliers informing you about advertising opportunities. You may send a mailshot to customers on the company's database to encourage them to order products from a new brochure. You may fax a press release to a gardening magazine to raise the firm's profile. You may telephone a designer to change the layout of a brochure before it goes to print. Your line manager may e-mail you, asking you to organize a corporate event for an important business client. You may meet with a colleague to discuss how a project should be progressed. You may deliver a presentation to colleagues showing sales revenue figures in a graph. Or you may draft a report for the senior management team based on research that you have carried out.

Activity 1.1

Whether you are undertaking your course of study by continuous assessment or the examination route, use the skills audit form (Figure 1.1) to examine the types of communications you use and who you communicate with in your job. Spend some time to self-assess your skills level in the areas outlined in the form. If appropriate, you may want to undertake some peer assessment by consulting your colleagues and line manager about their views. If you are not working you could consider how you communicate and with whom in your personal life. For instance, if you are seeking employment you may use the Internet to research jobs, you may write job application letters, attend job interviews and contribute to meetings at your local sports club.

Please see the activity debriefings in the Appendix 6.

Who are an organization's customers?

By now you will have realised that all the people you communicate with are your customers – not just the people who buy your employer's goods and services. You will no doubt find that you have been involved in communicating with people both inside and outside of your organization. You will have sent and received information to and from colleagues, suppliers and your firm's paying customers for a variety of reasons and in a variety of communication formats.

In the traditional sense of the word, *customers* are the people who buy a firm's products. To communicate with them effectively, an organization needs to know who they are, what they want from the firm's products or services, where they are located and the most cost-effective methods of communicating with them. By doing this, it will be easier to develop effective communications, such as advertising, sales literature, packaging and product instructions, that appeal to and are understood by the customer.

The consumer/user

The most obvious customer is the consumer or person who pays for a product or service. However, the person who pays for the product may not be the user or the consumer of the product. For example, a manufacturer of toys needs to communicate with both the children who will use with the product, so they will exert pressure on parents, and the parents themselves as they will be the purchaser/decision maker.

The decision-making unit

In business-to-business marketing, it may be relevant for an organization to communicate not only with the purchaser but also with others who could be involved in the decision to purchase. The other people involved in the purchase decision are often referred to as the *decision-making unit.*

	Syllabus Ref	Current Skill Level				Importance to Current Role				Likely Future Importance				YOUR COMMENTS
DEVELOPMENT AREAS:		None		High		Low		Vital		Low		Vital		
Write business letters and memos	4.1	0	1	2	3	[ ]	[ ]	[ ]	[ ]	[ ]	[ ]	[ ]	[ ]	
Write informal business reports	4.1	0	1	2	3	[ ]	[ ]	[ ]	[ ]	[ ]	[ ]	[ ]	[ ]	
Write formal business reports	4.1	0	1	2	3	[ ]	[ ]	[ ]	[ ]	[ ]	[ ]	[ ]	[ ]	
Write direct mail letters and material	4.1	0	1	2	3	[ ]	[ ]	[ ]	[ ]	[ ]	[ ]	[ ]	[ ]	
Write press releases and articles	4.1	0	1	2	3	[ ]	[ ]	[ ]	[ ]	[ ]	[ ]	[ ]	[ ]	
Write sales proposals and quotations	4.1	0	1	2	3	[ ]	[ ]	[ ]	[ ]	[ ]	[ ]	[ ]	[ ]	
Write copy for information sheets	4.1	0	1	2	3	[ ]	[ ]	[ ]	[ ]	[ ]	[ ]	[ ]	[ ]	
Write management briefings and notes	4.1	0	1	2	3	[ ]	[ ]	[ ]	[ ]	[ ]	[ ]	[ ]	[ ]	
Conduct one to one/group interviews	3.6	0	1	2	3	[ ]	[ ]	[ ]	[ ]	[ ]	[ ]	[ ]	[ ]	
Plan and lead group discussions/meetings	3.6	0	1	2	3	[ ]	[ ]	[ ]	[ ]	[ ]	[ ]	[ ]	[ ]	
Plan and conduct sales meetings/visits	3.6/7	0	1	2	3	[ ]	[ ]	[ ]	[ ]	[ ]	[ ]	[ ]	[ ]	
Negotiate sales, price and terms	3.6/7	0	1	2	3	[ ]	[ ]	[ ]	[ ]	[ ]	[ ]	[ ]	[ ]	
Phone to gather market/sales information	3.7	0	1	2	3	[ ]	[ ]	[ ]	[ ]	[ ]	[ ]	[ ]	[ ]	
Phone to make appointments/liaise with clients	3.7	0	1	2	3	[ ]	[ ]	[ ]	[ ]	[ ]	[ ]	[ ]	[ ]	
Plan presentations/ briefings/talks	3.5	0	1	2	3	[ ]	[ ]	[ ]	[ ]	[ ]	[ ]	[ ]	[ ]	
Prepare speaking notes/scripts for others	3.5	0	1	2	3	[ ]	[ ]	[ ]	[ ]	[ ]	[ ]	[ ]	[ ]	
Prepare presentations using IT (e.g. PowerPoint)	3.5	0	1	2	3	[ ]	[ ]	[ ]	[ ]	[ ]	[ ]	[ ]	[ ]	
Make presentations to groups	3.5-7	0	1	2	3	[ ]	[ ]	[ ]	[ ]	[ ]	[ ]	[ ]	[ ]	
Visually present statistical data/information	3.5	0	1	2	3	[ ]	[ ]	[ ]	[ ]	[ ]	[ ]	[ ]	[ ]	

Figure 1.1   Skills audit form

Create visual aids/images	3.5	0	1	2	3	[ ]	[ ]	[ ]	[ ]	[ ]	[ ]	[ ]	[ ]
Specify layout for promotional material	4.1	0	1	2	3	[ ]	[ ]	[ ]	[ ]	[ ]	[ ]	[ ]	[ ]
Specify layout for printed advertising	4.1	0	1	2	3	[ ]	[ ]	[ ]	[ ]	[ ]	[ ]	[ ]	[ ]
Use IT for word processing/DTP	5.1/2	0	1	2	3	[ ]	[ ]	[ ]	[ ]	[ ]	[ ]	[ ]	[ ]
Use IT to maintain information databases	5.1/2	0	1	2	3	[ ]	[ ]	[ ]	[ ]	[ ]	[ ]	[ ]	[ ]
Use IT to maintain financial information	5.1/2	0	1	2	3	[ ]	[ ]	[ ]	[ ]	[ ]	[ ]	[ ]	[ ]
Use IT/Internet to communicate	5.3	0	1	2	3	[ ]	[ ]	[ ]	[ ]	[ ]	[ ]	[ ]	[ ]
Plan and build a simple web site	5.3	0	1	2	3	[ ]	[ ]	[ ]	[ ]	[ ]	[ ]	[ ]	[ ]
Identify role/motivation of DMU members	1.1/3	0	1	2	3	[ ]	[ ]	[ ]	[ ]	[ ]	[ ]	[ ]	[ ]
Articulate Features, Advantages, Benefits statements for key targets	1.1/3	0	1	2	3	[ ]	[ ]	[ ]	[ ]	[ ]	[ ]	[ ]	[ ]
Identify and use secondary research data	2.2	0	1	2	3	[ ]	[ ]	[ ]	[ ]	[ ]	[ ]	[ ]	[ ]

Figure 1.1 (cont.)

For example, a firm that supplies computer systems to other businesses, needs to communicate with a variety of people who may not be customers but who may influence the decision to buy and therefore need to be communicated with.

The purchaser

A purchasing official may have sourced a new computer system and may ultimately place the order. As far as customer communications are concerned, it is important to make the purchaser's job easy, ensuring that up-to-date product, contact and after-sales information is easy to digest and that the ordering process is easy.

The initiator

The initiator or the specifier could be a member of staff or senior manager or even an external consultant, who sees the possibilities for new equipment to improve efficiency. The computer company must consider who these people might be and raise their awareness about its products, possibly via relevant trade press advertising, sales promotional material, exhibitions or public relations activities.

The user

The users in this example would be the staff who would use the computer system. These people may not influence the decision at the outset of the process but may be invited along to test equipment as part of a task group before the purchase decision is finalized. After the decision to purchase has been made, the good opinion of these people is vital if repeat business is to be transacted. The computer company could ensure good customer communications by providing clear user manuals and by providing training and help lines.

The influencer   — *canbicula —*

Influencers could be the technical staff who affect the purchase decision by supplying information about a variety of suppliers or by setting buying specifications. Or they could be staff in the finance department who could block the purchase decision with financial constraints. Similar to the situation with initiators, these *customers* need to be supplied with sufficient information about the product/service via whatever channels are considered suitable.

The decision maker   — *MD – Group Boad – Ops Director.*

These people are the most influential in terms of making the purchase decision. They may be senior managers or the managing director. It is vital to identify who these people are within a firm. The computer company's message could be communicated directly by a sales representative who might use some form of corporate entertaining to influence the purchase decision.

The gatekeeper   — *Commercial Secretary .*

Gatekeepers control the flow of information through an organization and may be switchboard operators or secretaries who are responsible for dealing with incoming calls, mailshots and trade journals that arrive by post. The computer company should communicate effectively with this customer in order to be able to reach others in the decision-making unit. Sales representatives need to be able to talk persuasively to the gatekeeper to obtain appointments or pass on information to the decision makers or influencers.

> ## Definition
> **Stakeholders** are people who affect an organization or are affected by its activities.

The stakeholders/publics

Most organizations also have a mix of stakeholders or publics, i.e. internal and external individuals or groups who come into contact with an organization or who affect or are affected by its activities. From a communications point of view they can be considered as important customers or target audiences with whom the organization must communicate.

It is important to appreciate the importance of knowing about an organization's stakeholders and why they might want to communicate with them. An organization may choose to communicate with these publics, such as the media or the local community, because it is good for its public relations image and ultimately good for business. Or it could be a legal requirement for an organization to produce an annual report for shareholders. It is often essential for an organization to form a close relationship with suppliers or distributors. Thus an organization may establish an Intranet to provide suppliers with up to date stock requirements or provide distributors with automatic access to orders to help them plan their distribution schedules.

In addition, most organizations wish to communicate effectively with current and potential employees to attract and retain the best staff in the marketplace. An organization's stakeholders might comprise the following (see Figure 1.2).

Let's consider the example of a small restaurant that serves food. Its stakeholders might be passing trade and regular customers who eat there. All forms of communication with them from the 'shop front', through the menu, advertisements or its web site, need to be considered to ensure appropriate and effective communication with customers. The business may be a family business or part of a large chain. Whoever has a financial share in it and a say in the running of it (e.g., shareholders) are stakeholders. Again, communications with this group need to be carefully considered to ensure the successful running of the business.

If the restaurant owners have a bank overdraft to help with the cashflow then the bankers are also stakeholders. Regular communication to show that the restaurant is operating successfully is necessary to show business expertise and may be important at a later date if the bank overdraft has to be extended.

Figure 1.2 *An organization's stakeholders*

Staff and even potential staff are stakeholders. It is wise to communicate with staff and find out what customers think of new additions to the menu. It also makes sense to inform staff of changes to the menu before they occur. How will they be able to answer customer questions about a dish if they have not tasted it and do not know what is in it?

If staff are happy they may tell others and encourage them to apply for positions that become vacant. A good reputation in the local community and with customers may also make future staff recruitment easy. Very few staff would like to work for a restaurant that had been prosecuted for breaches of hygiene regulations.

If the restaurant passed a local authority inspection with 'flying colours' or was recommended in a 'good food guide', or if the chef won a food competition, this could be the sort of information that a restaurant would want publicised. This could be via press or radio advertising or via the restaurant's web site.

The restaurant may want to extend opening hours to increase business but this could have a negative effect on people who live nearby. One way to address this conflict of interests could be to consult local people on what they would find acceptable or at least to communicate why it is important that the restaurant changes its opening hours.

Similarly, it is also important to keep in regular communication with the other businesses that the restaurant owners deal with, such as the meat supplier or the dairy that delivers milk. If a good relationship exists, suppliers might be more inclined to help if last-minute extra orders were needed.

Activity 1.2

Identify the stakeholders that a car manufacturer would communicate with. Use the list of stakeholders mentioned in Figure 1.2 and add to them if you can. Briefly explain what methods of communication might be used, what messages might be communicated and why it is important for the organization to communicate with these stakeholders.

Please see the activity debriefings in Appendix 6.

Internal customers

Consider your internal customers and how important it is that there is good internal communication in an organization. Think about how sometimes you are the customer and someone else is the service provider.

For example, when you receive your payslip from the finance department, you are the customer and expect it to be correct, to be delivered on time and the salary payment actually paid into your bank account. If there is a problem, you expect to be dealt with courteously and promptly. You do not expect to have to engage in lengthy correspondence to rectify a mistake. If you do receive information from the finance department – say, for example, about a new profit-related pay scheme – you expect it to be clearly written and well presented.

At other times you could be the service provider to your colleagues or line manager, for instance, when you are asked to find out the costings of producing a sales promotion item as part of a future promotional campaign. Your internal customers will expect you to have completed the task on time, accurately, and to present it clearly at the next planning meeting.

So internal marketing is about working together with colleagues and providing them with a good service so that, as a team, your organization achieves its goals.

Internal marketing

Just as individuals have internal customers, such as colleagues and line managers, that they have to deal with, organizations have internal customers in the form of their staff.

From an organization's perspective, internal communication is vital to internal marketing and the maintenance of employee motivation and company competitiveness. Simple methods of communication can be used to keep staff informed about new products/services, internal restructuring or how well (or not) the organization. In dynamic environments, where firms need to manage change effectively, communication needs to be harnessed to help staff adapt and become familiar to changes in their working environment.

According to Berry & Parasuraman (Berry, L.L, & Parasuraman, A. *Marketing Management*.1992) 'A service company can be only as good as its people: if they aren't sold, customers won't be either.' The point here being that most organizations provide at least some level of customer service as part of their product offering and increasingly it is seen as a way of differentiating products in an overcrowded market. Without a culture of internal marketing and effective internal customer communications, the employees within an organization face the following problems:

- Communication problems.
- Frustration and non-cooperation.
- Time-wasting and inefficiency.
- Stress and lack of job satisfaction.
- Poor quality of work.

All of these problems eventually lead to poor service to the external customer, which eventually leads to reduced profit in the long term.

To foster strong relationships and an atmosphere of shared values, communication and information should flow two ways. Information will obviously flow downwards from senior management to employees, but mechanisms should be put in place to ensure that it also flows upwards from employees to senior managers.

Consider the following statement and how this state of affairs can be achieved:

> When everyone in an organization understands their role in meeting customer needs, the organization can be described as customer-focused. (Smith. *Meeting Customer Needs*. Butterworth-Heinemann 1997)

The answer is, of course, communication.

It is therefore important for many marketers to market their department or services internally to colleagues and other departments. Problems can be raised by other people unaware of the marketing department's full range of services and the contribution it can make to the business.

Two-way communications

To encourage a two-way flow of information organizations can choose from a variety of methods to enable managers to hear the views and opinions of employees:

- Regular staff meetings and team briefings.
- Meetings with senior managers where the overall performance of the firm and future developments are discussed.
- Performance reviews/appraisal systems that enable staff to suggest how they could be empowered to do their jobs better.
- Suggestion schemes where employees are rewarded if their ideas are implemented.
- Works councils where staff can get involved in the running of the organization.

Future challenges for internal communications

The changing environment in which organizations operate means that it may be difficult for some organizations to communicate with staff in the traditional way, and pressures upon staff may mean that they are less inclined to be committed to the organization's values and culture.

Factors influencing change

- The combination of downsized organizations and flatter management structures has removed layers of management and this means that employees are nearer to the decision makers and the communication process is speeded up. However, staff who are less secure in their jobs and more pressured to work faster and harder are less likely to communicate openly with their colleagues and managers.
- The trend to teleworking, with more people working away from the office, means it is more difficult to create a corporate culture and sense of belonging where people feel happy to communicate on an informal basis.
- The merging of companies across the UK and elsewhere in the world is creating global organizations that do not have local identities and which cross over different cultures, languages and operating systems. This can make it difficult for senior managers to communicate effectively with employees.

Communicating with the extended organization

Good customer communication goes beyond your own immediate organization. The relationship your staff has with your organization's suppliers, distributors and the like, can have a critical impact on the service your customers enjoy. For example, The Body Shop (the retail chain that sells health and beauty products) ensures that its staff work closely with the firm it retains to distribute its merchandise by giving the distributor office space within The Body Shop factory. This arrangement ensures that close relationships and good communication are achieved.

A good working relationship with suppliers and other 'partners' can produce dramatic effects, such as:

- Innovation
- Improved performance
- Lower costs
- More holistic solutions to problems
- Better understanding of the needs of all parties
- New ways of working together
- More cooperation.

Improving customer communications

In the earlier parts of this unit, you looked at who should be communicating with whom. The next stage is to consider the ways you communicate with your customers.

The internal communications mix

Internal customer communications involve the effective use of memos, letters, reports, notices, e-mails, meetings, team briefings, telephone calls and presentations. Obviously some of these communication methods can be used to communicate externally. In this workbook we are making the distinction that external communications are those that are used to promote and sell the organization's goods and services, which we will refer to as the *external communications mix*. For guidance on using internal customer communication methods, see Unit 6 and Unit 8.

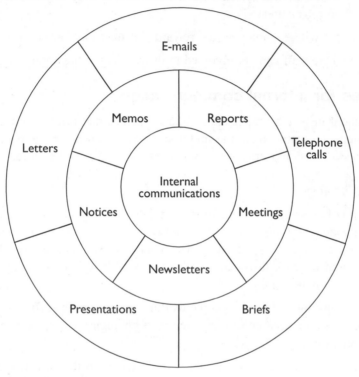

Figure 1.3 Internal communications

The external communications mix

To communicate with external customers, organizations use a range of activities that can be described as the *external communications mix*. These activities range from advertising, direct marketing and selling to public relations and the creation of a strong corporate identity. These activities are used to create brands, to inform customers about product improvements and to promote sales, and because most organizations are not interested in a one-off sale, communications are used to build an ongoing relationship with the customer. For guidance on how to use these communication activities, see Unit 9.

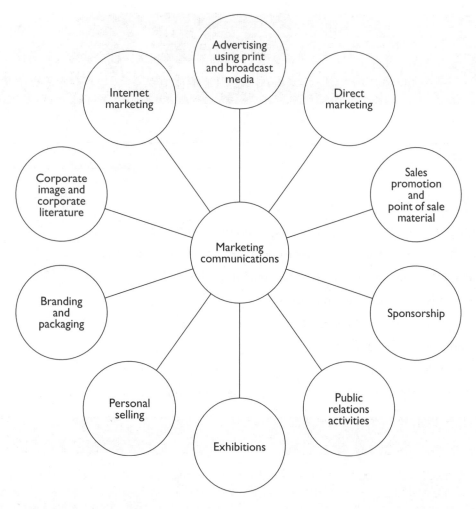

Figure 1.4 *The external communications mix*

Summary

In this unit you have studied the following:

- What is meant by the terms 'customer' and 'stakeholder'.

- The range of internal and external communications that individuals and organizations use to communicate with their *customers*.

- How internal communication and internal marketing can help achieve customer focus.

Further study and examination preparation

Go to the end of the book and attempt to answer question 2 parts a) and b) from the December 2000 examination paper.

Exam hint

Be prepared to answer questions where you have to identify the stakeholders or customers in a given situation. Ensure that you are able to distinguish between internal and external customers and able to determine the appropriate communication method and message that might be relevant in a given situation. Avoid attempting to rote learn the contents of this unit. Instead, familiarize yourself with the material so that the knowledge you have gained will give you an overview of the whole subject before you cover other topics in the book.

Objectives

In this unit you will:

- Examine the changing context of customer needs.
- Appreciate the role of communications in implementing customer care.
- See how customer communications help build customer relationships.
- Look at why customer care systems sometimes fail.

By the end of this unit you should be able to:

- Use communication skills to establish good customer care.
- Handle customer complaints effectively.
- Identify how customer care could be improved in a given situation.
- Devise appropriate customer communications as part of a customer care programme.

Study guide

This unit develops the customer theme from Unit 1 and focuses on how customer communications are a vital part of good customer care and customer service. It covers indicative content areas 2.1.2 and 2.1.3 of the syllabus. This unit also links to the Marketing Fundamentals syllabus, in particular with indicative content 1.1.1. and 1.4.2 and 1.4.2.

Both syllabuses deal with the issues around adding quality to product/service delivery in order to close the gap between customer expectations and their experience, and the importance of creating a dialogue with customers to promote a long-term relationship. However, the emphasis in the Customer Communications syllabus is on the practical aspects of improving interaction with customers. Consequently this unit deals with how customer service can be improved to meet customer expectations by improving customer interaction and communication with customers.

There is further reading that links to areas covered in this unit in Unit 1 and Unit 9 of the Marketing Fundamentals coursebook.

You should take one hour to read the unit and a further hour to complete the activities. At the end of this unit you are also directed to relevant examination questions.

Study tip

At the end of this unit you could check whether your place of work has specific policies or procedures for dealing with quality or customer care issues. Consider how these are implemented.

In addition, you could undertake an audit of the various ways that customers are communicated with and check whether they comply with stated customer care standards.

For example, if you work in a doctor's surgery you could look at the following:

- How easy it is for patients to communicate with the surgery.
- How patients' telephone queries and complaints are dealt with.
- What is the attitude of staff to patients when they deal with them face to face or on the telephone?

Relations with customers

Customer care, customer service, customer satisfaction. Are these merely buzzwords that organizations pay lip service to, or have we really entered a new age of customer focus? Customer focus, or putting the customer at the centre of the organization's operations, has always been central to marketing philosophy, but for a time it seemed that many firms in various industry sectors had forgotten the customer in their bid to maximize profits and minimize costs. However, the desire to meet the growing demands of customers and the need to keep up with more innovative customer-focused competition has forced many firms to re-examine how their customers are really treated. And even firms operating in markets that traditionally compete on price have been faced with the fact that it needs only one competitor to break rank and raise customer expectations for all to be faced with a compelling need to jump on the customer-care bandwagon.

The changing context of customer needs

Consumers wherever they come from, are far more likely to complain nowadays. This is simply due to the fact that in general terms, consumers are more widely travelled and more educated than ever before. Many consumers have developed sophisticated tastes and have higher expectations having seen the superior service standards in the USA and the innovative approaches to quality control that originated in the Far East.

As a consequence, images of deferential consumers from the Far East or of stiff upper-lipped British consumers are fast becoming old-fashioned stereotypes that do not apply to the modern, global society we inhabit. The trend is for more consumers to be more demanding than ever before.

In a Henley Centre research survey (in *Marketing*, November 1998), 56 per cent of people said they complained in person about poor services or faulty goods over the past year, a massive leap from 39 per cent in the previous year. The Henley Centre survey showed that consumers are more assertive and willing to take action against companies. This may range from complaining about faulty goods or inadequate service, or warning friends and family away from a company, to stopping purchasing from a company because it is viewed as unhealthy, unethical or environmentally unsound.

Furthermore, in 2001, a Henley Centre research survey of the insurance sector (Insurance Day, 2001) found that, despite the investment in customer relations by insurance businesses, customers are generally cynical about whether companies really listen to them. The facts support this: 20 per cent of general insurance consumers who have complained to their provider, only 5 per cent felt they had been dealt with satisfactorily. Worse still, out of 5 per cent of pension customers who complained, no-one was happy with the response.

However, things are changing slowly and organizations have begun to realize that they operate in a more competitive and litigious environment where they must respond to consumer demands. Most organizations also realize that it is far easier and cheaper to retain current customers than it is to cultivate new ones. Moreover, research shows that dissatisfied customers tend to spread the news of their bad experiences very quickly – something that affects not only an organization's image but also the bottom line in the long run.

Customer focus

The consumer trend to being less tolerant and more demanding transcends industry sectors. Consumers are less willing to accept shoddy workmanship from builders, lame excuses about unsatisfactory hotels from holiday companies, poor service from shop assistants, overbearing attitudes from health professionals or overcomplicated application forms from mortgage companies. In other words, or-

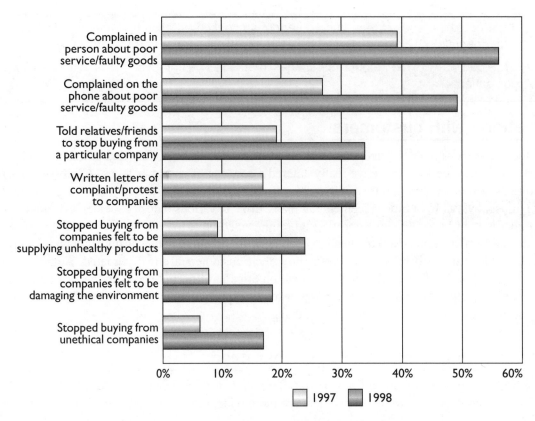

Figure 2.1 *The rise of the assertive customer. Reproduced with kind permission from Marketing magazine.*

ganizations need to focus on customers needs and expectations, not only in relation to the quality of products they provide but also with regard to their quality of service (i.e. the way customers are treated) and the ease with which consumers can access products and services.

Perhaps the most obvious culture change can be seen in British organizations that were previously nationalized companies with little or no competition. For instance, British Telecom and most of the utility companies that are now in the private sector have had to become more customer focused. They have had to improve product and service quality and change the way they do business, to focus on what customers want rather than on their own internal processes.

For example, British Telecom have changed the format and content of bills they send to customers so that they are easier to understand and have a clearer layout with better use of space, colour and fonts. Bills now also contain the kind of information that customers want, such as, how much each call costs and the telephone number called. Many utility companies providing essential services such as water, gas and electricity supplies, now have staff who are trained to be helpful when dealing with customer queries. Many have even changed the way they operate so that essential services are not 'cut off' when people move house and have changed their telephone systems so calls are routed to specific staff after customers have indicated the nature of their enquiry.

So nowadays more businesses try to do business in a way that is helpful to customers or is 'customer focused'. For example, an electrical retailer that previously used its own drivers to deliver goods such as washing machines and dishwashers, now puts the work out to contractors, who ensure that they arrange delivery to suit the customer. They now give time slots within which the delivery will take place, so customers do not have to take a whole day off work to wait for a delivery.

Consumerism

The pressure on organizations from consumers to be more customer focused has seen a rise in consumerism. The impact of consumerism can be seen in a more customer focused National Health Service (NHS) in Britain. This has come about after a long period of intense criticisms about levels of hospital care. The NHS has produced a 'customer charter' that lists the minimum service levels that patients can expect in an attempt to show its focus on patients' rights and expectations.

Rights and standards throughout the NHS

Access to services

You have the *right* to:

receive health care on the basis of your clinical need, not on your ability to pay, your lifestyle or any other factor;
be registered with a GP and be able to change your GP easily and quickly if you want to;
get emergency medical treatment at any time through your GP, the emergency ambulance service and hospital accident and emergency departments; and
be referred to a consultant acceptable to you, when your GP thinks it is necessary, and to be referred for a second opinion if you and your GP agree this is desirable.

Figure 2.2 *Example of a customer charter. (Taken from The NHS Patient's Charter and is reproduced with the kind permission of the Department of Health.)*

More organizations are using customer communications, such as newsletters, leaflets and even advertising, to respond to pressure groups that complain about products, prices, packaging, advertising or ways of doing business. For example, Shell paid for a high-profile newspaper advertising campaign defending its right to produce petroleum in Nigeria. Similarly McDonalds produced leaflets to explain that by sourcing its beef in North America the company did not damage South American rainforests.

Some firms have seized upon 'complaints' and turned them into opportunities to provide products and services that are more in tune with the market and have used their customer communications effectively to promote the product/service strengths via packaging, advertising or public relations. An example of this is the number of different organizations that have made 'green' claims in recent years.

However, it is important that if a firm gives in to public pressure, it should use its communications with customers to get the best publicity from the situation.

Case history

The Bank of Scotland's customer communications

An example where this did not happen was when the Bank of Scotland outraged many sections of its customer base when it announced a deal with a US television evangelist. In the face of angry customers it scrapped the plan to provide a telephone bank service for millions of his US followers, after he made outspoken attacks on gays, feminists, Muslims, Hindus and effectively insulted the whole of Scotland.

Initially the bank stood its ground even as many customers closed accounts, local authorities, charities and trade unions threatened to take their trade elsewhere and protestors handcuffed themselves to its headquarters.

Then, after senior management realized their blunder, they authorized an extensive media campaign of damage limitation.

However, during the campaign at an annual shareholders' meeting, the Bank's Governor appeared to only begrudgingly apologize for the fiasco, apparently seeming not to regret what the bank had done but appearing more to regret that people did not like what it had done. Thus an extensive media campaign to apologize and acknowledge public pressure was wasted because the people at the top of the company lacked a customer focus in communicating with an important group of stakeholders.

Ethical marketing

Ethical businesses are those where staff recognize that they have a social responsibility, i.e. they cannot conduct their business without due regard to broader social concerns. They may go one stage further than obeying the law or may even set themselves a voluntary code of practice where no law exists.

In the UK, strict employment law protects workers from exploitation but there is no law that prevents firms from sourcing supplies from countries where workers are exploited. An ethical business might respond to consumer pressure as part of its customer focus and only contract with suppliers that do not exploit their workers.

Case history

Lands' End

Lands' End supplies casual clothing by mail order. They use their catalogue to communicate with customers about their customer focus. They feature endorsements from satisfied customers, for example:

> When I tore my trousers on a railway carriage door I asked if you could repair them. Instead you replaced them immediately. You really do push the boundary of customer service further than anyone could reasonably expect.

They feature a statement about their business ethics:

> We contract only with suppliers who produce products of high quality and value, who ensure their employees are of legal age, work under safe and healthy conditions, are paid fairly and are not discriminated against.

They also provide a free copy of their Standards of Business Conduct via a freephone number.

Quality and customer care

Customer care and its close relation, quality, are not new ideas, only old ones that have been brushed down and spruced up. They help to remind organizations that they should not rest on their laurels in an increasingly competitive and unforgiving world.

Customer care and quality are linked in that both are concerned with getting things right first time. Quality management is usually associated more with production issues whilst customer care is more concerned with the organization's relationship with its customers and customer service issues.

Quality management is basically concerned with: establishing standards for a product or service; establishing procedures, production methods and service criteria to ensure that standards are met; the monitoring of actual quality; and taking action when quality falls below standard.

With customer care, the aim is to close the gap between customers' expectations and their experience. This is often achieved by finding out what the customer thinks and what they want in terms of product/service quality, packaging, delivery and after-sales service.

For some large service-delivery organizations, such as banks, it has been a case of realizing that customers need to be treated as people who matter and they have had to concentrate on delivering a personal service that makes people feel welcome.

For Lloyds Bank in Britain in the early 1990s, it was a case of laying down a service challenge to staff that set out a number of minimum standards. These included:

- Not letting the telephone ring more than four times before it is answered.
- The person answering should introduce themselves by name.
- Queues at tills should not have more than five people in them.
- Establishing various levels of product knowledge that staff should have.

Some organizations have considered the total product concept and have looked to add value. An example is the toy car manufacturer that packs the product in a box which folds into a toy garage.

Other organizations have gone further and have gone through a process of business process re-engineering. In these cases firms have looked at the whole transaction process a customer goes through from the customer's point of view in order to simplify it and make it easier. In the insurance industry this has revolutionized the way some firms operate so that services are no longer sold through intermediaries but delivered direct and therefore more cheaply to the consumer.

Delighting the customer

Some companies have gone to great lengths to get the detail right. For example, when Nissan dealerships take a car in for a service they provide a replacement courtesy car, check the car over and undertake repairs, clean it and leave a free air freshener inside. A few days later they telephone the customer to find out if there are any problems and to check whether the customer is happy with their treatment.

However, the most innovative companies have gone even further to exceed customer expectations. In many cases these organizations consider that most jobs have two parts – the mechanics of what needs to be done, and the people part. Maws, manufacturers of baby feeding products, established a customer care line to answer new mothers' queries. When one anxious mother called the number to ask about stockists for a product to soothe a crying baby, a highly trained member of staff manning the care line not only provided clear information about stockists and how the product should be used but also felt empowered to send out a complimentary pack of the product. Good business practice indeed, because these relatively inexpensive items have to be replaced every six weeks – and, of course, by exceeding customer expectations they won a loyal customer who is also prepared to sing the company's praises to other potential customers.

Customer delight will ratchet up standards – it is not a static relationship. If the customer is delighted by something for the first time, they eventually get used to the extra service. For example, delivering a fresh bowl of fruit to a hotel room as part of the service soon becomes expected and customer expectations rise even further.

Activity 2.2

Think of an incident when you have been delighted by the service you have received. It could have been when you have been doing your weekly shop at the local supermarket, or buying items at a chemist, or when you were making an enquiry at the bank, or when you were travelling on business. Explain how you were delighted and estimate the cost of the service improvement in relation to the cost of attracting a new customer.

Relationship marketing

The main idea behind relationship marketing is to build strong relationships with customers in order to retain them instead of concentrating efforts on recruiting new ones.

There are several factors which influence customer retention:

- High-quality products to encourage repeat purchase.
- Customers need to feel valued to be loyal. This can only be created by excellent customer service.

- Taking long-term marketing decisions, for example continuous improvement or innovation to keep ahead of customer needs.
- Frequent customer contact to establish customer profiles in order to ensure accurate customer targeting of goods, services and information.

Consequently relationship marketing is closely aligned with both customer care principles and the basic tenets of consumerism. From a customer communications perspective, the most important factor in relationship marketing is the creation of a dialogue between the organization and the consumer. This results in the consumer getting what they want and at the same time becoming a loyal customer who recommends others to the firm.

A good illustration of relationship marketing is the way supermarkets have established loyalty cards to encourage customers to collect reward points when they shop at stores. The advantage to customers is that after collecting so many reward points these are converted into money-off coupons. The advantage to the store is that when customers register for a loyalty card they provide the store with valuable customer information. This information is used to build up profiles of customers who use a particular store in a particular area. This can help individual stores to stock the products wanted by their particular clientele. So, for example, a store in a location with a large Jewish community would know to stock a range of kosher products.

Each time a customer uses the card to collect points from shopping, the customer's purchase history is added to. The value of this information is that past purchase history is the best indicator of future purchase behaviour. This helps stores with many marketing decisions, including, for example, planning appropriate targeted customer communications such as direct marketing and advertising campaigns.

Customer loyalty and retention

The growing realisation that keeping the customers you have is as important as customer acquisition has come about because of the costs involved in attracting new customers. This realisation has evolved into understanding a customer's *lifetime value*. By doing this, you can be selective about who you try to keep as well as who you want to attract.

Smith (*Meeting Customer Needs*. Butterworth-Heineman, 1997) believes that customer retention affects the bottom line and quotes the following facts:

- A 5% increase in customer retention could create a 125% increase in profits.
- A 10% increase in retailer retention can translate to a 20% increase in sales.
- Extending customer lifecycles by 3 years could treble profits per customer.

For example, a client who occasionally uses the services of an advertising agency to produce its low-cost press advertising but places all its high-value promotional literature and exhibition design work with a design consultancy is not a particularly valuable client to the advertising agency. However, the client that stays with the advertising agency and as it grows gives more work each year to the agency could be said to have a high 'customer lifetime value'.

The idea of 'cherry picking' valuable clients and directing more resources to these key clients has been used by many types of organizations. Financial services companies have used the idea well to target graduates with cheap loans and free bank accounts in the hope that these customers will buy a range of financial products over the years of their customer life, for example, personal loans, life assurance, mortgage and pensions. Obviously, by analysing customers and trends, organizations can target appropriate communications depending on the customer's lifetime value.

In business-to-business marketing situations, some organizations have structured their departments and staff, so that individual staff can be responsible for certain key accounts or clients. By having a single point of contact organizations find they can look after clients in a 'seamless' way.

One company that builds masts as part of the physical infrastructure for telecommunications companies does not have a large number of different clients, but its 'key' clients spend massive amounts of money. Consequently, 'key account managers' have been appointed to work closely with the staff from the client firms. They provide expertise and technical support beyond the physical product that they provide. Building this kind of client relationship almost builds in client dependency and enhances the relationship. Very generous credit facilities and reciprocal buying practices have been established so that clients do not want to put their business elsewhere.

Client communications are such that account managers regularly 'network' with clients to ensure that they are happy with the way contracts are proceeding and close relationships are built up. Regular telephone contact and progress reviews mean that any problems are resolved before they become serious issues. A high level of face-to-face, telephone and electronic contact means that account managers understand their client's business so that they can anticipate further contracts and cross-sell other construction and site management services to clients.

Activity 2.3

Consider a loyalty scheme that you are familiar with and describe how it works to the advantage of the customer and the organization.

Managing the customer relationship

Customer relations should not concentrate on handling complaints, i.e. putting wrong things right, it should be about quality issues and customer service improvements.

According to Bee, F & R, (*Customer Care*. Chartered Institute of Personnel and Development,1999), 'Customer care is not just a set of tasks, a list of do's and don'ts: it is a way of life.' They hold that customer care is important because:

- Satisfied customers take up less time.
- Satisfied customers cause less stress and bring job satisfaction.
- Satisfied customers tell other people which enhances your organization's reputation.
- Your customers are your business – without them there is no business.

Steps involved in establishing quality

- Establish standards of quality for a product or service.
- Establish procedures to ensure that quality standards are met.
- Monitor quality.
- Take control action when quality falls below standard.

Steps involved in improving customer service

- Measure standards by finding out levels of customer satisfaction.
- Analyse the feedback.
- Act upon the information and develop what people want, for example customer-friendly systems or getting the detail right.
- Train staff to ensure competence.
- Review processes and procedures to ensure they are customer-focused.
- Consider how much further you could go in terms of exceeding customer expectation.

What do customers want?

Customers certainly do not like any of the following:

- Rude staff
- Insensitivity and apathy to customer requests
- Delayed service
- Difficulties in getting through to a company (often unanswered telephones)
- Poor billing or letters that are inaccurate or do not make sense
- Misinformation i.e. different information from different staff.

All of these create an unprofessional impression. Research shows that when a customer has a negative experience with an organization, the customer will tell on average about eleven people, and nine out of ten people do not complain but take their business elsewhere.

In analysing customer feedback it appears that most feedback and complaints are not about actual products but seemingly peripheral issues, such as late delivery, the way the product does not pour easily from the carton, the way the customer was spoken to or given the wrong information. There are four key characteristics of good customer service.

A positive/proactive attitude

Customers do not want to be faced with apathetic staff who have to be asked the right question before they will be helpful and suggest a solution to a customer problem. They want staff who take responsibility for making things go smoothly and keep customers informed – customers do not want to chase staff to find out things.

Customer-friendly systems

Customers need payment to be made easy, user-friendly application forms and store layouts or computer programs to be designed with the user in mind. The organization's systems should be set up so there is a degree of flexibility, for instance, if a customer wants to change an order or cannot answer all the questions of an application form.

Knowledgeable/courteous staff

Customers want to be dealt with by trained staff who have a satisfactory level of technical knowledge. They also want friendly and courteous staff to deal with, who do what they say they will do and genuinely seem to care.

Product/service reliability

Products that work consistently. Services that turn up on time – every time.

Rules of good customer service

- Getting it right first time.
- Listening to customers to find out what they actually want.
- Communicating clearly and positively with customers.
- Making it easy for staff to help customers.
- Employing staff who are genuinely courteous.
- Encouraging staff to be fair, understanding and flexible in their response.
- Handling complaints in a constructive way.
- Investigating mistakes and learning from them.

Customer service skills

In many customer service situations, there are four ways that customers can be made happy and problems resolved:

- If customers are shown respect and understanding of things from their perspective.

- If customers are listened to.
- If staff ask what a customer actually wants.
- If staff are pro-active and offer suggestions or ways to resolve a situation.

This topic is developed further in Unit 5.

```
1   Smile; be polite, helpful and friendly.
2   Listen and show interest.
3   Satisfy queries positively
4   Do not guess, find out.
5   Work tidily and safely
```

Figure 2.3 *An extract from Asda's customer care policy*

Improving customer interaction

Good customer communications are a vital part of customer care. The communication may be face to face, in writing or on the telephone – whatever the method, it is essential that the communication is clear, concise, courteous, creates the right impression and conveys the correct message.

Creating a good image

You can create a good first impression with customers through positive action, such as:

- Good personal grooming.
- Smart clothes or uniform.
- Punctuality.
- A tidy and well-organized work environment.
- Smart reception areas.
- Establishing a consistent method for greeting people when they enter the organization.
- An overall positive image in all documentation such as invoices, application forms, instruction manuals, leaflets, posters, signs, company vans and shop windows.

Improving internal communication

Some organisations have had to spend time and resources in changing the way they do business to improve internal communication and so ultimately improve external customer service. One insurance company has changed its job roles so that clerks no longer deal with one aspect of a claim or a customer file but instead become 'case managers' who have full responsibility for seeing a process through and dealing with a customer at all stages of a claim. This approach has led to a 'seamless' process and directly contributed to a reduction in complaints and delays.

Other organizations have used technology to improve teamworking and internal communication. A new generation of desktop systems now makes small-scale videoconferencing affordable and easy to use. A single card, installed in a personal computer, can enable people to hear and see colleagues face-to-face wherever they are in the world and exchange and amend documents on screen.

In addition, more organizations are investing in 'knowledge networks' or 'knowledge management' to make the most of skills and experience that exist in an organization. This usually means establishing a database to store company procedures, templates of forms, file notes and projects so that staff anywhere in the firm can access current information and examples of past project work to improve the way they do their jobs.

Communication tools such as mobile telephones, pagers, voice mail and call routing are used so that personnel can be reached wherever they are working. Similarly more staff are allowed to work at home or on the move by using remote data access through lap tops or computers at home.

Staff at a large consumer electronics company, with 64 bases in 30 countries, found internal communication between international sites and the head office in Japan was difficult. There had been little face-to-face or even phone communication in the past, which had lead to poor working relationships and delays which in turn affected production and distribution. To overcome language and time differences, fax communication and personal videoconferencing meetings have been used with great success.

Activity 2.5

Find out what the following 'flexible office solutions' are and how they can help improve customer service:

- Intelligent telephony services.
- Message and voice processing.
- Personal videoconferencing.

According to Smith (*Meeting Customer Needs*. Butterworth-Heineman, 1997) 'Good customer service often goes beyond your own organization. The relationship your organization has with suppliers, retailers, distributors and other members of the 'demand chain' have an important effect on the service your customers enjoy.

Smith advocates that everyone in the demand chain should be capable of delivering a quality service and that this can be achieved through training, good communication, support and a shared commitment to the customer.

Activity 2.6

You work in the export department at a bottling plant for a famous label drink and are having problems contacting distributors and retailers in one of the overseas sales regions by telephone. You are concerned that they are not receiving the latest product and sales promotion information because of different office opening times and time differences between the two countries. How can you ensure that they are fully kept fully informed?

Making it easy to do business

By making it easy for customers to do business, you can improve customer service and the way your organization is perceived by its customers. If the business receives a high volume of incoming calls, one way to achieve this could be by using telecommunications technology to improve customer telephone response. You could enhance call response by:

- Using 0800 numbers that allow customers to call for free, so improving convenience and demonstrating customer care.
- Having customer care lines to assist after-sales service.
- Ensuring that incoming calls are queued and answered in order.
- Giving information to those waiting to reduce the risk of callers hanging up.
- Allowing callers to leave messages using voice mail.
- Using integrated voice response order-processing systems to answer calls automatically and take details, e.g. some gas and electricity companies use systems that mean customers can access information or leave meter readings by keying certain digits.

Ultimately all systems and procedures impact on the external customer. For most organisations there are five key processes that need to be considered from a customer's viewpoint:

1. Sales and ordering.
2. Accounts and invoicing.
3. Delivery.
4. After-sales.
5. Customer complaints.

If you are trying to improve any of these areas you could ask yourself the following questions to help you identify how you could improve customer service.

Sales and order systems

- How easy is it for a customer to make a purchase or place an order?
- Do customers receive confirmation or information about their order, for example, if there are delays?
- How quickly are orders processed?
- Can you deal with non-standard requests?

Accounts and invoicing systems

- How accurate are invoices?
- How are queries dealt with?
- Can customers use a variety of ways to pay, e.g. in cash, by cheque, by direct debit.
- What credit arrangements are available and is the information easily available to customers?

Delivery systems

- Do you deliver when and where people want?
- How do you inform customers about deliveries?
- Are deliveries reliable in terms of time expected and condition of goods?
- What sort of quality check are made before/after delivery?

After-sales

- Do you make it easy for customers to contact you?
- How well do you follow up requests e.g. for repairs, for further information, for a follow-up visit?

Complaints

- Do you get any? What do you do with them (do you have a recording mechanism)?
- How easy is it for customers to complain?
- How do you resolve complaints, what system is in place and what really happens when someone complains?

Activity 2.7

Think of four different ways that different types of businesses have enhanced customer service with technology.

Case history

Changing behind the scenes processes to improve customer service and communication

One financial services organisation wanted to increase personal loan sales by improving customer services. Personal loan applications had originally been handled by post, using a time-consuming process that occupied a large team working with separate IT systems. By establishing a 'direct' telephone operation and a computerized credit scoring system, the loan application and approval decision process was reduced from 7 days to one 12-minute telephone call, thus improving customer satisfaction levels.

Telephone operators can now deal with customers personally, instead of taking details of an application and passing it to a different work area. This gives staff greater satisfaction and the customer an immediate response. In turn, staff have the opportunity to build a relationship and rapport with the customer and as a result sales of additional products, such as loan insurance, have increased.

New integrated customer service systems using the organization's database, mean that accounts can be set up and tracked for the period of the loan. This streamlined process means that staff can deal with enquiries more efficiently.

In addition, new electronic filing systems mean that traditional paper-based filing systems are becoming a thing of the past. These new systems save space and money by converting bulky files to compact desktop systems. They improve customer service because the risk of losing documents is reduced; the time it takes for staff to find documents and respond to enquiries is also decreased.

Furthermore, new document management systems ensure that information and documents are available when and where they are needed, wherever they are located. It means that application forms and associated documents, such as, proof of residence or past bank statements can be scanned and converted into electronic form. Staff can annotate documents and pass them to colleagues as and when needed, without ever having to get up from a chair and physically sort through file notes and documents.

Activity 2.8

1. You are the manager of an estate agents' responsible for a team of six negotiators who regularly deal with customers buying and selling houses. The team deals with customers on the telephone and those who visit the estate agency office.

    To improve standards of customer care you decide to involve staff in determining best practice for dealing with customers.

    To assist staff in formulating a protocol for best practice, draft five minimum standards you would expect to achieve when dealing with telephone calls from customers.

2. You overhear a customer complaining to one of the negotiators that the property details sheet for his house contains incorrect room measurements, incorrect room descriptions and a number of spelling mistakes.

    The member of staff's response to the customer is that he is not responsible for preparing the property information sheet and that prospective buyers will find out what the house is really like when they view it.

    In advising the member of staff how to provide good customer service, outline five main points that you would make to him about the above situation.

Why do customer care systems sometimes fail?

There is no doubt that thousands of organizations providing products and services implement customer care programmes and yet still have customers who receive poor service and complain about it.

The problem often lies in allocating a specific department for customer care instead of training and empowering all staff to deal with customer care issues.

A common problem is that companies impose customer care programmes on staff without explaining the reasons behind them, or do not allow staff who deal with customers every day to influence how customer care is implemented.

Other problems occur where firms have organized supposedly customer-centred systems and processes designed to enable staff to help customers but prospective customers are asked so many personal questions with no relevance to the actual query that they are put off from doing business with the organization.

In other cases organizations move from a localized branch network where staff may know customers quite well, to a round-the-clock service provision supported by centralized telephone services in a bid to give customers improved access to services. Unfortunately, customers may then find that they spend a long time explaining a particular problem or enquiry to an anonymous person and if they have to call again they are faced with another anonymous voice to whom they have to explain the whole thing all over again.

Customer service can also fail if it is commoditized through call centres with staff on short-term contracts. Often these staff fail to see the company's goals as they are often more concerned about their job security. It is also difficult to see how staff could be encouraged to take customer care seriously if senior managers do not treat their internal customers/staff appropriately.

Many staff feel that customer care is something that senior managers pay lip service to because they do not allocate adequate resources to it or establish any reward or recognition system aimed at customer care standards. Some companies persist in thinking that technology is the answer to tackling customer care issues. There needs to be a balance between using telephone technology to speed up response and put customers through to the right department without trapping them in voicemail jail. Technology on its own does not improve customer service if there are no humans available to help solve customers' problems.

In the final analysis, if the product breaks or does not work or the service does not arrive or does not do the job it was asked to do, no amount of apologies, discounts or gestures will change the situation, so quality still remains a key aspect of any customer care programme.

Complaints

Benefits of complaints

Most organizations that supply products and services find that there are occasions when customers are not satisfied and have need to complain. As part of their approach to customer care issues, some organizations have established customer service departments or introduced policies to handle complaints so that complaints are dealt with in a consistent and appropriate way.

The advantage of recognizing that things do go wrong and that customers do complain is that instead of seeing complaints as an unfortunate occurrence, they can be examined to help identify ways of improving products and services.

Resolving complaints satisfactorily usually means that customers become more loyal in the long term because they appreciate that they have been listened to.

Organizations that recognize that it is useful to encourage customers to complain because it provides valuable feedback usually take active steps to obtain this feedback. (See Unit 3 for more guidance in this area.)

Handling complaints

There is obviously no one way to deal with complaints as the approach must be tailored to the circumstances. However, there are a number of general approaches that can be adapted to help deal with difficult situations where customers are dissatisfied and a complaint needs to be handled in a sensitive way. Here is a list of helpful approaches:

- Listen and say nothing until the customer has stated their grievance.
- Give the customer your name so they are assured that you are committed to resolving the problem.
- Use appropriate body language to show empathy with the customer.
- Use an empathic tone of voice.
- Use diplomatic phrases to calm angry customers, for example, 'This is obviously an unsatisfactory situation' or 'I'm sorry you're upset about this situation'.
- Apologize for the fact that there has been a problem – this does not mean you are accepting full blame.

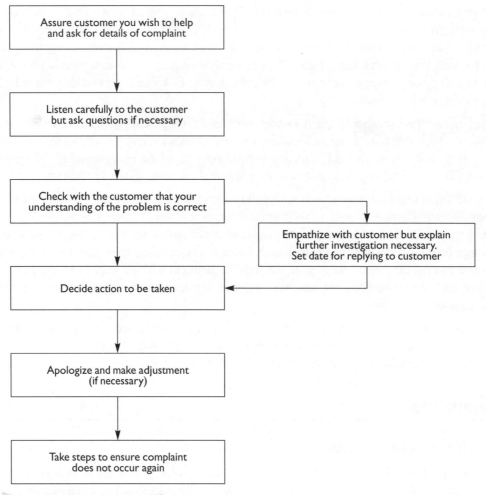

Figure 2.4 A complaints procedure

- Do not interrupt the customer and use effective listening skills to get an overview of the problem and show that you are taking the customer seriously.

- Clarify the problem by checking details and making notes so that you can fully investigate the complaint.

- Be positive, not defensive. So, for instance, you could thank the customer for telling you about the situation because you need to know about the problem if it is to be rectified.

- Tell the customer what steps you are going to take so that they know they have not just sounded off and wasted their time.

- In cases of serious allegations you may need to explain that you cannot take the matter at face value and that you must investigate to verify the allegations.

- Call for management help with customers who remain angry or dissatisfied.

Activity 2.9

Read the scenario below, identify the areas where Orange could improve their customer service and explain how they might improve their customer communications.

A customer purchases an Orange mobile telephone and is promised connection to the service later that day. Unfortunately the customer is unable to follow the complicated instructions in the user manual and rings the help line telephone number. The customer tries to get through to the help line number for three consecutive days but finds that it is constantly engaged. She eventually contacts the head office but there are no staff available to help because it is a weekend. However, the switchboard operator transfers her to the customer help line. A call centre operator answers her call but he is unable to help because the customer was not allocated a security code number when she bought the telephone. However, the call centre operator promises to pass on the matter to head office to be dealt with after the weekend.

After the weekend the customer has not been contacted by anyone from the head office so she decides to contact them again. She complains bitterly to a person in the customer service department about the overcomplicated manual and the service she has received. The member of staff provides a lengthy explanation about how a shortage of staff means the help line is constantly engaged. The customer becomes irate and says that she is not interested in Orange's staffing problems. She demands help with using her telephone, an apology for the way she has been treated and a discount on her bill to make up for the number of telephone calls she has made. The member of staff refuses to apologize, stating that it is not his fault that there have been problems. He explains that he has no authority to agree a discount on her bill and that it is not the company's policy to give discounts. However, he is able to give her the security code to enable her to use the telephone and clarifies the misleading instructions in the user manual. At the end of the call the customer can use her mobile telephone but she is still angry about the way she has been treated.

How to encourage customers to complain

Make it easy for people to complain by publicizing your complaints procedure. Stay close to your customers – regularly find out what customers think by asking them.

Put yourself in your customers' shoes by mystery shopping to find out what customers think.

Don't deflect complaints, find out what the customer expected and what can be done to put something right.

Summary

In this unit you have studied:

- How customer expectations have increased.
- The importance of having a customer focus.
- How consumerism and ethical marketing have changed the way companies do business.
- What is meant by 'customer care' and 'customer delight'.
- How relationship marketing improves communications with customers.
- How customer interaction can be improved.
- How to handle complaints.

Further study and examination preparation

Go to the end of the book and attempt Question 2b) from the June 2000 examination paper and Question 2c) from the December 2000 paper.

Exam hint

Be prepared to describe how and why customer expectations have changed and think of examples from your own industry sector.

Consider how an organisation's image might be affected by poor first impressions. Think of some practical examples of this.

Use the examples and the activities in the unit to help you consider how you can apply your knowledge of customer care issues to a variety of contexts and situations.

Finding out about customer communications

Objectives

In this unit you will:

- Explore the role of marketing research in communications.
- Examine various research methods and sources of data.
- See how data can be used to improve customer communications.

By the end of this unit you should be able to:

- Determine the type of research that could help improve customer communications in a given situation.
- Describe various marketing research methods.
- Devise a questionnaire.
- Evaluate research data to make customer communication decisions.

Study guide

This unit covers indicative content areas 2.2.1, 2.2.2 and 2.2.3 of the syllabus and develops your understanding of how marketing research can be used to determine customer communication decisions. It should take you one hour to read through this unit and a further two hours to complete the activities.

This area of the syllabus links with indicative content 1.2.1 and 1.2.2 of the Marketing Fundamentals syllabus. However, where the Marketing Fundamentals syllabus looks at how marketing research to assist in a whole range of marketing mix decisions, the focus on this area of the Customer Communications syllabus is on how marketing research can be used to influence customer communications decisions.

For a more detailed study of topics that are linked to this area (but will not be tested on the Customer Communications examination), such as, commissioning research, sampling, data analysis and organising marketing research, you should look at Unit 2 of the Marketing Fundamentals workbook.

Study tip

Think about any occasions when your opinions have been canvassed by an organization and consider the methods used to collect the information. In addition, collect samples of any questionnaires that you have been sent and assess their design and effectiveness.

How marketing research helps customer communications decisions

Marketing research helps organizations supply the correct marketing mix and can be used to help organizations find out about the best way to communicate with customers. Organizations use research to find out the answers to a range of questions relating to customer communications, such as:

- How effective are promotional activities such as advertising campaigns, sales promotions or web sites?
- What are customers' perceptions of company literature?
- What are levels of advertising recall or brand recognition?

- Are customers satisfied with levels of service and the way staff respond to them?
- How well do staff deal with telephone enquiries or customer complaints?
- What benefits do customers perceive the product/service provides, and how can this be successfully communicated in the future?
- Do we communicate well with our staff and how could we improve our internal communications?
- Are we reaching the right decision makers with our promotional material?

Ideally on a strategic level, organizations should carry out regular communications audits to see how they are understood and perceived by key decision makers. A communication audit can compare actual perception against current communications and can highlight key communication activities that are needed to achieve communication objectives.

For example, if a communication audit revealed that the true performance of an information systems company should be improved because the client company's senior management team had a poor view of the product's performance and the company's standing in the marketplace, then this information could be used as the basis of deciding a communications plan. This may outline what has to be communicated (for example, how well the company is doing in the marketplace with regard to sales, other leading clients, kite mark awards, annual profits, training plans, expansion plans, etc.) and how it should be communicated (for instance, via product updates and financial information in company literature and in client-account meetings or on the firm's web site).

In addition, information about customers can be used tactically to help target operational communications plans. For example, an airline's customer database with details of frequent flyer purchases could be used to target customers with customised sales promotion offers to encourage customer loyalty. Smith (*Meeting Customer Need*s. Butterworth-Heineman, 1997) gives the example of an advertisement used by an airline to show how it can precisely target business customers.

'This man flies with us regularly on business. He took a family holiday in Spain during the Barcelona Olympics. His last flight to Munich was during the World Athletic Championships. The promise of a free family ticket to the Sydney Olympics should keep him loyal to us.'

Data collection methods

Data collection methods depend on the type of information required. Two distinct categories exist:

- *Primary data* is new data specifically collected for a project through field research. Field research is actively involved in the marketplace, usually involving direct contact with groups of consumers.

- *Secondary data* is data that already exists and can be collected by desk research. Desk research may already exist within the firm and has to be accessed through reports and figures, or it may be more general information published by external sources.

Secondary data sources

This type of data can be collected from internal sources such as sales reports, financial data and internal marketing data. Information on response rates to a mailshot, coupon redemption figures or the previous year's results of testing one copy approach against another for advertising or direct marketing can be valuable sources of information when evaluating customer communications and promotional activity. In addition, sales staff out in the field may file reports on customer perceptions of the latest advertising campaign or the new brochure, and these are also relatively low-cost methods and immediate sources of information.

Activity 3.1

You work in the marketing department of a mail order company that sells fashion items via off-the-page advertising in various national newspapers and magazines. How would you find out which of the newspapers or magazines generates most orders.

Internal databases with customer purchase history can also be invaluable in determining the type of promotional material that should be sent to customers.

Secondary data can be collected from competitors. Looking at the way the competition communicates with its market from press articles, advertising campaigns, in-house newsletters and annual reports can be a very rich source of information on what is happening in the market you operate in.

External secondary sources such as published government information are unlikely to be of use in relation to customer communications. However, research published by Mintel, Jordans, Key Note Publications and directories for certain industry sectors can be useful when looking at overall trends in, say, media spend and promotional activity. Unfortunately, any new published research is already slightly out of date and is unlikely to be specific enough to help you identify how you can measure or improve the way your organization communicates internally and externally.

Vast amounts of secondary research can be conducted on the Internet. You can get general marketing and media spend information from web sites such as **www.tbcresearch.com**, **www.ebusiness.uk.com**. More global information can be obtained from web sites such as **www.asiasource.org** or **www.euromonitor.com** and specific company communications information can be obtained from specific company sites. For example, if you were interested in promotional activity for sports apparel in various countries, you could access web sites such as **www.adidas.co.uk** or **www.reebok.co.uk** and select the country and the language you wanted to access the web site in. Alternatively you could obtain ongoing research from subscription web sites such as **www.lexis-nexis.co.uk** or **www.enterprise.co.uk**, run by the British newspaper, the Sunday Times in conjunction with a number of other companies.

Primary data sources

This type of data can be obtained through various methods, including observation, experimentation, in-depth interviews and surveys.

Observation

Observation can help organizations find out about customer communications by looking at competitor promotional material or exhibition stands or using mystery shoppers to monitor the way that staff deal with customers. Similarly, mystery shoppers can be used on a firm's own staff to monitor customer communications. For example, after a period of training residential care home managers in customer care skills on such topics as how to greet prospective residents and what to say when showing people round, the senior management of a company decided to send a number of mystery shoppers to the homes to find out how each home manager communicated with prospective customers.

Experimentation

Experimentation can help assess the impact of variation in any promotional activity that is undertaken. For example, an animal protection charity wanted to assess whether it should use a 'shock approach'. It sent a fund-raising mailshot to one half of the customer database with a shocking photograph of animal cruelty and to the other half just sent the letter to assess which approach was most successful. Similarly, copy variations can be tested in advertising and direct marketing activity.

Other methods of experimentation can be used to measure the value of company literature or advertisements. For example, if a company runs a press advertisement in two different newspapers, each containing a different code, the responses quoting each code could be measured to identify which media is the most effective.

> ## Activity 3.2
>
> You are the manager of a city centre hotel that caters for people staying overnight on business. How would you find out about the quality of your hotel's customer communications, such as how people are treated when they telephone to make a reservation, how they are greeted at the front desk when they arrive and how staff deal with complaints?

In-depth interviews

In-depth interviews can be used to probe people's attitudes and motivations about any aspect of the marketing mix offering. They can be used to find out customers' views on a wide range of communication issues, such as sales promotions, advertising concepts, product names, packaging, brand images and corporate identities.

Individual interviews or in-depth interviews are informal and more conversational than questionnaires and allow respondents to talk in an unconstrained way. Respondents' deeper attitudes can be elicited by using projective techniques such as word association and sentence completion tests. For example, when the Midland Bank recently changed its name to HSBC, it is likely that they used this method to find out how the new name would be perceived and if it would work in the marketplace.

Focus groups are usually led by a trained discussion leader or moderator and will contain about five to eight people from the target audience. These discussion groups can be shown draft storyboards which show the draft stages of a 30-second television commercial. This is a useful way to check that the advertising proposition and message is appropriate and appealing before entailing the expense of actually shooting a commercial.

The idea behind getting a group of people together in a focus group as opposed to interviewing individuals is that the discussion is likely to become more wide-ranging as people make comments and others in the group either agree or disagree. Sometimes the discussion can appear to go off at a tangent, and that is where the moderator brings the group back on track. This approach can be very useful in determining customer attitudes to the way that an organization communicates with them. For example, a fashion mail order company asked a discussion group about their reaction to the spring/summer catalogue. They found out that the customers thought that the photographs of cheaper dresses made the items look much better than they were in reality. As a consequence, customers were often very disappointed when they received their orders and this explained the high rate of returns of cheaper items photographed in exotic locations.

Case history

Orient Pacific Century Market Research Services – running focus groups in Asia

Focus groups are one of the methodologies used by Orient Pacific Century, especially in areas of brand image monitoring and brand positioning, with products and services that are more complex or emotive in nature and therefore require qualitative data. The strength of the focus group methodology is in depth whereas professionally designed structured surveys provide breadth of information.

There are tremendous benefits with using focus groups in Asia due to its strong oral tradition. Talking and discussing comes naturally, whether it is in the coffee house or on the mobile phone. The exchange of information by word of mouth is central not only to Asian culture but also the way business is done. Business means building up a relationship and only when people have met and talked over an extended time do relationships move to the level of a more open exchange of views that is central to good business. The same applies for researching consumer opinions and this can mean that the warm-up period tends to be longer for focus groups in Asia.

The additional benefit of the focus group in countries like China, Taiwan, Indonesia, Thailand, Malaysia and the Philippines is that these countries are multicultural. Many consumers in Asia are at least bilingual and more often than not people can talk and converse in certain dialects but find reading or writing in those dialects more difficult. Translating questionnaires often leads to changes in the 'meaning' of questions, resulting in misunderstanding and invalid results. The focus group setting can reduce many of these difficulties.

When running focus groups in Asia there are certain considerations that need to be taken into account. Compared to people in the USA, Asian people are less open and have been conditioned to keep their opinions to themselves. So the moderator of a focus group has to be very skilled at making participants feel comfortable and encouraging participation.

The moderator also needs to be aware of the different ethnic and religious backgrounds of participants and having language skills is a definite plus. Breaking up your focus groups according to gender, age and social class should be considered carefully. More so than in Western countries, it is considered very rude in Asia for a younger person to even suggest they have an opinion different from that of an older person or one who is more 'senior' or 'important'. To a lesser extent, the same occurs with females in a group of males. Especially in places like Thailand and India, it is essential to keep sexes segregated.

Seating arrangements need not be an issue if you have divided up your groups. But unlike Western-style focus groups, which invariably involve people sitting in a circular arrangement without a table in front, the Asian style is to provide desks or tables for participants. Part of this is due to culture. In many Asian countries a barrier in front is a welcome physical defence. Without this many group members would feel uncomfortable and their openness would reduce.

Material reproduced courtesy of Lexis-Nexis

Surveys

Surveys, which collect data through the use of questionnaires, are the most common method of primary research. They can be used to collect both quantitative and qualitative data depending on the structure of the questionnaire and the contact methods chosen. A survey asks questions of a number of respondents selected to represent the target market. Below is a selection of factors that can be measured through a questionnaire:

- Finding out which media customers are exposed to in order to plan media buying.
- Measuring pre-advertising or PR campaign awareness of products/ services.
- Measuring post-campaign awareness to assess the effectiveness of advertising or PR campaigns.
- Finding out attitudes to brand names, promotional campaigns, sales promotions and other incentives.
- Rating your organization's performance against the competition.
- Finding out about customer expectations of service and what kind of information they require from the organization.
- Finding out whether customer service and customer communications, such as speed of delivery, helpfulness of staff and waiting times when customers telephone, are satisfactory.

Activity 3.3

The head teacher and deputy head teacher at a school are under pressure to attract more pupils in the next academic year. They would like to produce a brochure that contains information they imagine prospective school children and their parents would be interested in, such as examination results, sporting successes, information about school trips and concerts, as well as about the staff and class sizes. They want to find out if the contents of the brochure are relevant and interesting to their target audience before it is printed and distributed. Suggest how they might find out this information.

Contact methods

Surveys can be conducted by contacting respondents by telephone, mail or face to face.

Telephone surveys

These are a fast, convenient way to access a large number of respondents. Computer-assisted telephone interviewing can be used to guide the interviewer through a sequence of questions which appear on a screen answers are then keyed directly into the computer for analysis. For instance, Nissan dealerships contact a selection of customers who have had their cars serviced. When they contact the customer they ask about the level of satisfaction with the car's condition and about how quickly staff contacted the customer with a price quotation and how helpful the staff were on the telephone and in face-to-face encounters in the dealership.

Postal questionnaires

These can be inexpensive and reach geographically dispersed samples but can have low response rates. Customers may be encouraged to respond if there is some incentive to do so. In business to business situations customers may be very pleased to respond because they feel that their feedback may improve the product/service offering and the way the organization communicates with them.

Face-to-face contact

Personal interviewing is a popular method of collecting information and if sales staff do it as part of their sales job in business-to-business sales situations it can elicit valuable customer feedback. However, it can be time-consuming and expensive for an organization in the consumer market to employ staff to ask questions of passers-by.

Online contact

Online surveys are becoming more popular because of their relatively low cost and because it is one of the easiest ways to obtain feedback from customers who are spread over a large distance, including customers in international markets. However, language and cultural differences may mean that translators have to be used and some questions may have to be changed to deal with market differences.

Respondents can be contacted directly in the comfort of their own homes and answer questions in their own time. Organizations can contact their database of customers and tailor the questions to respondents. They usually keep the questionnaires quite short, in line with the kind of brief communication that e-mail is associated with. Incentives for taking part in online surveys are often offered. For example, British Airways Executive Club offers frequent flyers who take part in surveys the chance to win a free flight or holiday to an exotic destination.

Case history

Air Miles harness the power of Internet market research to obtain greater customer market intelligence

Air Miles, a wholly owned subsidiary of British Airways, operates a multi-collection loyalty currency and has over 6 million collectors on its database and over 100 collection partners including Shell, NatWest Bank, Sainsbury's supermarket and Vodaphone. Customers collect Air Miles and can exchange them for flights or part-payment on flights and holidays booked through Air Miles.

Air Miles has become a leading pioneer in the adoption of market research on the Internet. In late 1999 Justin Alderson, the Market Research Manager at Air Miles identified the need to research quantitatively its online user community about the Air Miles web site, www.airmiles.co.uk.

The survey, using Confirmit, a web-based information retrieval, processing and reporting application, was piloted in December 1999 to a representative sample of 600 members of Air Miles' online community. The pilot had two key objectives: firstly to establish whether or not people would respond and fill in the questionnaire; secondly, to discover whether the questionnaire would be successful in collecting market intelligence that could improve the web site and ultimately increase user activity.

The response rate was overwhelming. A staggering 45 per cent responded to the survey and encouragingly 90 per cent of respondents indicated that they would be willing to take part in future questionnaires. This response rate compared very favourably with traditional off-line approaches such as face-to-face or telephone interviewing and postal questionnaires. In addition Alsderson was encouraged by the number of users who commended

---

Air Miles for taking the time to listen to their opinions. Here is a selection of user comments:

> Thanks for taking an interest in the opinions of your users.

> This is the first online questionnaire I have completed. I am impressed with the way you are seeking customer feedback.

Initial technical concerns were unfounded as users commended on how easy it was to follow the link from the e-mail to the online questionnaire. Filling in the questionnaire online also posed no problems to the respondents. Alderson's decision to deliver the survey using personalised questionnaires through the e-mailed link approach (as opposed to pop-up questionnaires on the web site) was commended as respondents found it less intrusive. The survey results highlighted that the questionnaire had been accurately built and the questions pitched at the correct tone and level.

From the success of the pilot, a quarterly Website Tracking study was implemented. The decision was made to conduct ongoing research to ensure that the company is constantly on the pulse of its customers and ensures that its web site meets their information and service needs.

The first wave of the web site tracking programme began in early 2000 and a larger sample of 1500 individuals was chosen for the survey. For each subsequent survey, a fresh sample of individuals was chosen. 'It's essential to ensure that our customers do not see us as bombarding them with questionnaires and that we research new individuals each time to ensure objectivity,' added Alderson.

46 per cent of the sample responded and the company gained valuable opinions of its web site. They found that customers would like to see more ways to collect Air Miles on the site and greater online booking functionality and special offers. Over the last year Air Miles launched a new-look web site with online collecting opportunities and booking.

Air Miles have since used further online studies to research across all areas of its business including collecting opportunities and how customers want to spend their miles.

Justin Alderson give five top research tips:

- Use all available channels of communication between you and your audiences.
- Remember it's a two-way process – don't just talk at them – listen and let them speak.
- Keep your surveys short, simple and to the point.
- Take on board their opinions.
- Keep the communication channels open.

Questionnaire design

If you are producing a questionnaire that respondents will read and complete on their own, it is important to consider the design and layout of the questionnaire.

When designing a questionnaire, some attention should be paid to the layout so that there is plenty of white space and clear type to make it easy to read. Simple tick box options should be used where possible, although where relevant you can include an 'if other please specify' category so that you do not miss crucial alternative customer information. By paying careful attention to layout and restricting it to one page in length, you can make a questionnaire seem quicker to complete than it really is.

When designing questionnaires, it is useful if there is an introductory statement that outlines the objectives of the survey. Response rates can be improved if there is some incentive to encourage the customer to hand in a completed questionnaire. This could be as simple as a discount voucher, a free sample or entry into a prize draw. However, incentives alone will not encourage respondents to complete a questionnaire if it is not designed to be brief and easy to complete.

Respondents should be thanked for taking the time to complete the questionnaire and you should make it easy for them to return it, possibly using a Freepost address.

Questions should be sequenced in a logical order and grouped by subject, for example under headings such as About you, About your family, Media habits, etc. It is advisable to ask personal questions at the end of the questionnaire so that the respondent is not put off by initial personal questions asking about earnings and age.

You should be careful to ask only absolutely necessary questions, otherwise you run the risk of the respondent getting bored answering unnecessary questions.

Questions should usually follow from the general to the specific. If you are designing a questionnaire for mortgage customers, it is likely that you would first ask if the respondent has a mortgage, then proceed perhaps to ask for how long and then to ask more relevant detailed questions about their understanding of company information about mortgages and buildings insurance. This approach is particularly important if you are conducting face to face surveys where, for instance, you may only want to question people living in rented accommodation and who do not have mortgages, in which case you need to ask questions about this at the beginning.

Types of questions

You can ask open questions that invite an opinion and leave the respondent free to choose how to answer. For example, you could ask, 'What do you think of our delivery times?' but you will find that these answers are hard to collate and quantify.

You can ask closed questions that warrant a yes or no response or a rating on a scale, for example, 'Have you ever had any goods delivered late?' Or you could ask the respondent, 'How would you rate our delivery service – excellent, satisfactory or poor?'

Multiple choice questions are closed in the sense that answers are predetermined but they introduce choice from a list of responses. For example, you could ask the question 'How did you hear about us?' You could then offer a selection of options with a tick box beside them. The respondents could tick one or more boxes to indicate how they heard about your organization. These options might include: through a friend, through an advertisement or through a leaflet that was posted to me.

Rating scales help to quantify opinions and attitudes. These take several forms:

1. How did you feel the brochure description compared to the hotel accommodation you stayed in during your holiday?

    Accurate ☐ ☐ ☐ ☐ ☐ Misleading

2. Indicate in order of importance (1 being most important) the additional features you would like to be part of your holiday package:

    (a) Free 24-hour emergency health care line.

    (b) Free breakdown service with your car hire.

    (c) Free sports facilities.

    (d) Free childminding service.

    (e) Free guidebook and map of the resort.

    (f) Any other feature (please specify and denote order of importance).

Types of research

Marketing research methods can produce qualitative and quantitative information.

Quantitative research

Quantitative research seeks to measure or quantify information for statistical analysis. It involves asking a sufficiently large number (sample) of people a number of questions in order to draw general conclusions.

For example, you may design a questionnaire in which there is a question that asks if the packaging on a product provides them with sufficient information. This question would elicit a simple yes, no or don't know answer. If you questioned 500 people and 400 people answered no, there would be an overwhelming 80 per cent majority who feel that the customer communications need to be improved as far as packaging/ labelling information is concerned.

Qualitative research

Qualitative research explores attitudes, perceptions and ideas. As it asks for opinions it is difficult to obtain the information from simple closed style questions, so it usually involves face-to-face interviews with individuals or small groups. However, qualitative information can be elicited from open style questioning on surveys, though this is hard to collate and quantify when surveying large numbers of people.

For example, with qualitative research you may ask people 'In what way do you think the labelling on the packaging should be improved?' With this style of question, you could get as many different answers as the number of people you asked. Although you would build up a picture of what the labelling should say, it would be difficult to collate the information because each answer would be expressed differently.

However, you can use a combination of closed questioning to find out if there is a majority in favour of the labelling being changed and an open question which asks how it should be changed but limits people to choosing one of four different ways in which it could be changed. For example, you could ask them to select from options which might include: larger print; more information about additives; full explanations about environmentally friendly claims; or clearer information about storage and sell-by dates.

How questionnaires can be used to improve customer communications

Questionnaires can be used to measure how well an organization meets customer needs. For instance, after a car service, a dealership could contact the customer by telephone to find out how the customer heard about the dealership, how the staff treated the customer, how long the customer had to wait, how the car looked after the service (its presentation) and if the service record details were accurate and complete.

Figure 3.1 shows an example of a short survey developed for a leading chain of sports and racquet clubs that have recently opened in the UK and Europe. This survey is handed to new members after their first visit. The incentive for completing it is entry into a draw for free subscription fees for six months. The survey seeks to identify how well the club communicates with new members.

Case history

Mothercare

Mothercare cardholders are sent a short one-page questionnaire with their monthly account statement. At the top of the questionnaire a brief letter states that Mothercare have many special promotions and in-store events and that they would like cardholders to be the first to know about these so that they can benefit from cardholder discounts and offers. The letter then asks cardholders to complete a brief questionnaire with questions about contact details (this includes asking for the customer's e-mail address) and about the children the person has living with them.

Through this field research the company is collecting valuable customer information. This primary data can then be added to secondary data that Mothercare already holds about the cardholder's transactions. This enables the company to utilize research data in order to target appropriate communications to customers.

The Andrew Boyd Sport & Racquet Club New Members Survey	Yes	No
The Sales and Marketing Department of the Andrew Boyd Club would be very grateful if you could assist us in improving the way we communicate with our members by taking just a few minutes to answer the questions below. All completed questionnaires will be entered into a prize draw for six months' free subscription.		
Please tick the relevant boxes to indicate your answer and use capital letters where you are writing.	Yes	No
1. Have you read our new members' pack?		
If answer to question 1 is no, go to question 2. If yes, then please tell us how you rate it from the choices below. Please do not tick more than one box.		
It is easy to read and will enable me to make the best use of club facilities.		
It contains too much information, much of which is not relevant to me.		
It would have been better to put all the information in one booklet.		
It is hard to follow and I was not clear which facilities I can use for my grade of membership.		
Any other comments please indicate below.		
2. Have you found it is easy to find your way round the club, following the signs and directions in the club and the locator maps in the main areas?		
3. How have staff have treated you on your first visit? Please tick one box only.		
Friendly and helpful in dealing with my queries.		
Went out of their way to ensure I was comfortable and could find what I wanted.		
I felt I could not ask for help because they appeared unapproachable.		
I was not sure who worked here and who did not.		
Any other comments please indicate below		
4. What are the main benefits to you for joining the club? Please tick one box only.		
It will improve my social life.		
It will help me get fitter		
It is the best way to get same level tennis/squash partners to play against		
It is the best way to relax		
Any other comments please indicate below		
5. Since joining the club, which types of any promotional activity relating to the Andrew Boyd Club have you been exposed to?		
Press advertising		
Radio advertising		
Outdoor advertising e.g. large poster sites, bus shelters and sides of taxis.		
Articles in the magazines and newspapers		
Mailshots		
Banner advertising on the Internet		
Any other methods please state below:		
6. Do you feel that the image projected in our promotional activity matches the reality of being a member?		
7. If no to question 6, what is the reason for your answer?		

Figure 3.1 *Example of a short survey which seeks to identify an organization's communications with its customers.*

How the questionnaire feedback could be used

The questionnaire could elicit some useful feedback about the joining packs and if and how they need to be changed so they are more readable and informative. It will also provide information about how comfortable new members feel and if the signage and other graphic information around the club help new members to find their way round. It will provide useful information about customer service and staff attitudes. Finally it will provide some quantitative and qualitative information about current promotional activity, and if it promotes an accurate and appropriate image of the club.

Pilot questionnaires

It is advisable to pilot test a questionnaire first within your department and then among a representative target audience to ensure that it is easy to complete and elicits valuable information. At this stage you may realize that some questions are not vital and identify others that need to be asked.

One-off or continuous research

All the types of research that have been described so far can be undertaken on a one-off basis to find out specific information at any one time. Some research is conducted on an ongoing basis and can be useful to monitor trends.

Panels of people representing certain customer groups can be set up and regularly asked for information about such things as their media exposure and what advertising they have seen. Some organizations, such as service providers or computer firms, set up user groups to discuss issues and obtain feedback from customers on a regular basis.

Activity 3.4

A bank manager has set her staff certain standards relating to product knowledge. She expects staff to be familiar with all the bank's financial services. How can she find out if staff can deal satisfactorily with customer enquiries about a new mortgage product that has been introduced?

How promotion and communication research can help

Having undertaken research, it is important that the information is used to inform decision making and make improvements as indicated by the feedback.

For example, consider the situation where a client responsible for brand X complains to a senior manager in an advertising agency, that the account manager who works on brand X, rarely makes contact with a progress review.

In this context, the senior manager would use this 'informally obtained' information to improve the service provided and quite possibly this would ensure that the client does not take his business elsewhere.

Below are a number of different situations that illustrate how marketing research can be used in different customer communication contexts.

Using research data to improve business-to-business communications

Assume you are the marketing manager in a firm about to launch a new service. You have decided to appoint a marketing communications consultancy to produce promotional material. You shortlist a number of consultancies to pitch for the work. After the pitch presentations you appoint one of the consultancies.

One of the unsuccessful firms then contacts you for feedback to find out why they did not get the job. This firm would, in fact, be conducting marketing research with the aim of improving its performance when pitching for future work. As the potential customer, you could provide valuable feedback about the way the firm could improve – how staff answer the telephone, how well their staff deliver client presentations and how effective their promotional brochure is, for example.

Using marketing research to improve e-marketing communications

Assume you are the Marketing Manager of a chain of cinemas. You have just run an advertising campaign to promote the introduction of a web site where cinema-goers can find out about forthcoming films and can book seats online. You could use marketing research to evaluate the success of the campaign by finding out how many people accessed the site after the advertising campaign finished. You could then use the web site to find out from customers if the content of the web site was relevant and its design appealing. You could also monitor the number of online registrations and bookings to see if it was a viable form of customer communications.

Using research methods to solve internal communications problems

Assume you are the Chief Executive of a manufacturing firm with several factories in different locations. Reduced orders last year meant that several hundred redundancies were made. Staff were angry that they were not informed about the redundancies and initially heard about them through the local media.

You now intend to reorganize a number of departments and restructure supervisory and management positions within the firm. You believe you need to implement a structured communications programme and you are also considering introducing a staff newsletter but are unsure what it should contain. Within this context you decide to undertake some in-depth interviews with a random selection of staff to find out how best to improve internal communications.

Using research methods to monitor promotional activity

Assume you have run a sales promotion and advertising campaign to re-launch a newly refurbished restaurant. The press advertisements in two different newspapers contain a '£5 off the cost of a meal' voucher which customers need to bring when they eat at the restaurant. To measure the effectiveness of the campaign, you have ensured that the voucher which appeared in one newspaper is coded differently to the one that is in the other. As customers redeem their vouchers you take a record of which newspaper advertisement generated the better response. You would also take the opportunity to evaluate how much extra custom the campaign has brought

Using research methods to measure customer feedback

Assume you are responsible for organising your local CIM branch seminars. You are interested in finding out if branch members are happy with the service they receive. To obtain your customers' feedback, you leave a 'happy sheet' on each chair and ask everyone to complete and hand them in to you at the end of each seminar. The happy sheet you have designed asks a number of questions relating to the quality of the speakers, the presentation style, how they heard about the seminar and the service at the venue. Each answer can be graded using a rating scale ranging from excellent to poor.

Activity 3.5

You are the Marketing Manager of a group of residential care homes for elderly people. You wish to plan a client communications strategy for next year. You already distribute leaflets to people you believe influence the purchase decision and also undertake various advertising strategies/campaigns. To help you decide what promotion and communications activity you need to organize, you have asked managers to record how people hear about the residential care homes. Based on the feedback in the table below, which you have received in the last six months, how would you communicate with prospective clients in the next year?

Source of information	Number of enquiries
Advertisement in the telephone directory	258
Advertisements in the local newspaper	3
Posters displayed in GPs' surgeries	6
Entry in the residential care home directory	0
Leaflets distributed to district nurses	241
Leaflets distributed to social workers	300
Posters displayed in local libraries	25
Information on the company web site	1

Summary

In this unit you have studied:

- The role of marketing research in making customer communications decisions.
- How data can be collected.
- The different types of survey contact methods, looking in particular at the role of online surveys.
- How to design a questionnaire.
- The difference between quantitative and qualitative data.
- The need to pilot questionnaires.
- How marketing research can help develop and improve an organization's customer communications and promotional activity.

Further study and examination preparation

Go to the end of the book and attempt question 3b) from the June 2000 paper examination paper and question 6a) and 6b) from the December 2000 paper.

Exam hint

For the examination, be prepared to apply your understanding of how marketing research methods can help an organization develop or improve its customer communications.

One way to put theory into practice is to consider how your own organization collects information and uses it to improve its customer service or the way it communicates with stakeholders.

Also spend some time investigating how the Internet can be used to obtain customer feedback and practise your questionnaire design technique.

Objectives

In this unit you will:

- Examine the process of communication.

- Recognize the barriers to successful communication.

- See how an understanding of customer behaviour can help in the development of customer communications.

- Relate communications theory to the buying process.

By the end of this unit you should be able to:

- Produce a simple model of the communications process.

- Identify how and where barriers to communication occur.

- Use a planning framework in the development of customer communications.

- Apply communications theory when developing communications material.

Study guide

This unit provides an overview of the communication process and an insight into how to be an effective communicator. It covers indicative content areas 2.3.1, 2.3.2, and 2.3.4 of the syllabus. It should take you about one hour to read through this unit and a further hour to work through the activities.

The section on consumer behaviour and buyer behaviour in this unit links with indicative content 1.2.10 in the Marketing Fundamentals syllabus and the topic is covered in more detail in unit 2 and unit 7 of the Marketing Fundamentals workbook.

Study tip

After reading this unit you could identify a major item that you have purchased recently. Think about the steps you took before actually making the purchase decision and why you chose that product in favour of others in the market. Consider how you found out about the product and any other information that you obtained about it before buying it.

The purpose of communication

In marketing, you communicate with others for the following reasons:

- To inform or persuade.

- To obtain a decision or request action.

- To get something done.

- To maintain relationships or respond to a previous communication.

The pressures of modern-day living mean that when you communicate in business it must be clear, accurate and efficient so that time, effort and money are not wasted. Successful communications occur when the person communicating has a clear purpose or objective which is achieved as a result of the communication. To help you understand what actually happens when you communicate, here is a simple model of the communication process.

The communication chain

Communication is a *chain* of events which has *five* distinct dimensions (see Figure 4.1).

1. The sender has the need to communicate.
2. The need is translated into a message (encoding).
3. The message is transmitted.
4. The receiver gets the message (decoding).
5. The receiver interprets the message and provides feedback.

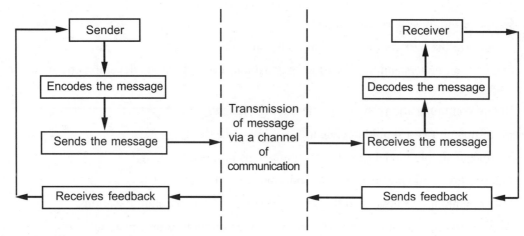

Figure 4.1 *The process of communication*

1. The need to communicate is *intrinsic,* but the *perception* of a message will be unique, therefore in the process of *conceiving* an idea, you will inevitably make assumptions and leave out details that seem unimportant. However, others will not perceive in the same way, therefore you must appreciate the *needs* of your recipient, their possible interpretation(s) and *plan* your message accordingly.

2. Messages may be *expressed* in a number of different ways depending on the purpose of the communication, subject or topic to be related, the needs of the recipient and your own personal skills in communication. In the process of *encoding* you will select bits of information and organize them for transmission. The first step is to decide what and how much to say; if a message contains too much information it is difficult to absorb, but if you do not include enough, it will not meet with the expectation of the recipient and may leave room for misinterpretation.

3. The *medium* you choose for transmission will depend on the message to be conveyed, location of the recipient, speed, convenience and degree of formality required. The usual internal methods are memo, report, telephone and face-to-face interaction.

4. Technological advances in electronic office equipment such as computer-based systems for sending electronic mail copies of documentation have made it possible to send communications from one location to another quickly and effectively.

5. *Decoding* is the interpretation of the message that has been received and will have been successful if the recipient has absorbed the message and assigned to it the meaning which the sender intended.

6. *Feedback* (or lack of) is the response that the recipient sends back to the sender and is a key element in the communication process as it enables the sender to *evaluate* the effectiveness of the message. Feedback may take the form of verbal (telephone call, face-to-face interaction, etc.), non-verbal communication or action (body language, etc.) or written messages.

Feedback is the key element that creates a *cycle* in the communication chain, enabling the information that is sent to be reviewed when it is received back and on this basis further communication initiatives or corrective action can be taken as necessary.

Barriers to successful communication

Distortion

It is possible to lose the meaning of a message during the communication process. This can occur at the *encoding* stage, where the sender puts their thoughts into a message. It can also occur at the decoding stage, where the recipient attempts to grasp the meaning of the message. This breakdown in communication can be caused by the sender not translating his message into appropriate language, with the result that the wrong message is sent or it is not understood by the recipient.

Although there may be instances where people deliberately choose to distort the message and understand only what they want the message to say, the most common reasons for the meaning being lost in the 'handling' of the message are as follows:

- Using the wrong words.
- Using jargon or technical words that are not understood.
- Using a foreign language or an accent that is not understood.
- Using words or pictures that have more than one meaning.

Distortion can occur with an advertising message where there is ambiguity in the message, whether this is intentional or not. For instance, if the people who write and design an advertisement that is used in international marketing, are from one culture and the recipients of the message are from another, there may be problems in how the message is interpreted. For example, Shell's advertising slogan 'To put a tiger in your tank' caused problems in Taiwan where people attach a religious significance to tigers and therefore had a different understanding of the message being conveyed.

Noise

Noise, such as distractions or the interference that occurs as the communication is being encoded, transmitted and decoded, can obstruct the transmission of the message. There are many different types of noise that can render a message inaccurate, unclear or even mean that it is not received at all.

Technical noise

Technical noise can occur while the message is being transmitted; for example, when a poor telephone connection means the caller's voice cannot be heard or a fax machine breaks down.

Physical noise

Physical noise can occur while the message is being transmitted; for example, people talking, traffic or noisy machinery could render a speaker's voice inaudible during a presentation.

Social noise

Social noise creates interference in the transmission and decoding of messages. It is caused when people are prejudiced against others because of their age, gender or social class. For example, a young woman delivering a presentation on corporate funding to older businessmen may be perceived to lack credibility by some of the audience who are prejudiced because of her age and gender.

Psychological noise

A person's emotional state or attitude could interfere with message transmission. A person's anger or hostile attitude can create psychological noise. For example, a customer whose goods have not been delivered may be unable to hear the reason why the goods have been delayed because he is so angry about the situation.

Other barriers

Perceptual bias can occur where the recipient of a message makes assumptions and selects what they want to hear. This can result in the wrong message being received. For example, if a doctor has told a patient that their condition is not serious as long as they change their diet, the patient might choose to hear only part of the message and not take in the message about changing their diet.

Information overload can occur if the recipient of the message receives too much information or information that is too technical. The result is that the key messages are not conveyed or understood. For example, when a new member of staff is given a very detailed demonstration of how several pieces of equipment work in a short space of time, it is likely that they will become confused and remember very little about what was actually said.

Contradictory non-verbal messages can occur if the person encoding a message says one thing but their body language says something else. For example, if a person wears casual clothes and a baseball cap to a job interview in a formal business environment and says that they think they would fit into the organization, they are conveying mixed messages to the interviewer.

Language can be a barrier if two people speak different languages and cannot understand each other.

Case history

UK factory hosts Japanese delegation visit

A UK manufacturing company hosted a delegation from an associate company in Japan. The Marketing Manager was given the task of arranging the first day's activities, which were to include a two-hour presentation about the history, structure and objectives of the firm, a tour of the main manufacturing site and lunch followed by a brainstorming session on how the two companies could forge closer links and benefit from future joint projects. However, little consideration was given to the communication barriers that arose during the visit:

- Cultural differences in the way Japanese people greet others, their degree of formality and taste in food.

- The language barrier in that many of the delegation did not speak English and none of the host company spoke Japanese.

- The unfamiliar technical environment and organization of the company, which meant that the jargon and abbreviations specific to the host company that were used in the presentation, made the presentation incomprehensible to most of the delegation.

- The noisy manufacturing site meant that during the tour most of the visitors could not hear what was being said to them.

- The lengthy presentation meant that the visitors who understood English had 'information overload'. Most lost concentration and could not take in the overall message.

- The delegation did not feel confident or comfortable with contributing to the brainstorming session.

For future visits the marketing manager thought of a number of ways to eliminate the communication barriers:

- Employing an interpreter.

- Researching cultural differences and using this information to provide appropriate refreshments and use appropriate greetings, seating arrangements, etc.

- Ensuring that no jargon or colloquialisms are used by speakers.

- Using small groups to tour the factory at a quiet time so visitors can hear what the guide is saying.

- Using a shorter presentation to prevent boredom and information overload.

- Using a different presentation approach, with visual media, such as slides or video and Powerpoint software.

- Increasing interaction with the audience with question and answer techniques to check understanding.

- Providing a pack of information in English and Japanese, containing key points about the company, such as its structure, objectives and current operations.

- Avoiding the brainstorming session as it may be too ambitious an exercise. Replacing it with a social event where individual host managers can be 'partnered' with visiting managers and interpreters used to help exchange views in a less threatening context.

Avoiding barriers to communication

Communication barriers cause mistakes and can damage the business relationship with external customers. With internal customers, communication barriers can lead to conflict (at worst) and irritation (at best), neither of which are a good recipe for internal marketing and customer care.

To overcome possible communication barriers, careful thought needs to be put in before encoding messages so that the full message is conveyed. Gaps in messages are usually caused by making assumptions about how people will 'decode' the message.

Avoid jargon or technical words that may not be understood and try to avoid ambiguity.

Ensure that you understand your target audience as this is key to avoiding barriers to communication. The accuracy and precision of your message is important if it is to be decoded correctly. An understanding of your target audience's needs should mean that you are able to have the same 'mental image' about a product or service that your customers have.

For internal communication with staff, you could provide training to eradicate unnecessary social and psychological noise that can be created when people make assumptions about customers or allow themselves to react inappropriately when customers make complaints.

When communicating with customers it is essential not to create information overload and to be aware that only part of the message may be heard. You may have to repeat a message many times before it is heard fully.

It is also important to establish credibility so that customers feel you and your message is trustworthy and internal customers believe in what you say.

By taking some time to consider how a communication might be received you are more likely to shape a message that will not be misinterpreted or misunderstood. In other words, by carefully shaping your message and considering the effect it might create, it is more likely that the communication will be successful.

Activity 4.1

Read the following case study and identify the barriers to communication and the problems they are causing in the workplace.

Sally Strict, the office manager at XYZ, is nearing retirement and considers herself to be 'of the old school'. She likes the girls on her administration team to appear neat and tidy and to do as they are told without question.

One day they are short-staffed and the recruitment agency agrees to send a temporary administrative assistant to work for a week. Sally had asked the agency to send someone for two weeks but the telephone line had been so crackly that the message had not got through.

When Peter Patel, a young business studies student who liked to get work experience during his vacations, was sent by the agency to the XYZ office, Sally was shocked by his appearance. She wondered how a young man with dyed hair and earrings would ever be able to cope with the work done in her department.

She spoke to him in a sarcastic tone and said: 'You'd better make yourself busy – that is if you know anything about office work.'

Peter was very irritated by her hostile attitude. However, he knew that she and the rest of the department were under a lot of pressure to get work completed. He was sure the office manager would appreciate his hard work and he decided that if she did not, then he would just walk out and leave them in the middle of all the work they had to complete.

Later in the day the department received a large number of orders that had to be processed immediately and this would involve all the team staying late.

During the afternoon tea break, Sally, who had by now realized that Peter was an efficient and hard-working member of the team, said: 'So how are you getting on now?'

Peter immediately assumed that she was being sarcastic and 'having a go' at him. He smiled politely and said: 'Fine, thanks.'

Sally was relieved that he had not taken offence at their initial meeting and was glad to see him settling into the office.

A few minutes later, Peter put on his jacket and walked out of the office. He was determined that he was not going to stay at XYZ to be insulted by the office manager.

Effective communicators

Successful business communicators have the ability to transfer and receive information using the most appropriate channel. They eliminate barriers to communication and proceed without prejudice, bias and unsuitable language in line with the needs of the recipient. They possess the following attributes:

- *Credibility* – they are highly believable and trustworthy in terms of the content of their communication/message with which you, as a recipient, feel completely comfortable. Indeed, this is vital for successful managers and those involved in the leadership of others.

- *Precision* – this is linked to the first point. It is not only related to the ability to articulate words, sentences and phrases into a meaningful communication but also helps to create a communication experience whereby the recipient(s) share the sender's 'mental picture'.

- *Perception* – a successful communicator will be able to anticipate and predict how their message will be received and therefore shape it accordingly. The response of the recipient(s) (which may be presented in written format, verbally or non-verbally) will then be assessed by the sender and if necessary further communication will take place to adjust for misunderstandings.

- *Control* – linked to the point about perception is the feeling that you should now be getting, which is that successful communicators are able to control their message to a great extent and also to generate (mostly) the required response, if appropriate.

- Finally, one of the most important (natural) skills possessed by successful communicators is that of congeniality – the ability to be pleasant and friendly, in written, verbal or nonverbal communication, even if the message is serious and possibly very bad news.

Activity 4.2

Explain how each of the following can create a barrier to communication and use an example for each to indicate how the impact of noise could be reduced.

1. Lack of credibility (4 marks)
2. Perceptual bias (4 marks)
3. Information overload (4 marks)
4. Contradictory non-verbal signals (4 marks)

Planning the business message

Professional communicators decide the purpose of their communication at the outset. By being clear about their intention, they then know if they have achieved their objective at the end of their communication.

Business communications tend to be planned, formal, impersonal and succinct. The degree of planning involved in the communication depends on the purpose and context of the communication. For example, you may carefully plan a sales call to a prospect, since you may need to deal with any objections that the customer may raise. However, you are unlikely to do this when you want to arrange lunch with a colleague, even though there may be several important matters you wish to discuss with him. In this situation you may not make detailed notes of the issues but your planning may extend to making a mental note of them.

A planning framework

The PASS framework is an easy to remember mnemonic that you may be familiar with. To assist you in the planning of messages you should also consider the communication *mode* you intend to use, as the communication format and media you use will be important in determining the structure and style you adopt.

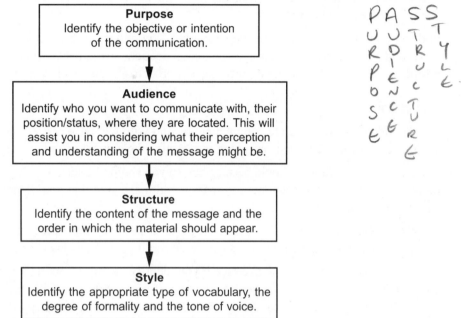

Figure 4.2 *A planning framework*

Identifying the purpose

There are an infinite number of reasons why you might communicate in business. Generally, in internal communication situations, you will be informing colleagues, line managers or subordinates about something, responding to a previous communication, obtaining a decision or requesting action. In external markets you may be trying to raise awareness in the media, persuading customers to buy or stimulating some other response, such as ordering a catalogue or ringing for more information.

Barker (1999) recommends that you do not confuse your document's purpose with its subject. He says that if you were writing about a new piece of equipment, you could write about it in many ways. The way you choose will depend on your purpose and what you want your document to do.

According to Barker, possible objectives of a product include:

- Justifying the cost of buying it.
- Comparing it with similar products.
- Telling the reader how to operate it.
- Listing the options for using it.
- Detailing its technical specifications.
- Explaining how it fits into an existing network or system.

Each purpose will generate a completely different document. The document will only be useful if it addresses the purpose clearly.

Acknowledging the audience

For internal communications the position of the person you are communicating with and how well you know them will determine the style of communication you adopt in terms of the detail, complexity and words used. In addition, the purpose of the communication and the urgency of the matter will determine which communication format and media you will use.

In order to tell a colleague that you will not be available for lunch for another hour, you may just call into their office or telephone them. In contrast to this, you may write a memo or send an e-mail to inform staff about a change in the time and place of the weekly sales meeting.

In writing a press release to announce some important news about the company you work for you may draft two versions of the press release. One may be tailored for the national press and one may be targeted at the trade press. However, if you had a particular contact in the broadcast media whom you wanted to inform, you may consider using the personal touch and actually telephoning the contact with the information.

In developing advertising to your target market, you will need to consider the characteristics of the target audience in terms of their age, gender, education, social background and lifestyle when composing the words and deciding on the visual approach and the media you will use.

Structure

Having identified why you are communicating and with whom, you need then to consider what you are going to say and how you are going to organize the content of the message.

Business communications should be succinct, so you should be selective with the content you choose to include. Use relevant, accurate information and make sure that you do not overload the recipient with too much information.

Having selected the material for your message, you need to decide how you will organize it. The way you group material together and how you sequence it determines the shape of the message.

It may help you to structure the message if you identify the most important point and follow with the supplementary information you need to include. If you are dealing with particularly complex material it may be helpful to present the simple information first and build up to the more complex argument or points you wish to make. You may feel it is important to present information in chronological order, particularly if you are dealing with a series of events or a complaint about a number of issues.

Whatever structure you adopt, you should note that it is easier to read an argument that follows a logical progression and quicker for people to absorb information that is grouped together in chunks with relevant headings.

Style

The style you adopt in any message is governed by the words you use, the way you structure sentences and the tone of voice you adopt.

The way you use vocabulary is a personal choice. The English language is very rich and you may often have several words to choose from that will convey the same meaning. However, you should consider your audience and their familiarity with the words you use. It is not always appropriate to avoid jargon or technical words, especially when you know your audience is familiar with them and where it is important for you to establish credibility and common ground with your audience.

By changing the structure of sentences you can place emphasis on certain words and by altering the order of words you can produce greater fluency or flow.

The tone of any communication conveys the overall effect. You can create an overall impression of friendliness and informality with the greeting you use, simple wording and colloquial expressions. For example, the following sentence has a friendly, informal tone: 'Thanks for lunch yesterday. It was useful to go through the client list and I will make appointments to see each of them a.s.a.p.'

Alternatively, you can convey a formal tone by giving instructions, using technical wording and an impersonal tone. For example: 'The figures indicate that sales staff need to cut the cost of expenses by x per cent. Consequently all journeys over x miles should be agreed by the Sales Manager.'

By emphasizing points, by appealing to the recipient's emotions, repeating selling points, using reassuring terms and asking questions that lead the recipient to a series of benefits, you can create a persuasive message. For example, the following statement has a persuasive tone: 'How can Home Care help you? With Home Care you can be assured of quality care in the comfort of your own home. No more struggling with the cooking and cleaning . . .'

Activity 4.3

Rewrite the sentences below, avoiding the use of jargon and cliches, and correct any unnecessary wordiness.

1. The practicability of planning to meet possible future service requirements should be explored.

2. The supplies manager has been at pains to explain that the availability of the product is diminishing rapidly.

3. Inflationary land prices have rendered it an uneconomic proposition to relocate the production operation.

The mode of communication

The communication format (whether that is a written report or an oral presentation at a meeting) or the media (whether that is the telephone or electronic means or some form of advertising media) that you use to transmit your message will influence its structure and style.

In addition, when communicating internally, you will need to consider the purpose of the communication and the audience you wish to communicate with, to help you decide the correct communication format. For example, there will be some occasions when it is suitable to put a notice on the notice-board to communicate with colleagues and at other times it will be more appropriate to send a memo or organize a face-to-face meeting.

For external communications there will be occasions when it is suitable to send a fax message and at other times it will be easier and more confidential to send an e-mail.

Where you need to raise awareness about an issue or a new product, your choice of media will influence the style you will adopt.

For example, if you were trying to raise awareness about the dangers of driving without seatbelts you could either use a press campaign or a radio campaign to communicate your message. However, the treatment of the message would be different in each case. For radio, you could use sound to communicate an emotional message of a family talking about the death of a loved one. For the print advertisement, you could go into more detail as you would not have the same time constraints as a short radio commercial. So you could include more facts and figures about the number of car accidents caused by not wearing a seatbelt. Such a detailed message would be totally inappropriate if it was read out loud in a radio commercial but could be absorbed by people reading it in their own time and at their own pace.

How the PASS framework can help in planning messages

If you needed to raise awareness among teenage girls in one city in your country, about the dangers of smoking, the PASS framework could be your starting point to help you decide what you want to say and how you should frame your message.

For example, by considering the 'purpose' of the communication task you would be clear about the message you needed to convey, i.e. to warn of the dangers of smoking.

By considering the 'audience' you would ensure that you concentrated on teenage girls. This may influence the language you use, i.e. not technical or medical language. For instance, sending text messages is very popular amongst teenagers so you could use that type of language to give your message impact and credibility.

As the style and structure of a message are greatly influenced by the communication method you are going to use, you would consider this aspect next. Assuming you were restricted to a tight budget,

Figure 4.3 A print advertisement can contain more detail than a radio or poster advertisement

you may consider that posters or outdoor advertising could be an economical medium to use. However, you would also need to consider where you would place your posters. Relevant places could be community and sports centres that young people use. Or outdoor poster sites at cinemas and shopping centres or transport advertising on buses and underground trains or at 'adshel' bus stop sites, could be used.

The next consideration would be the 'style' of the message that would suit your target audience. You would have to ensure that your style was not patronising. You could even use a celebrity who appealed to this age group. You would need to consider the restrictions of the poster format and the best design of the poster in terms of layout, type face, colours and imagery that could be used.

The structure would be the final consideration. This would mean looking at how you are going to convey your message. You would have to be selective with words and group the material in a sequence that is logical. In other words you would have to focus on the most important point and make that first. This could be fairly straightforward task when determining a short poster-style message.

Thus the PASS framework can help in planning messages.

Relating customer behaviour to external communications

Understanding how customers behave and what influences their purchase behaviour helps determine effective and relevant communication and promotional activity. When designing and implementing communication plans it is important to consider who your customers are, what their lifestyles are, their educational background, the type of jobs they do, their income levels and their attitudes.

Influences on consumer behaviour

One approach is to consider a customer as a 'black box' with a variety of inputs that influence purchase behaviour. Some of these inputs or stimuli are SLEPT (social, legal, economic, political and technological) factors over which you have no control. However, consideration of these factors can

50

help you to communicate with your customers. For example, at a time when the cost of borrowing money is low because of low interest rates, a financial services company might want to invite current mortgage customers to extend their mortgage. In drafting a mailshot to communicate this message to customers, you would probably want to make reference to the economic situation as part of your selling message.

Other influences that affect purchase behaviour are controllable factors, such as your organization's marketing mix offering. So, for example, the knowledge that in the washing powder market on-pack price promotions and money off influence customers to change brand (at least in the short term) may be a vital piece of information when manufacturers are planning customer communications.

There are several other buying influences that affect consumer behaviour.

Social influences

Through research into your organization's customer base you should be able to identify a profile of your target audience which enables you to develop the right messages and tone of voice in communications that will appeal to them.

The following are powerful social influences on consumers:

- *Social class* in terms of a person's job, income, educational background and social status, which may influence the newspapers people read, where they spend time socializing with friends and the type of holidays they go on.

- *Stage in the life cycle* in terms of whether a person is single and has high disposable income or is married with young children and therefore spends large amounts on household products.

- *Culture* in terms of religion or ethnic grouping, which can affect people's food choices, the clothes they wear and the magazines they read.

Individual differences

The following are some of the influences that shape people's individual tastes/needs:

- *Motivation* affects people in different ways. Some people are highly motivated by status and therefore tend to buy expensive brand-named goods that are a 'status symbol'. Others are more interested in self-fulfilment and prefer to spend their disposable income improving themselves, for example, learning how to play a musical instrument or to speak a foreign language.

- *Personality* can affect a person's consumer behaviour. Although everyone has their own distinct personality, there are specific traits that are identifiable in some groups of consumers. For example, if you ran a travel agency that specialized in adventure holidays, then your advertising would be designed to appeal to people who could be described as having an 'independent' personality.

- *Beliefs/attitudes* relate to a person's opinions. So, for example, The Body Shop appeals to consumers who have strong beliefs that testing products on animals is wrong. The Body Shop communicates this message in all its advertising, packaging and in-store promotions.

Lifestyle

Lifestyle refers to how consumers spend their free time and what they spend their disposable income on. For example, if you were marketing a magazine that focused on health and fitness for men, then you would want to target men whose lifestyle was oriented around keeping fit, playing sport, being a member of a gym and going on activity holidays. This customer profile or visual image of your target audience would enable you to develop communication messages and strategies that would appeal to them.

The relevance of customer behaviour to customer communications

Having a basic understanding of the influences on consumer behaviour can help you identify or understand your target audience when drafting customer communications material, such as press releases or mailshots, and can help you to decide what to say at an internal meeting or a sales presentation or when planning sales promotion offers.

So, for example, if you are writing a mailshot with the objective of encouraging people who enjoy surfing as a hobby to book an activity holiday in a coastal area known to be good for surfing, your understanding of customer behaviour would help you convey your message. With your understanding of customer behaviour, you would know that people who enjoy surfing tend to buy magazines and equipment related to their hobby. That would probably lead you to renting a database from a specialist retailer or undertaking a joint project with a relevant magazine.

Your understanding of stages in the life cycle and social class would help you refine your knowledge of your audience. You would also have a mental picture of your audience's personality type, what motivates them and their attitudes/beliefs.

Your knowledge and research into this target market might lead you to identifying people who are aged 18 – 35, with a high disposable income, who are slightly rebellious and are keen on self-fulfilment, i.e. they want to improve their surfing ability and skill. They may also have strong beliefs about pollution and be keen to visit clean beaches.

By giving consideration to customer behaviour you would have a strong starting point for developing material to communicate with this customer group. It would provide you with a focus on your message and how you should frame it.

Communication objectives and the buying process

Consumers are generally recognized as going through a number of stages as they proceed from initially identifying that they have a need for something to the point of purchase (see Figure 4.4). Sometimes consumers can proceed through the various stages in a matter of seconds, when they buy on impulse. Typically, consumers are unaware that they are going through a process, it just happens subconsciously.

Using the AIDA model (see Figure 4.4) you can see that customer communication strategies and messages can be tailored to fit in with the buying process that a consumer might go through.

For example, when consumers purchase a car, they will go through various 'problem-solving' stages. Communication messages to prospective car buyers therefore need to be staged to match their progression through the decision-making process.

The buying process

Need recognition/problem solving

Consider the case of a young woman who decides she needs to buy a car as she has moved to a new job that is not convenient for public transport. She may also consider that she would like a car because all her friends have one. At this stage she has recognized she has a need.

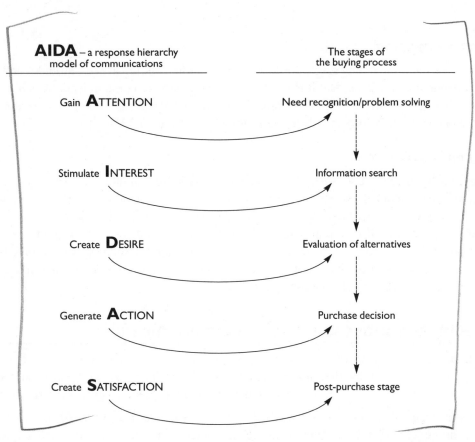

AIDA – a response hierarchy model of communications

Gain **A**TTENTION

Stimulate **I**NTEREST

Create **D**ESIRE

Generate **A**CTION

Create **S**ATISFACTION

The stages of the buying process

Need recognition/problem solving

Information search

Evaluation of alternatives

Purchase decision

Post-purchase stage

Figure 4.4 Relating communication objectives and messages to the stages of the buying process

As far as customer communications are concerned, car manufacturers may tailor their messages to young people to trigger their need/desire to own a car. They may appeal to a young person's desire to have freedom and a good time. Knowing the attitudes and lifestyle of the target audience is key to developing communications that have appeal. This corresponds to the *attention* stage of the AIDA model. Communications should be designed to grab the target market's attention at this stage.

Information search

The next stage after recognizing a need/problem would be for the young woman to search for information relating to the prospective purchase. At first she may be in a state of heightened attention, where she is more receptive than ever before to information about this product category. She will look at poster sites and magazine advertisements for cars with a new interest. She may listen to friends' conversations about their cars.

Next she is likely to undertake an active information search about different types of cars. Her sources of information may be friends/family and memories she has about various cars she has driven. She will also look at advertising, read consumer magazines and car programmes, talk to salespeople and even perhaps have a test drive.

The implications are that car manufacturers need to take advantage of every opportunity to communicate with prospective customers and have product information widely available in the media and in car showrooms. In addition, they need to have cultivated a strong brand image and other satisfied customers in the target market. This corresponds to the *interest* stage of the AIDA model, indicating that communications should be designed to create interest.

Evaluation of alternatives

After searching for information, she is likely to evaluate the various car models and makes that are on the market. The communications task for the car manufacturer at this point is to get the brand into the customer's 'choice set' and to want the product. This corresponds to the creating *desire* stage of the AIDA model. However, research should have identified what exactly the target market desires in terms of the product's main attributes. Having identified the most important attribute, it is essential that this *unique selling point* is communicated clearly to the target audience.

The purchase decision

Having got to the intention to buy stage, the consumer's personal circumstances, attitudes and beliefs will affect the purchase decision. But it is at this stage that customer communications, whether they are through advertising or the face to face approach from a salesperson, should move the consumer to the purchase decision. This corresponds to the action stage of the AIDA model.

Post-purchase evaluation

Having bought the product, consumers will either be satisfied or dissatisfied, depending on their expectation of the product and the product's actual performance. Even at this stage, communications with the consumer are important in order to foster a favourable opinion of the product. This is mainly because customers tend to discuss purchases with friends/family, and so word-of-mouth advertising becomes a powerful communications tool. In addition, a favourable memory of the product may influence a repeat purchase decision in future years. At this point it is possible to add a final communications stage to the AIDA model, creating *satisfaction*.

How the buying process relates to communications

If, for example, you were marketing nicotine supplements, such as, chewing gum, patches, tablets and fake cigarettes, as a healthy alternative to smoking and to help smokers give up, you could use your knowledge of the buying process to help you produce appropriate customer information.

Looking at the stages of the buying process in Figure 4.4. you see that you need information that would gain the target audience's attention, in the first stage of the buying process. This could be public relations activity to raise awareness of the health and economic reasons for giving up smoking.

The next stage is to stimulate interest when people are at the information search. Advertising in relevant magazines, newspapers and on television and radio could help at this stage to provide information about the different products that are on the market. The audience needs to know what products are available to help give up smoking and reduce the 'craving' for nicotine.

At the evaluation of alternatives stage, it is important to have plenty of material about your products at the places where purchases can be made. This could involve having leaflets on the customer counter in chemists or pharmacists. It could involve having free trial products available in health or consumer magazines or even at the point of sale. It is important at this stage that *your* product (rather than the competitors') is visible when potential customers are evaluating their options.

At the purchase decision stage, the call to action could be generated by sales promotion offers that just help tip the buyer's decision in your favour rather than the competition's. Ideally you would have a persuasive sales person to advocate the benefits of your products but this would probably not be possible in a consumer situation. However, you could target the retailers with appropriate information so that they recommended your brand in favour of other brands.

Activity 4.5

Using the AIDA model and the model that illustrates the buying process, complete the table below to indicate which promotional tool a car manufacturer might use at each stage.

The buying process	AIDA model of communication	Promotional tool
Need recognition	Gain attention	Poster sites
Information search	Stimulate interest	Talk to sales people
Evaluation of alternatives	Create desire	Unique selling points
Purchase decision	Generate action	Product details
Post-purchase decision	Create satisfaction	after sales/word of mouth

Summary

In this unit you have studied:

- The purpose of communication.
- How communication occurs.
- How and why barriers to communication occur.
- How to overcome communication barriers.
- How to plan customer communication activities.
- How customer behaviour and the buying process relate to customer communications.

Further study and examination preparation

Go to the end of the book and attempt question 4b) from the December 2000 examination paper.

Exam hint

Practise drawing a simple model of the communications process as this sometimes crops up as one part of a question on the communications process. Ensure you can apply your understanding of it to practical questions relating to communication barriers. Consider the variety of contexts where communications barriers occur, for example, in interviews, in advertising and in any written messages.

Be prepared to apply your understanding of the PASS framework to the development of communication activities, for example, writing a letter, a report or an advertisement.

Ensure you understand how the stages of the buying process and the AIDA response hierarchy of communications model relate to using different types of communication to target consumers effectively.

Objectives

In this unit you will:

- Appreciate how non-verbal cues can add to or detract from communications.
- Understand how to be a better listener.
- Build on your telephone communications knowledge.

By the end of this unit you will be able to:

- Use non-verbal communication effectively in a variety of situations.
- Be a better listener in all face to face interactions and when using the telephone.
- Make and receive telephone calls in a professional manner.
- Deliver effective presentations.

Study guide

This unit covers indicative content areas 2.3.3 and 2.3.7 of the syllabus. It provides you with a basic understanding of the role of non-verbal communication and active listening and extends your knowledge in the areas of telephone use and the delivery of presentations. It will take you a minimum of one hour to work through this unit and a further hour to complete the activities.

Study tip

Choose two countries that friends, family or colleagues have visited. Find out if there are any differences between them in relation to how non-verbal communication is interpreted.

Communication skills in marketing

Effective verbal, non-verbal and listening skills are essential in marketing as there are so many face to face and telephone interactions when you need to use good oral skills and be able to listen to verbal and watch for non-verbal cues.

Verbal communication

When speaking with customers, whether face to face or on the telephone, it is important that what you say is perceived as helpful, welcoming and appropriate to the situation. It is easy for a culture of internal orientation to become established in an organization. This is evident when staff become so focused on internal procedures that they do not respond appropriately to customer queries or requests. They may answer customers in such a way as to irritate or annoy customers because they feel that their custom is not valued.

Sentences that drive customers away

'I'm in the middle of something' or 'x's busy – could you call back?'

'There's nothing we can do – it's company policy.'

'We're closing – you'll have to come back tomorrow.'

'You'll have to give me your account number before I can help you.'

Tone – how you say things

The tone that you use can be either intentionally or unintentionally inappropriate and can infuriate customers. An apathetic, droning or listless tone of voice can convey the message that you don't care or are not interested in the customer and their problem/query. A rushed tone can make you sound impatient with the customer. In fact different tones of voice can change the meaning of the same words. By changing the inflection in your voice, you can say the words 'Your statement is ready now' in an angry way, sarcastically, apologetically, shyly and even in a humorous way.

Customers obviously want to be greeted or spoken to by someone whose tone of voice sounds interested, helpful and patient and, if appropriate, sounds apologetic and sincere if they have been treated unfairly or a mistake has been made.

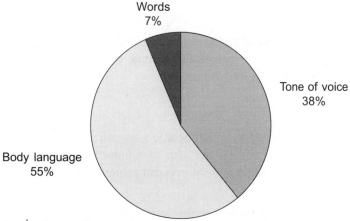

Figure 5.1 *How we receive messages*

Voice characteristics

Consider the expression 'Oh, that's just great'. A different message can be conveyed depending on how the voice is used to express the words. For example, said in a friendly tone of voice when someone has received something they are pleased with, it conveys a friendly, grateful message. If the same expression is shouted at someone, it could be a sarcastic message that in fact they are not pleased with something and things are not in fact 'great'. The same words said quietly in a deep and husky voice in an intimate situation would convey a completely different message. So the tone of voice, volume and pitch that are used can affect the message being conveyed.

Non-verbal communication skills

Non-verbal communication consists of:

- The body language you use, such as eye contact, facial expression, posture, gesture and physical space.
- The impression/atmosphere you create by your punctuality, hospitality, manners and personal appearance.
- The voice characteristics you adopt – tone, pitch and volume.

Non-verbal communication can convey messages without words or add meaning to whatever words are being used.

Eye contact

The look in someone's eyes can have a variety of meanings. In a romantic scene, the way an actor looks into the leading lady's eyes conveys a very different meaning to the way a person can stare in defiance or in a challenging way. In a business context, avoiding eye contact can convey disinterest or shiftiness but making positive eye contact while you are delivering a presentation shows that you are relating to and connecting with your audience.

Facial expression

Your facial expression and coloration can convey various meanings. A flushed face can indicate embarrassment, while the colour draining out of your face can indicate shock. Pursed lips can reveal your irritation at something, a frown can show disapproval and a smile can indicate happiness, approval or a welcome.

Posture

If you adopt an upright posture, it can show you are attentive and the opposite can show you are disinterested. If you were lounging in your seat when your Managing Director walks past, it could indicate that you do not respect the individual.

If you sit hunched up in your seat in a group, it could either indicate a lack of confidence or hostility.

Gesture

Your gestures might include a clenched fist to indicate anger, or a shrug of your shoulders to convey that you do not really care, or you may tap your fingers and, without knowing it, indicate that you are impatient with the person or the situation you are in.

Physical space

Sitting on a big chair behind a big desk so that people who enter your office have to sit on a lower chair opposite you, with the desk as a barrier, can communicate your authority and the level of formality you expect from others. Alternatively, you can achieve informality in meetings by using a horseshoe-shape layout.

Physical space also refers to the invisible line that surrounds people and is referred to as *personal space*. By breaching someone's personal space you can intimidate them and be perceived as over-bearing and insensitive.

An accepted move into someone's physical space in Britain is the friendly handshake. In Europe and other countries, kissing on the cheek may be acceptable. Different countries and cultures have different norms.

The impression/atmosphere

You can create a favourable impression in a business situation with a smart appearance in terms of your clothes and personal grooming. If you are punctual and use the appropriate greeting, for example a formal handshake, particularly when meeting new business contacts, this can influence whether you are seen to be acceptable by conforming to the norms of business behaviour.

Similarly, your hospitality can be judged not just by the words you express but if you are seen to be helpful and considerate to visitors. This can include taking their coats, checking that they are warm/cool enough, whether they need a drink and ensuring that your body language is positive, for example, smiling rather than looking at your watch as if you are in a hurry to get rid of them.

You can create a different impression with different types of body language. Consider the difference between a nervous cough, a bored sigh and a snigger. You can also use your body language to indicate that a meeting has finished by edging out of the door, getting up from your chair or gathering up your paperwork.

Using and interpreting non-verbal communication

You can use non-verbal communication to your advantage in meetings, interviews, negotiations and presentations to do the following:

- To create a positive impression.
- To show that you fit in with the culture of an organization.
- To convey enthusiasm and confidence.

By recognizing the messages intrinsic in the non-verbal communication displayed by others you can do the following:

- Recognize other people's true feelings.
- See potential problems.
- Read situations better and modify your message accordingly.

Negative body language

By using inappropriate body language you can make your customers angry. For example, if you give a customer a blank stare because you are preoccupied with a personal matter, the customer will probably feel that you are intentionally making them feel uncomfortable or that you are not interested in what they want.

By holding your head down and avoiding eye contact or being busy talking with colleagues, you will also convey the message that you are not interested in the customer.

Similarly, if you are talking with a customer and fidget in a distracted way, such as drumming your fingers on a desk or playing with a pen, this could also give the impression that you are not interested in dealing with the customer.

If a customer asks you a question and you shrug your shoulders, this could indicate that you do not know the answer, and that you do not care.

Positive body language

You can also use body language in a positive way. Simply by making eye contact with customers you show interest in them and what they have to say. A friendly smile can make you seem approachable, and simply by moving in the direction of a customer with a slight inclination of the head you can indicate that you are available to help, without actually saying anything.

International body language

Even though body language is common to everyone, there are still cultural differences and language subgroups which, if you operate in the global marketplace, you should learn.

Here are some examples of cultural body language differences:

- Southern Europeans and people from the Middle East stand close together when they are talking whereas people from Britain stand at arm's length and people from Oriental cultures stand even further apart. So don't be offended if someone from another culture appears to 'invade your personal space' or be backing away from you. Accept the difference and do not step back/forward (depending on the situation) as this could cause offence.

- Even if your gaze is meant to be sincere, avoid staring into a Japanese person's eyes. In Japan long stares are regarded as bad manners and people prefer to keep their gaze fixed on the neck.

- Never wink at anyone in Hong Kong as it is considered to be impolite.

- In the Middle East and Far East always present things to people with the right hand and do not use your left hand for eating as it is regarded as 'unclean'.

- Japanese people bow rather than shake hands.

- Nodding your head means "no" in parts of Greece, Yugoslavia and Turkey and shaking your head means "yes".

- Never show the sole of your shoe when you are in an Arab country as this is considered to be a grave insult. However, eye contact is important in the Arab world.

- Do not blow your nose at a business meeting with Japanese people and always present your business card with both hands.

Activity 5.2

You are responsible for internal communications within an import/export company with offices around the world. The firm has recently moved to team working within departments, which means that managers hold regular briefings with their teams. Write a memo to managers giving guidance on the importance of appropriate body language when briefing teams.

Listening skills

Good listening skills are important in marketing, simply because you will use them during meetings, interviews, negotiations, other people's presentations and when you are in a selling or briefing situation.

You need to work at your listening skills so that you possess all the necessary and relevant information, avoid wasting time and maintain good relations with both internal and external customers. Listening skills are particularly important if you are dealing with a customer who is trying to air grievances.

Many people imagine that listening is something that just happens. However, it is important that you distinguish between hearing and listening. *Hearing* is what might happen when you have the radio playing in the background whilst you do something else. *Listening* means engaging your mind and your memory, and you are active in selecting information, organizing, interpreting and storing it.

Listening skills are a vital part of customer care. By using effective listening skills you can obtain all the necessary and relevant information you need to find out what customers want or what they are not happy with. Listening is an active, not a passive activity. By checking what a customer has said and paraphrasing it, you can check that you have understood exactly what they mean. This avoids confusion and wasting time.

In many situations where you are dealing with unhappy customers, listening skills are very important to understand the problem. Often customers will go into great detail about a number of things that they are not happy with. However, it is usually one thing in particular that they want rectified. A good listener can select the most relevant information and decide what can be done about the situation.

Barriers to listening

Your thought processes operate four times faster than most people speak, and as a listener you may become bored and allow your mind to wander. You may regard what is being said as dull or irrelevant and close your mind, thus missing vital pieces of information.

You may have prejudices or fixed ideas about things and, if you are listening to something with which you disagree, you may react by pretending to listen but 'tuning out' to the message or becoming angry and distracted from the message that is being communicated.

You may be listening to someone who is talking about something technical that you do not understand, with the result that you stop following the conversation and may become too embarrassed to ask questions.

You may be listening to a great number of facts and figures and lose track of what is being said because of information overload.

How can we be better listeners?

1. Through active listening you can actively concentrate on what the person is saying and make a conscious attempt to understand. You could even make selective notes of the key points that have been made.

2. By being a patient listener and letting the person speak without interruption.

3. By being open-minded and guarding against prejudice and stereotyping so that you do not 'tune out' from the message.

4. By seeking clarification you can check with the person what they have said, paraphrasing in your own words.

5. By being sympathetic and showing empathy, particularly if you are listening to a complaint. You can demonstrate this with appropriate body language, such as making eye contact, nodding your head in agreement or making encouraging sounds/statements, such as, 'mm-hmm', 'that's interesting' and 'I understand'.

6. By being helpful, particularly in a complaint situation. You need to resist the temptation to argue and look for solutions to the problem instead.

Activity 5.3

A colleague has been promoted and will have to interview staff in future. He lacks interview experience and asks for guidance on listening in interviews. Suggest four ways in which he can be an effective listener in interviews.

Using the telephone

Advantages of using the telephone

With all the various methods of communication available to people, the telephone remains a popular tool for the following reasons:

- It provides quick, easy access over long distances (even if the recipient of the communication is not available it is usually possible to leave a message either with a colleague or on an answer machine/voicemail system).

- It is a relatively cheap means of communication.

- It is interactive (it provides a two-way form of communication).

- It is possible to protect the time of others by deciding whether or not to put the caller through.

- It is easier to hide your emotion on the telephone if you wish, because people cannot see your facial expression and body language.

- It is much easier to terminate a conversation with someone on the telephone than if you are in a face-to-face situation with them.

Disadvantages of using the telephone

- There is no permanent record of the communication and it is therefore difficult to verify the contents of a telephone call unless you record it.

- There is no opportunity to judge body language, which can make negotiation situations difficult. Equally, some customers may not feel confident doing business this way, particularly with important or complex financial decisions, such as buying mortgages or pensions.

- You can become involved in a 'telephone tennis' situation, where messages go back and forth and the caller never actually gets to speak to the person they want to communicate with.

- The truth of a situation, whether someone is actually in a meeting or not, is difficult to gauge.

Planning telephone calls

The most effective approach in using the telephone in terms of saving time and money is to adapt the PASS planning framework, to ensure you make effective and efficient telephone calls.

Purpose

Plan your call and be sure of the purpose of your call. This will guide you in deciding what you have to say. Have all the relevant information to hand, such as the correct telephone number. And, for example, if you were trying to arrange a meeting, you would need your diary. If you were ringing to query an invoice, you would need the original letter with the quote and the invoice that you received.

Audience

Consider who you are contacting, as this will influence what you say and how you say it.

Structure

In planning your message it may be helpful to make a checklist of points you wish to make as a reminder for use during the telephone conversation.

Style

When making a business call you may adopt a different style to the one you use for personal calls. The style you adopt is made up of the words you use, the way you order sentences, your pronunciation and your tone.

You may indeed adopt a telephone voice that close friends and family do not recognize. You do not need to do this but you should communicate in a clear, organized and succinct way. You may need to spell out words, using other words to indicate the letter you mean where there may be confusion. For example, you may say 'F' for foxtrot, not 'S' for sierra to distinguish like-sounding letters. You may also group numbers together, if you are communicating a telephone number or reference number of some sort. For example, you may read out a telephone number as zero, one, six, one, and then pause before reading out the rest of the number.

In business calls you should avoid slang or over-familiar words, such as 'OK', 'yeah', 'ta ra then'.

You should be confident when making a business telephone call, or at least sound confident. One of the advantages of telephones (at least those that are not videophones) is that the recipient of the call cannot see you. When someone is slightly nervous on the telephone, they sound hurried and use careless speech. Consequently you should speak slightly more slowly than your usual pace. This is also important because the recipient of the call cannot lip read, so it is important that you pronounce words clearly.

The tone of voice you use in telephone conversations is very important, as your body language cannot be seen. (See Figure 5.1.) You can overcome the barrier of not being seen by adopting the tone of voice that is relevant to the message being communicated. (See *Voice characteristics* on page 58.) You should also vary the tone of voice you use, as a relentless monotone can give the impression either that you are boring or that you are bored with the conversation.

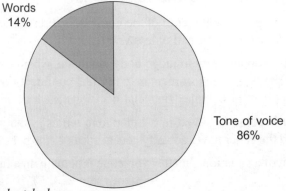

Words 14%

Tone of voice 86%

Figure 5.2 How we receive messages by telephone

Guidelines for making effective telephone calls

Once you get through, greet the person who answers, identify yourself, your company and ask for the person you wish to speak to. At this point you may have to give a brief outline of the purpose of your call.

Having made sure that you are speaking to the right person, make your call in a courteous, clear and concise way. You should be prepared for the person you need to speak to not being available and be able to give a shortened version of the message you wish to communicate. Alternatively, if it is not appropriate to précis your message, you should politely ask for the recipient of the call to ring you back.

Guidelines for receiving calls

Organizations have their own procedures for answering the telephone, so you will find that this section provides some guidelines which may have to be amended to fit in with your own organization's system.

Whatever procedures are set down for staff to follow, it is essential that a friendly and efficient image be conveyed to anyone who contacts the organization.

Callers should not be left waiting while the telephone rings. Some organizations stipulate how quickly the telephone should be answered. It is inappropriate for a caller to be left waiting for several minutes while information is being retrieved. It is equally unacceptable for a caller to be passed around several departments or to be made to feel as if they are an unwelcome interruption. Good telephone technique is vital for the maintenance of good public relations.

Putting a customer on hold

Ideally, customers should not be left hanging on the line. If you consider it is going to take some time to get the right person on the line, it is better to take down the relevant details so that the right person can contact the caller later. If, however, you do need to put the customer on hold, then you should ask for their permission first and briefly tell them why you need to do this. If you have been finding out information while the caller was put on hold and you go back to them, it is only good manners to thank them for holding.

Callers are rarely asked if they mind being put on hold. What usually happens is that when callers draw breath at the end of a sentence, they are summarily sent to telephone limbo and forced to listen to music, while the person on the other end of the line tries to transfer them or consults their files.

Transferring a call

Customers become intolerant when they are transferred over and over again, and particularly when they have to explain their situation several times.

The best approach, if it is possible to do so, is to explain why the call needs to be transferred and to whom. You should also ask if the customer minds being transferred. Before you hang up, make sure there is someone to pick up the call. Before the customer talks to the person they have been transferred to, you should briefly outline the nature of the call, so that the caller does not have to repeat details again.

Taking messages

It is very important to get the details of a message right first time. This is where your listening skills will be very useful. It will mean taking the time to clarify the caller's name, company, telephone number, the nature of the call and the action required.

You need, therefore, the right equipment, such as a pen and message notepad, to hand. Most organizations have pre-printed pads where you complete the relevant boxes with a tick to indicate the action required. Always print your name on the message pad so that the recipient of the message can come back to you if they need to clarify any details.

Answering calls

The circumstances may vary:

- *Answering your telephone extension where calls come in through a switchboard operator.* The caller knows the company they have reached and you only need identify yourself by giving your name. For example: 'Good morning Andrew Kelly speaking, how can I help?'

- *Answering the telephone on behalf of a department.* You could give your name and the name of the department. For example: 'Good morning, Technical Support, Andrew speaking, how can I help you?'

- *Answering the telephone on behalf of the company.* The caller needs to be given the company name and perhaps your name. For example: 'Good morning, Pine Box Productions, how may I help you?'

The greeting should be used to demonstrate friendliness. The telephone should be answered within a certain number of rings; three to five is normal.

You need to be prepared with the right equipment so that you can deal with the enquiry or instructions given to you during the telephone conversation. This will vary depending on your circumstances but usually comprises at the very least: pen, message pad, company extension list, notepad and diary.

General guidelines for using the telephone

- Answer the telephone promptly.
- Smile when you first pick up the telephone.
- Begin with an appropriate greeting.
- Identify yourself/your department or the organization.
- Establish the caller's needs.
- Speak clearly.
- Speak slowly.
- Avoid jargon.
- Be courteous.
- Be concise.
- Take messages accurately and pass them to the appropriate person where necessary.
- Listen carefully and do not interrupt the customer.
- Show empathy and understanding.
- If dealing with an angry customer, do not argue with the caller or offer lame excuses.
- If you undertake to do something for a customer during a telephone conversation, do it, don't just hope they won't come back.
- Give the caller a name, department or extension number to enable them to pursue the matter if they need to call back at a later date/ time.
- End the call effectively so that the caller knows what action is to be taken, what has been agreed or when someone will come back to them.
- Close the call politely with an appropriate greeting and thank the caller for calling.

Conference calls

The technology exists to have several different people in different locations talking to each other at the same time. While these conversations lack the impact of a face to face meeting, they can be a convenient and relatively inexpensive method of getting people together for instant feedback.

However, it can be difficult to avoid situations where everyone speaks at once and the conversation flow is often inhibited by the lack of non-verbal cues.

Activity 5.4

Effective use of telephones

You are the Marketing Manager for a chain of hotels. Write a memo for circulation to all reception staff about the effective use of telephones. In particular, you should focus on the appropriate way to deal with incoming calls, the transfer of calls and message taking.

Presentation skills

Types of presentations

For most marketers it is an inevitable part of their professional career to give speeches or presentations. In the early part of your career you could be asked to give an informal briefing to colleagues on a recent training course or a demonstration on how a piece of equipment works. As you become more established you may find yourself going through the results of a campaign to a group of managers, giving colleagues a progress update on a project, putting forward your proposals to a client or even delivering a sales pitch.

Planning an effective speech or presentation

As with all communications, the PASS framework is a relevant planning framework and will help you plan the content and delivery of your presentation.

Purpose

The planning of the presentation begins with objectives. Consider the purpose of the presentation, why you are delivering it and what you hope to achieve. At the end of the presentation you should be able to determine if you have achieved your objectives.

Audience

To help you decide on the message you want to deliver and how you should deliver it, you should consider who is your intended audience. Consider what their needs are in terms of what they need to know, how long you have with them, the size of the group and the type of room they will be in.

Structure

Knowing what your purpose is and what your audience's requirements are will help you decide on the structure of your presentation. You should decide on the key points, the order that they should go in and how you will link the material together.

Style

To determine the style of the presentation you will have to decide the level of formality and involvement that is appropriate. For a small group you could deliver a presentation on a complex matter in a fairly informal way with a high level of participation from the audience. You also need to decide if you are going to use visual aids.

Composing the message

Decide what you are going to say, having first, if necessary, researched your topic. List the points you *could* include and select those that you *must* include. Allocate time to each point and develop a sequence.

You should try to make your presentation conversational rather than trying to learn hundreds of words off by heart. One way could be to write out your talk in longhand, reduce it to shorthand notes and reduce that to crib cards. Your delivery should then be based on the crib cards.

Another approach is to imagine that your audience will get your message from a picture. Once you have an outline picture, then you can take people into the detail by creating a series of smaller pictures by breaking down the argument more simply.

To develop this approach you could use a mind map. The idea is that you draw a circle with your topic heading in it and from that draw branches that are labelled with four or five key areas. Then draw a branch off each of these branches to indicate other detailed points. For example, if you were giving a presentation about the opening of a DIY store your mind map might look like the diagram in Figure 5.3. You could then use prompt cards to remind you of the key areas and sub-points from your mind map.

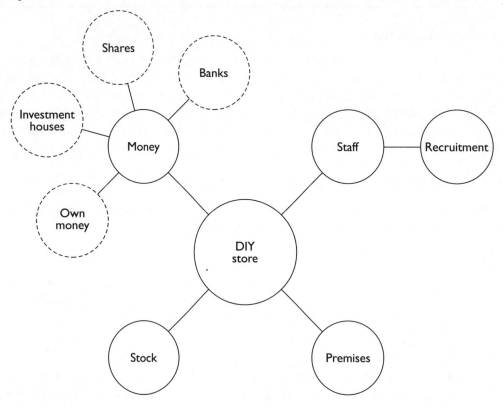

Figure 5.3 *Example of a mind map*

Whatever method you use to compose the content of your message, you should plan your talk so that it has a beginning, a middle and an end. A well-known quote that describes this approach is as follows: 'Tell them what you are going to tell them, then tell them, then tell them what you told them.'

Preparing for the talk

You should ensure that you have prepared the stage management aspect of the presentation. If it is a large, organized conference that you are speaking at, then this will be done for you. If not, then you need to check the following:

- The layout of the chairs and tables (for a small group a horseshoe shape is often better than lining people in rows).
- That there are enough chairs and tables for the audience.
- That you will be visible from where you are going to stand.
- That there is a lectern or table for your paperwork.
- That the equipment for visual aids works.
- That the lighting is adequate.
- That the room is tidy and has adequate heating/ventilation.

Delivering the talk

A good presentation can be broken down into message, body language and voice. According to Eileen Sheridan in an article in *The Guardian (2001))*, 93 per cent of our communication with others is non-verbal. What you actually say makes up only 7 per cent of the picture.

Body language

The nerves that some people feel before delivering a presentation are usually connected with having to stand up in front of an audience that is totally focused on you. You should try not to be seen to be nervous by having control of your body language. You should aim to do the following:

- Don't look tense – relax your jaw muscles and smile (be careful if you are delivering bad news, though).
- Stand upright with your shoulders relaxed.
- Do not fold your arms across your chest.
- Don't hunch up/bend your head down to read from your notes – just refer to them occasionally.
- Maintain eye contact with the entire group – don't stare at one individual or one section of the group. This can be difficult if you arrange the group in a horseshoe shape.
- Avoid gesticulating wildly or other distracting mannerisms, such as jangling change in your pocket or scratching.

Voice

Except in specific circumstances where you might need to use an authoritative tone, you would normally use a friendly tone to deliver a presentation.

You should consider practising your talk to calculate how long it takes you to get through it. One problem to avoid is an attack of nerves that tempts you into the 'racehorse' syndrome of getting your head down and charging through to the end of the presentation. Take care to consciously slow yourself down.

You can use pauses not only to slow down the pace but also to place emphasis on important points. You also need to give people time to absorb the information in any visual aids you use.

Try to vary the pitch of your voice. Another technique for slowing yourself down is to modulate your voice. If you make your voice rise and fall, as you do when you tell a joke or a story to others, you are less likely to end up with a fast monotone that sends the audience to sleep. This will enable you to put emphasis on certain words or parts of your speech. You also need to sound energetic and enthusiastic to convince people that you are worth listening to.

Use of visual aids and technology

Visual aids, such as overhead projector slides or acetates, pictures, slides of still photography or flip charts, can be used to give variety and impact to a presentation, particularly when you are presenting lists or numerical information. However, they should be produced to a high standard or they can give rise to a negative reaction.

If you are using visual aids, you should be careful how you use them. Check that you have pens to use on the flip chart or that the stand works. Check that you can focus the overhead projector. Always check that all the audience can see visual aids.

When you use visual aids, do not stand in front of them and obstruct the audience's view. Do not read from them verbatim – it is better to talk around the issues that the visual aid encapsulates. When you have finished with the topic, remove the visual aid so that it does not distract the audience.

We work in an age of specialized software such as Powerpoint, video walls and a plethora of acoustic equipment that can enhance a presentation. Used sensibly, these tools can bring clarity and add impact to a presentation. But it is essential to remember that technology is an aid, not a crutch. Unlike a brief television commercial, a successful speech is rarely a triumph of style over content. If you do not get the words right, your audience will quickly lose interest.

Tutor day task	We need 7 groups - so if 20 people could be 6 groups of 3 and 1 group of 4.
In your group analyze the candidate answer ▌ to identify the positive & negative aspects ▌ to suggest suitable teaching strategies to overcome common problems shown in answer	You have 30 minutes to look at a question, so if you are group 1a, analyse the candidate's answer to q1a on last session's paper and identify the positive and negative aspects of the answer and suggest suitable teaching strategies to overcome the problems shown in the answer. I'd like to stress that these are fairly common answers ... Could you use flip chart paper to put down your main points and appoint one person to be scribe and another to present on behalf of your group. After the half hour is up we will come back for a plenary session to see what all the groups have to say.

Figure 5.4 A slide and the speaker's notes

The use of video walls at conferences is growing as companies want their brands and the people speaking on their behalf to appear larger than life. Unfortunately for presenters, it means that every nervous lick of the lips and gravy stain can be seen in close-up. They can also have an unfortunate effect on people's clothing. Clothing with big patterns, very bright colours and glittering jewellery can blur and produce a strobe effect. The presenter can also blend into the background if the colour of their clothing is the same as the background.

Always assume that the technology you plan to use for your presentation is going to fail. If your speech does not stand up on its own without the technology, you should question whether the script is good enough.

Verbal skills

To help you decide on how you should deliver your talk, you should consider how people listen and take in information. People tend to take in information at the beginning and at the end and only snippets throughout.

So it is a good idea to pepper a presentation with devices that bring the audience back to you. You can do this with metaphors or analogies (comparing something to something else that everyone is famil-iar with; for example, the business was an acorn but has now grown into an oak tree) and anecdotes or examples (stories from real life). These can be very effective tools, but do not overuse them or you might confuse your audience.

As a general rule, use punchy sentences and avoid unnecessary jargon. Beware of jokes. They can be hard to carry off as they require excellent timing. Also, you risk offending your audience.

You need to connect with your audience, so use vocabulary that fits in with them. You can add emphasis by using the following devices:

- Repetition, for example, 'This campaign has increased our turnover by £500,000 – that's right, half a million pounds!'.

- Rhetorical questions, for example, 'You may ask me what are we going to do about it but I am asking you "What are you going to do about it . . .?"'.

- Quotations, for example, 'As Martin Luther King said: "I have a dream . . ."'.

- Statistical evidence, 'A dissatisfied customer tells nine other people about their dissatisfac-tion . . .'.

Questions and feedback

The great advantage of presentations is that they are interactive. You can sense how your message is going down with your audience and even get instant feedback. However, you may find it very disrup-tive to handle questions during your presentation. If this is the case, you should say that you would be happy to answer questions at the end. You should then leave time at the end for questions and com-ments from the audience.

Techniques for handling questions/feedback

- Repeat any questions so that the audience can hear and be involved in this part of the session.

- If the question or comment is relevant, then either answer the question directly or thank the person for their contribution.

- If the question is rambling or unclear, try to clarify and retrieve one simple question from the narrative.

- If the question is irrelevant, you could say that it is outside the scope of the presentation.

- If the question is hostile or you don't agree with the points made, accept as much as you can of the points made but do not get drawn into a long argument.

- If you cannot answer the question, admit that you cannot but enlist the help of the audience, or you could say that you will get back to the person once you have had a chance to look into the matter.

Evaluating objectives

At the end of the presentation, consider whether you persuaded people to do something or make a decision about something, or did you sell something, clarify something, change people's minds about something, inspire people to think about something in a different way – in other words, did you achieve your objectives?

Activity 5.5

You have been short-listed for the post of Communications Manager at a privatized electricity company. As part of the selection process you have been asked to do a presentation on the importance of effective internal marketing and internal communications to the success of the organization. Draw on your experience to explain how some organizations improve their internal communication systems. Draft the notes that will form the basis of your presentation.

Summary

In this unit you have studied:

- The role of communication skills in marketing.
- How to use and interpret non-verbal communication skills effectively.
- How to be a good listener.
- Why the telephone is an important marketing tool and how to use it appropriately.
- How to deliver dynamic presentations.

Further study and examination preparation

Go to the end of the book and attempt question 2a) and 5bi) from the June 2000 examination paper and question 4a) from the December 2000 paper.

Exam hint

Do not rote-learn the body language section but be prepared to apply your understanding of it in questions that are set in a variety of contexts, such as managing staff, in interviews, dealing with customers and delivering presentations.

Be prepared to answer questions on the use of listening, telephone use and presentations that apply your knowledge to marketing situations.

Objectives

In this unit you will:

- Develop your understanding of why meetings take place.
- Look at the different types of meetings that occur.
- See how to manage meetings effectively.
- Become familiar with meetings terminology.
- Examine meetings documentation.
- Understand the role of interviews and negotiations in communicating with others.
- Appreciate the different stages of interviews and negotiations.
- Recognize different negotiation techniques.

By the end of this unit you will be able to:

- Manage and lead meetings effectively.
- Prepare appropriate meetings documentation.
- Lead and contribute to interviews and negotiations.
- Demonstrate good questioning skills.
- Demonstrate appropriate interpersonal behaviour in negotiations.

Study guide

This unit covers indicative content area 2.3.6 and 2.3.7. The first part of the unit develops your understanding of meetings, how to lead them effectively and the documentation associated with them. The second part of the unit covers the topic of communicating in interviews and negotiations. The unit will take one hour to read and a further two hours to complete the activities.

Study tip

Use any opportunities at work where you attend meetings to take notes on how they are managed and how people interact. Develop your skills at meetings by asking a colleague or supervisor to evaluate how you lead and contribute to meetings.

If, in your current position you do not take part in interviews or negotiations, you could ask your line manager to arrange for you to sit in on an interview or negotiation so that you can evaluate the process and its effectiveness.

Meetings

Meetings are an assembly of people for the purpose of discussion. They occur face-to-face or remotely by using satellite communications or video conferencing. Meetings are an extremely useful means of communication but while they present good opportunities for obtaining immediate verbal feedback and demonstrating or observing non-verbal feedback, they can present problems if they are not organised and planned for.

The advantages of meetings are that information can be exchanged and an immediate response can be had. Any feedback or questions can be dealt with immediately. With face-to-face meetings, body language and tone of voice are very much evident and people can interpret these signs or use them to add to the communication process. Sometimes non-verbal communication and tone of voice can be distorted when using communications technology to have a meeting.

Meetings can be informative, can help build teams and can improve motivation. Meetings are also a good way to convey sensitive and confidential information.

However, if people have to attend too many meetings and/or attend meetings that are badly organised and do not achieve their objectives, they can be jaded by their experience and will resent the time spent, which they may feel they could have used more productively.

Reasons for meeting

In marketing meetings can be used to do the following:

- Reach decisions after discussion.
- Convey information, e.g. to update people about the progress of a project.
- Obtain formal approval of decisions or make group decisions.
- Exchange of ideas, e.g. about how a campaign should be developed.
- Discuss marketing plans.
- Review an advertising campaign.
- Plan corporate events.
- Review the progress of new product development projects.

Types of meeting

Meetings range from informal discussions to formal meetings and can be about any number of matters.

Informal meetings

Informal meetings could just comprise two or more colleagues talking in the course of their work or as they go about their business but can be extremely fruitful in terms of conveying information and even making decisions and coordinating work.

Examples of informal meetings:

- Team briefings or departmental meetings.
- Meetings with clients to present work or provide an update on work.
- Meetings with prospective clients.
- Task group meetings to plan projects, decide on who does what and make decisions.

Formal meetings

In formal meetings people are appointed to specific roles, such as chairperson and secretary, follow a particular procedure for conducting the meetings and use specific terminology about the proceedings. Formal meetings have a written agenda which participants follow, involve circulating minutes after the meeting as a record of what has occurred and tend to have a formal seating arrangement with the Chairperson at the top of the table.

Examples of formal meetings:

- Company board meetings or annual general meetings (AGMs).
- Large union meetings.
- Social club meetings with a constitution, e.g. a tennis club.
- Branch membership meeting, e.g. local branch of CIM.

Managing meetings

Meetings require careful planning and organisation. Problems can occur if people arrive at a meeting with different objectives about what is to be achieved. If the meeting is not well organised and run to time, time can be wasted and people can become demotivated, even hostile. Information should be clearly conveyed before, during and after the meeting so that there are no misunderstandings. If contributions to the meeting are not handled properly so that everyone has a chance to contribute but the discussion is kept within the parameters of the agenda, then it lead to aimless discussion and/or a small minority dominating the meeting.

There are several ways to ensure that a meeting goes well:

- Consider whether a meeting really needs to be held.

- Establish clear objectives.

- Draw up a list of relevant participants and invite them to attend.

- You may need to invite participants to provide you with items for discussion and/or draft a list of matters to be discussed in the form of an agenda.

- Ensure participants are clear about the following: the meeting's purpose, the date, start and finish time and venue.

- Distribute the agenda (you will read more about this later in the unit) and any additional material to participants in advance of the meeting.

- Decide who will lead or chair the meeting.

- Decide who will keep a record of proceedings.

- Visit the venue before the meeting to check the layout and facilities.

- Ensure that the meeting starts and finishes on time.

- Ensure that there are no interruptions.

- The chairperson should follow the agenda and take control of any conflict in the meeting.

- The chairperson should summarise the key points or decisions made as the meeting progresses and keep the meeting moving from item to item.

- The chairperson should also notice when people want to contribute and encourage quieter participants to contribute.

- The chairperson should put any decisions to the vote.

- The meeting should be closed formally to ensure that participants know that it has ended.

- After the meeting accurate and impartial minutes should be circulated to participants and other relevant people.

Activity 6.1

In your absence your colleague is to lead a product development meeting to check the progress review of product x. Your colleague, who is a very quiet person has asked for some guidance on how best to lead this informal project meeting.

Constituting a formal meeting

A formal meeting is only properly constituted if it is convened (called) according to a set of regulations (statutory or otherwise). The main issues are as follows:

1. A meeting must have a chairperson who oversees its conduct and progression.

2. A meeting must have a quorum, i.e. a minimum number of persons who are physically present, as stated in the regulations.

Formal meetings are completely different from informal meetings in their organization and procedure. A set of strict rules and conventions is followed and formal documents are required before the meeting takes place.

Formal meetings procedure

Formal meetings are usually organised according to specific procedures and conventions.

Motions

A motion is a proposal put before the meeting in order that it can be discussed and relevant decisions made. However, not all items on an agenda are proposals which must be voted on. An agenda item may just be information that needs to be communicated to the rest of the meeting. If the motion is approved or *carried* by the meeting, it then becomes a *resolution* or decision. The procedure for dealing with a motion means that the proposer must speak first on the matter, followed by the seconder. Discussion against the motion usually follows, but the *right of reply* means that the mover (person speaking for the motion) has the last say before the item is put to the vote.

Rules concerning motions mean that they should be feasible and not *ultra vires* i.e. outside the power or scope of the meeting. Motions need to be worded so that ambiguities do not exist. For example, a motion stating 'That a ban on smoking be introduced' is too vague because it does not state exactly where the ban extends to and when it should take effect.

A motion may be put forward to the meeting and, although participants or members of the meeting may agree with it in principle, they may want to change the wording slightly so that it is more precise. Alternatively they may believe that the fine detail of the proposal should be changed. If this is the case then an *amendment* or change may be put forward. If it is seconded the amendment will be voted on. There may well be several amendments and these will all need to be voted upon.

If enough people vote for an amendment, it becomes a substantive motion. At this point it is voted on again and becomes a resolution if it is carried. Even then a resolution can be changed slightly by the inclusion of extra words, referred to as an *addendum* and a *rider*.

Procedural motions can be made and are aimed at making meetings more effective. So if a speech is going on too long, the chairperson may use the procedural motion 'That the question be now put' to hurry business along.

If the motion 'That the meeting proceed to the next item of business' is carried, the meeting stops discussion on that item and goes on to the next item on the agenda. Often this happens because agreement on the subject seems unlikely and so it seems better for the matter to be left for the present.

An item on the agenda can be postponed with the motion 'That the discussion be adjourned' and if it is adjourned 'sine die', no date for when the matter should be discussed again is specified.

Points of order

Points of order are interruptions in the meeting, voiced when participants feel that the regulations are not being adhered to. For example:

- The meeting is not *quorate* – there are not enough people present as stipulated in the rules to form a quorum.

- The speaker is not *speaking to the agenda* – that the item being discussed is not on the agenda.

- The subject is *ultra vires* – outside the powers of the meeting.

- The speaker should *address the chair* – all remarks should be addressed to the chairperson rather than allow a situation where discussion occurs between other participants at the meeting.

Voting

Decisions are made through voting, usually by a show of hands (open voting), or by a general voice vote, where it is judged whether yes or no is said the loudest or even by secret ballot.

The results of voting may be declared in the following way:

- Passed *unanimously* – everyone voted in favour.
- Passed *nem con* – no one voted against but only a few have voted for the proposal with the majority abstaining.
- *Lost* – the majority voted against.
- *Casting vote* – the chairperson is given an additional vote to break the deadlock of an equal number voting for and against a proposal.

Terminology of meetings

There are a number of vocabulary items that are often exclusive to meetings, such as the following:

- *Proposer* – speaks about the statement/argument that they have proposed.
- *Seconder* – supports the proposal.
- *Quorum* – the minimum number of people that must be present at a meeting.
- *Motion* – a proposal to be considered at the meeting.
- *Amendment* – to the proposal which will have to be voted for and, if carried, accepted.
- *Collective responsibility* – a rule by which all participants agree to be bound by a decision.
- *Adjourn* – this means that a meeting will be held over to another time or date.
- *Constitution* – a set of rules by which the members of a group are expected to abide.
- *Ex officio* – an individual given rights and powers by reason of the position he or she holds.
- *Mover* – an individual who speaks on behalf of a motion.
- *Opposer* – an individual who speaks against a motion.
- *Point of order* – drawing attention to the breach of rules or procedures.
- *Proxy* – this means on behalf of another person, e.g. proxy vote.
- *Resolution* – a motion that has been carried.

Meeting documents

The main meetings documentation comprise: the notice, the agenda and the minutes. These are used for formal meetings and sometimes also for informal meetings.

The notice

The notice will be prepared and circulated before the date of the meeting, according to the constitution of the company and any other regulations with which the organization may have to comply.

If a large number of participants are to attend, it may be impractical to communicate with them all individually, therefore notices of the meeting may be placed on notice boards as a main channel of communication, especially if these are regularly accessed by potential participants.

Where individuals can be contacted directly, the following channels of written communication may be used:

1. An invitation printed on a card or note.
2. An internal memorandum.
3. A personal letter.

If the agenda (described below) is already drawn up and available for circulation, it is usually included with the notice to enable the participants to study its content before the meeting.

The minutes of the last meeting (also described below) may be attached to the notice so that any issues in respect to the points made can be stated in advance of the meeting, especially if the minutes of the previous meeting have to be approved as a matter of procedure. Figures 6.1 and 6.2 give examples of notices.

NOTICE OF ANNUAL GENERAL MEETING

Notice is hereby given that the Annual General Meeting of Anyone Limited will be held at The Anyplace Hotel, Anywhere Road, Anywhere on 10 June 200X at 10.30 am for the following purposes:

1. To receive and adopt the Reports of the Directors and Auditors and the Accounts for the period ended 31 March 200X.
2. To declare a final dividend.
3. To re-elect Mr J Sugree as Managing Director of the company.
4. To transact any other business.

By order of the Board
Mr B Keating
Company Secretary

Figure 6.1 *Notice of a formal AGM*

MEMORANDUM

TO: The Marketing Task Group.

FROM: Roy Keane

DATE: 19 September 200X

The next Marketing meeting will take place on Thursday 25 September 200X at 2.30 pm in the board room at head office.
As usual the meeting will be reviewing current marketing projects and will also be discussing matters relating to developing the company's marketing plan, so please forward dates to me in advance of the meeting which indicate when you can be away from normal office duties for a 3 days block. In addition, if you have any other items you would like putting on the agenda please contact me on 0161 448 7212 no later than Monday 21 October 200X.

Figure 6.2 *Notice for an internal meeting.*

The agenda

This is the schedule of 'things to be done', i.e. the subjects to be discussed, which is prepared by the secretary after having enabled all participants to propose items for the agenda. Although an agenda is not an obligation for the conduct of a meeting, it is a useful tool for guiding the discussion and ensuring that the full scope of the meeting is covered.

Once the agenda has been set, it is then discussed with the chairperson in terms of suitability of subject matter and order of items which the meeting will follow.

The agenda will then be distributed to all the participants so that they are aware of the subject matter of the forthcoming meeting and the order of proceedings, together with any supplementary material that needs to be considered and the minutes of the last meeting. This communication process enables the participants to prepare themselves in advance and also to decide whether their presence is necessary for the full duration of the meeting.

Copies of the agenda are either sent out with the notice of the meeting or distributed to participants as they arrive at the designated location.

A special agenda is prepared for the chairperson, which contains more details than the document circulated to the participants and the names of any particular participants that will be making a special contribution (e.g. presenting a report), with space for the chairperson to make notes on the meeting for personal reference.

Agendas normally contain the following items:

1. Apologies for absence – announced by the chairperson once the meeting has been officially opened and the time and date recorded by the secretary.

2. Minutes of the previous meeting – the chairperson will ask members whether the minutes represent an accurate record of the previous meeting and if so, he/she will sign them as such.

3. Matters arising is an opportunity for participants to declare views or report back on developments since the last meeting.

4. Correspondence from parties outside the meeting may be read and considered.

5. The main agenda items are then opened and discussed in turn, with the chair trying to keep the meeting moving ahead (particularly if a time constraint was imposed at the start) and aiming to reach a consensus on the main points. The types of items discussed will reflect the nature of the meeting, which may be to produce plans, solve organizational problems, deliver reports or feedback, debate proposals or to reach decisions.

6. Any other business (AOB) is stated and discussed. If an item is of relevance to the general discussion or appropriate for the meeting, it may be raised under this section. If the issue is considered unimportant or unsuitable for the present meeting, it may be carried over to another or a separate meeting called.

7. Date of the next meeting is discussed and agreed and the chairperson closes the meeting by thanking the participants for attending the meeting.

Finally, agendas will vary from meeting to meeting and may be a reflection of the following:

- Degree of formality required for the meeting, which will determine the style of layout in the agenda and state the procedures to be followed.

- Length of the meeting, which will be determined by:

  - The number of subjects to be discussed.

  - The complexity of the subject matter.

Snack Attack

The Quality Sandwich Delivery Service

MARKETING MEETING

AGENDA

19 September 200X at 2.30 pm
in the boardroom at head office.

1. Apologies for absence.
2. Minutes of the last meeting.
3. Matters arising.
4. Evaluation of radio advertising campaign.
5. Update of database software.
6. Discuss product development for Winter hot soup range.
7. Motion: 'That the company purchases two new delivery vans before the Christmas period'. Proposed: Paul Rapaporte Seconded: David Surinam
8. Company Marketing Plan Arrangements
9. Any other business.
10. Date of next meeting.

Figure 6.3 *An agenda*

The *chairperson's agenda* is different to the one described above in two respects:

1. Each item on the agenda has additional notes which are pertinent to the discussion that will take place in the meeting and for which the chairperson should be suitably prepared with background information or sensitivity in handling material presented and discussed or points raised.

2. A right-hand margin, which is wide enough for the chairperson to make notes during the meeting, is incorporated into the layout of his/ her personal agenda.

The *duties of the chairperson* are as follows:

1. Keep the meeting to the agenda and in good order so that the business can proceed smoothly.

2. Be unbiased and fair in allowing the members and participants to make their contribution without taking too much of the meeting's time.

3. Allow only one person at a time to address the meeting and take a decision on the sequence of speakers if more than one wishes to make a contribution.

4. Ensure that all issues and points of debate are addressed to the chairperson, thereby avoiding the deterioration of the meeting into fragmented groups or arguments.

5. Conduct the voting if this is deemed necessary during the meeting or at its conclusion.

6. Keep an overall sense of the meeting according to the agenda and the logic of the discussion.

The minutes

These are a written record of the transactions that took place and should be as accurate as possible, reflecting the duration and general tone of the meeting.

The minutes are usually taken by the secretary, who should have them typed and distributed as quickly as possible after the meeting as they are an important channel of communication and source of reference.

Research and Development Group
Minutes

Minutes of the Meeting held in the 'Panelled Room' at 'Building Headquarters', Bromley, Kent on October 15th 20XX at 4 pm.

Present: T. Stones (Chair), A. Peters (Secretary), L. Simons, K. Andrews, J. Clarke

1 Apologies for absence.
   Apologies for absence were received from J. Thyme, L. Young and P. Ankers.

2 Minutes of the last meeting.
   The minutes of the last meeting were taken as read and signed as a true record.

3 Matters arising.
   Further to item 2, the Chairman has received a report of the new innovation currently in prototype stage and will circulate a copy to all members before the next meeting.

4 Proposal to cut the budget by £1 million to be phased in over a period of three years.
   All members present argued for a strong statement to be issued to the M.D. on the consequences for new and existing projects as a result of this budget cut and seek clarification if jobs are also to be lost in this process.

5 New Product Development.
   Len Simons and Ken Andrews presented a visual report on the new products to be commercialized by the end of the financial year.

6 AOB.
   Jane Clarke raised the need for a new laser printer. Angela Peters will receive literature and circulate this to members of the group before the next meeting.

7 Date of next meeting.
   The next meeting of the R&D group was scheduled for January 10th 20XX at Building H.Q.

   Signed X   T. Stones (Chair) Director R&D. Date Nov. 10th 20XX

Figure 6.4 *Resolution minutes*

The style or format used to present them, i.e. narrative or structured in some way, should reflect the type of meeting and needs of the participants.

There are three types of minutes:

1. *Resolution minutes* – these are minutes where only the resolutions are recorded and therefore do not reflect the tone of the meeting or specific points made leading to the resolution.

2. *Narrative minutes* – these are a brief summary of the meeting which led up to the resolution (decisions) and include the comments made by the participants which have gone on record as their judgement of the arguments preceding the resolution.

3. *Action minutes* – these minutes indicate the specific courses of action that need to be taken as a result of the resolutions made in the course of the meeting and the individuals responsible for the action items.

ITEM 7: The task group discussed the proposal to purchase two extra delivery vans.

JD felt that the business development work in the two new industrial estates in the East of the city had resulted in several new contracts that would be coming on stream in the next few weeks and this would put undue pressure on the current vans.
HG also admitted that the run up to Christmas would be very busy and extra resources would be needed.
GW complained about the extra cost and suggested buying one van as an interim measure. By a majority of 5:1 it was agreed that two additional vehicles should be purchased by the end of the month.

Figure 6.5 *Narrative minutes*

However, if the discussion went another way then action minutes might look like Figure 6.6.

Item No	Topic	Action
7.	Proposed purchase of two additional vans. It was agreed that the purchasing manager should look into the costs of leasing compared with purchase .	SW to cost options.

Figure 6.6 *Action minutes*

Activity 6.2

You have been asked to participate in your company's management training programme. Prepare for the first topic 'Effective Meetings' by drafting explanatory notes on:

1. The role of meetings

2. The different types of meetings which occur in business situations.

3. Leading meetings

4. The documentation used in meetings

The role of interviews and negotiations

Interviews tend to be planned and usually have objectives. Negotiations are often quite a formal process in which two or more parties come together to form an agreement.

At present you may not interview or negotiate with people (in the formal sense of these activities) as part of your job. However, it is very likely that in the course of your work or private life you will be interviewing and negotiating with people in an informal and almost subconscious way. For instance, when you arrange a social event with colleagues or discuss a quote with a supplier, you are often indirectly and informally negotiating about matters in order to come to a suitable agreement. Similarly when you need to obtain an update on a project or discuss a problem with a colleague you are often informally conducting an interview.

This unit looks at the more formal aspects of the interview and negotiation process, as these are activities that you are likely to become involved with in your dealings with customers, colleagues, subordinates or suppliers as you progress through your marketing career.

Purpose of interviews

Interviews are a good way to exchange information and obtain an immediate response. Interviews are generally one-to-one communication situations where you can usually determine if the information you have communicated has been received or you can deal with questions and objections immediately.

In this respect there are fewer opportunities for misunderstandings or for communication barriers to exist than in other situations. It is usually easier to appreciate the underlying message being communicated and easier to read body language in face-to-face interviews.

Interviews are also useful opportunities to adopt appropriate body language to convey your message and to convey a range of emotions, from sympathy and support to enthusiasm and trustworthiness. In an interview you can use various questioning styles to gain a better understanding of what is being said.

Face-to-face interviews are good for improving working relationships between clients and suppliers; hence the phrase 'It is nice to put a face to the voice'. Interviews provide opportunities to develop the social side of business communication that makes doing business easier and more pleasant.

However, because interviews involve complex communication processes and require both interviewers and interviewees to demonstrate good communication skills, there are plenty of opportunities for interviews to be less effective than they might be. Common problems relate to insufficient planning, inappropriate body language, not controlling the content, the pace, the tone, the atmosphere and the timing of the interview, not asking the right questions and not listening sufficiently.

Types of interviews

There are various types of interviews used for different purposes.

Selection interviews

Interviewers use selection interviews to find out if job applicants are suitable for a job. Interviewees will also want to use the opportunity to find out about the job, the organisation and the terms and conditions on offer.

Interviewers will usually prepare for the interview by familiarising themselves with the job applicant's curriculum vitae or application form, the job description and the person specification. On the basis of these and other documents, the interviewer will draw up a list of questions.

Staff are usually trained in an organisation's 'house style' or approach to selection interviews. To get the best out of the selection interview situation various issues need to be considered:

- Candidates should be given a favourable impression with an appropriate welcome, for example, offering refreshment, showing them around the workplace, introducing them to other staff, explaining the procedure for the day.

- The physical layout of the room where the interview will take place is appropriate – perhaps without the physical barrier of a desk between interviewer and interviewee.

- The process needs to be fair, so that all applicants get an equal chance and that interviewees are given a chance to ask questions.

- The interviewer should adopt the right tone in terms of putting candidates at ease and asks open questions that encourage candidates to talk freely.

- The pace and duration of the interview should be controlled and appropriate notes taken to help with the selection process.

Appraisal interviews

These are used to give feedback on an individual's performance and to identify training needs. Interviewees may wish to find out how they are doing, in order to improve their performance and raise issues about their job role. Sometimes appraisal interviews are used as the basis of a salary review.

Because appraisal interviews deal with the sensitive issue of appraising performance they can be difficult for both interviewer and interviewee. They work best where the organisation has a set procedure and trains both parties in how the process should be managed.

Issues to consider from a communications perspective relate to the interviewer's skill in preparing appropriate questions and comments for the interview, being objective rather than showing bias in favour of the interviewee or being unduly critical. The tone will depend on the situation. If the appraisee's performance is poor then a firm but supportive tone is appropriate. The interviewer needs to be constructive and indicate clearly how the appraisee can improve performance.

Interviewers will need to be able to ask appropriate questions, listen carefully to answers and also make brief notes of salient points in order to be able to complete any necessary documentation at the end of the interview. This means the interviewer has to be focused and concentrate carefully to ensure that the interview is effective.

If the appraisee disagrees with the performance assessment, the interviewer needs to be careful that the interview does not degenerate into an argument. This requires control and before the interview careful preparation of strategies for dealing with negative responses.

Counselling, grievance and disciplinary interviews

Unless properly trained as a counsellor, most managers who counsel employees do so as a first stage to identify and resolve personal or professional problems that may hamper performance. Most managers would try to use the situation to offer support and encourage a subordinate to seek help and guidance from appropriate professional sources. Sometimes counselling is the first stage before an organisation deals with an employee's performance through its disciplinary procedure.

Most organisations have set procedures which provide a clear set of instructions about what managers should do if employees have a grievance about how they have been treated. All grievance interviews need to be treated seriously and time should be taken after the interview to investigate the problems raised. A follow-up interview is necessary to help resolve the situation.

Disciplinary interviews are used to take action against an employee who is habitually late, has a poor work performance, breaks workplace rules, such as health and safety regulations, or refuses to do work as instructed.

The first stage of a disciplinary interview may be to establish facts and investigate an incident. This may be followed-up by a second interview to discipline the employee. Disciplinary interviews are also potentially sensitive occasions which can become unpleasant. In conducting them, the interviewer has to be clear on how the interviewee's behaviour has to change and what will happen next if this does not happen. Interviewers should remain objective and anticipate that the interviewee may be resentful about being disciplined.

The interviewer needs to be authoritative without being authoritarian, should have the full facts with supporting evidence and should be objective and fair.

Customer interviews – complaints handling

Handling complaints can be difficult when customers are frustrated and possibly angry. (See Unit 2 and Unit 5 where there are relevant sections on handling complaints and effective non-verbal communication.) In some situations complaints may arise in an ad hoc way as part of a normal day – in others, you may be dealing with someone by prior appointment.

With ad hoc situations, although there may be a variety of things that customers could complain about, you should be able to anticipate the main categories and to develop certain strategies and approaches for particular situations.

Before an appointment with a customer, you should familiarise yourself with the case and be prepared to deal with the complaint, whether that is to make clear that there is no substance to the complaint or to put things right if there is.

As with all interviews, the advantage of face-to-face communication with a customer is that you will be able to deal with questions or objections immediately and be able to use the situation to diffuse an angry situation. You will need to use your skills of diplomacy and tact to calm a customer at the same time as being objective and calm. As long as you are trying to be genuinely helpful you should be able to resolve the situation.

Your tone and your ability to read the customer's body language and use your own to good effect should enable you to communicate effectively and sympathetically. The interview situation will also mean you can clarify exactly what the problem is and sometimes this is only apparent after careful questioning.

In certain situations you may not be able to resolve the situation there and then. In that case you need to be clear about when the customer will hear from you and you need to make sure that you have all the person's contact details so you can indeed contact them.

Planning the interview

The key to success in conducting interviews that are efficient and constructive comes from being in control throughout the event and this is largely a function of careful planning.

1. Before the interview, spend a suitable amount of time thinking about the purpose and aims of the interview, whether this is to select an applicant, solve a problem or negotiate for a contract or pay claim and so on.

2. You should reflect on the nature of the discussion to be facilitated in the interview process and draw up a list of points which will help to guide the interview proceedings and ensure continuity and completeness.

3. The discussion should largely go backwards and forwards from the interviewer to the interviewee so that the interviewer maintains the position of controlling the proceedings.

4. The interviewer also has the responsibility for setting the general tone of the interview, which will reflect the relationship of the parties and the nature of the discussion.

5. The interviewee will have a general purpose for attending the interview, i.e. to obtain or pass information. However, they may also have a personal agenda in attending the interview which is not explicit and, whilst it may be wasted effort to speculate on this issue, it is useful to consider the possible reaction of the interviewee to the discussion that will take place during the interview and to plan further points of action, if appropriate.

6. Choose an appropriate location and time and collect all necessary background data that will set the structure for the interview.

7. During the interview, listen carefully for facts and feelings expressed by the interviewee. This will help you to make an assessment of the real issues under discussion and the personal qualities and judgement of the interviewee, which may be significant in appreciating the overall value of the interview.

8. You should also make notes on critical issues during the course of the interview and close with a summary of the main points raised, highlighting any further action to be taken. If possible and suitable, finish on a positive note.

9. After the interview, spend a few minutes making additional notes that may be useful for reference later, whilst the meeting is still fresh in your mind. This may also be the best time to draft a short response in the form of a memo or letter to the interviewee, to thank them for attending the interview and enclose a summary of the discussion and outcome, if applicable.

Your final task is to put into action any items that needed to be resolved as a result of the interview.

The interview process

There are five generally accepted stages to the interview process.

Preparing for the interview

The approach that will be taken during the interview should be planned beforehand. This will mean setting the objectives of what should be achieved and considering the needs of the interviewee as well. However, if you are a skilled interviewer you should be flexible enough to respond to questions and input from the interviewee as well as sticking to your 'interview plan'.

You should review all available information in preparation for the interview and have all necessary paperwork to hand and in good order for easy reference during the interview itself.

You should make any necessary physical arrangements, such as organising seating arrangements for the interview room, refreshments, waiting areas and timings so that there are no undue delays or overbooking of rooms.

Opening the interview

At the beginning of the interview you should ensure that you set out the purpose of the interview so that the reason for it is clear and the interviewee is made aware of what is to be achieved.

You should set the pace and tone of the interview at the outset. For instance, if you are dealing with a grievance interview where an employee is making serious allegations about another member of staff, then it is in keeping with the gravity of the situation to start proceedings in a serious tone of voice. If it is a complex situation, such as a series of complaints about different aspects of the service your organisation provides, then you could deal with each complaint at a fairly slow pace so that you can check that you have a proper understanding of all the matters being discussed at the outset.

Conducting the interview

It is important that the interviewer adheres as much as possible to the interview plan to ensure that the original objectives are achieved. This means retaining control over the information gathering and giving process whilst also being flexible enough to respond to situations and information that arise in the course of the interview. For example, in an interview situation you may need to ask more probing questions to find out exactly what was involved in the interviewee's last job; or in a disciplinary interview, you should respond appropriately to an interviewee's admission that they are suffering from a serious illness which has led to poor work performance.

The interviewer should also ensure that the interview does not go over the time set aside. It is also important that you adopt and interpret body language appropriately. Non-verbal cues can indicate an interviewee's feelings, such as irritation or enthusiasm. For example, in an interview where a member of staff is raising a grievance and appears to be getting angry, you could interpret their body language to forestall an angry outburst in order to keep the interview on a calm and professional level. Similarly you may need to use non-verbal signals to show your empathy or desire to hear more where an interviewee may appear to be hiding information or seems reluctant to give you all the facts.

An important interviewing skill involves listening in order to evaluate the interviewee's responses. Active listening means paying special attention and deliberately making an effort to understand what the interviewee is trying to say. Although there will be certain things you need to say in an interview, usually more time should be spent listening to the interviewee than speaking yourself. It is particularly important to keep an open mind and guard against prejudice to avoid 'tuning out' of the message being communicated. You may also need to check your understanding of what is being said by paraphrasing what the interviewee is saying. Although you may want to make a note of certain points, keep your concentration on the interviewee rather than your notes.

Your questioning skills are an important aspect of the interview. You should use different questioning styles for different purposes.

You can use closed questions. However, because these require a 'yes' or 'no' response they do not encourage the kind of free flowing conversation that is usually required in most interview situations.

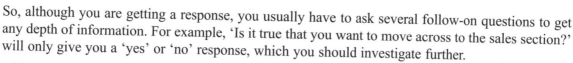

So, although you are getting a response, you usually have to ask several follow-on questions to get any depth of information. For example, 'Is it true that you want to move across to the sales section?' will only give you a 'yes' or 'no' response, which you should investigate further.

Although there are occasions when you need to ask a closed question to verify information, it is often much better to use open questions that encourage the interviewee to frame responses in complete sentences. Open questions tend to start with words like 'why', 'what', 'how', 'when'. For example, 'Why are you interested in moving across to the sales section?'

When you have received a response to a question, there are times when you need to get further clarification or probe deeper to find out what the interviewee really means or if what they are saying is accurate. If the response to an open question is fairly bland such as, 'Because the work looks more interesting', you can obtain more evidence to back up what is being said, with a probing question such as, 'What in particular do you think is more interesting about the work?'

Two-part or multiple-part questions such as 'Have you got any sales experience and if so tell me about the kind of clients you dealt with and your approach to them?' can be confusing. While this question can be used in selection interviews to give interviewees focus about the direction you want them to go in and tests their ability to handle large amounts of information under pressure, it often leads to the interviewee forgetting the original question and digressing onto other subjects. It is often better to keep questions fairly straightforward and follow up with supplementary questions to lead into subjects you want to discuss. Multiple questions would certainly be unsuitable in a disciplinary interview.

You should guard against leading questions in selection interviews that guide the interviewee to agree with you or give the answer you want to hear. For example, asking 'Don't you agree that working in sales would be a more interesting proposition than working in the finance department?' will not supply you with a meaningful answer.

However, you could use a leading question to encourage an interviewee to see your point of view in a disciplinary situation. For example, 'Can you see that by being late every day, you are leaving the rest of the team to do your work?'

Closure

You should control when the interview closes. If the time available has run out or you have reached your objective or it is obvious that you are unable to achieve all the objectives on this occasion, then you should signal the close of the interview.

You can do this by summarising what has been achieved or the 'state of play' and provide any decisions or information about what is to happen next.

In some instances you may need to use your body language to signal that the interview is coming to a close. As you thank the person for their time and explain what you are going to do next, you could gather a few papers together, or you could shake their hands and start to show them out. This is important in interview situations where you can see that the interviewee is not sure that the interview has come to an end.

Follow-up

After an interview you will need to spend some time considering the information that you have obtained. You may need to make notes or organise the notes you made in the interview. At this stage you should decide any action to be taken and implement your decision.

Types of questions

1. Open-ended questions allow interviewees to express themselves in detail, as they are able to form opinions and explain these, for example asking a panel of customers: 'What do you think about our new products that were launched last week and you have tested in the home?'

2. Closed-ended questions require short answers or simple 'yes', 'no' or 'don't know' type responses. For example: 'Have you acquired our latest catalogue and price list?'

3. Probing questions tend to follow open questions when the interviewer wants to find out more about what the person has just said. Often a good way to get interviewees to justify what they have said.

4. Restatement questions enable the interviewer to check that they have:

   ◆ Not misunderstood a piece of factual information given in response to a question.

   ◆ Informed the interviewee correctly.

For example, 'You stated that you do not use our executive lounge because it is always overcrowded. Is that correct?'

Activity 6.3

An airline company is holding an open 'recruitment' day and is hoping to attract customer service staff for its call centre. Managers from various departments will be holding first stage interviews.

1. Write a memo that provides managers with a checklist outlining the five stages of an interview process. Briefly explain what each stage involves.

2. Explain the benefits of using open and probing questions.

Negotiations

Negotiations are interviews designed to achieve agreement that is acceptable to both parties. In situations of this nature, the mutually acceptable deal often involves the agreement to provide a product or service at a particular time, at a particular price and in a particular way. Negotiation is not supposed to be about winning or losing.

Forsyth (*The Negotiator's Pocketbook*. Management Pocketbooks, 2000) says that negotiation has many purposes, for example in:

- Persuasive communication and selling
- Purchasing
- Dealing with staff
- Arbitration
- Many business or personal transactions, from buying a computer to agreeing when and where to meet for dinner

Forsyth believes that everything is negotiable – everyone is a negotiator.

Negotiation phases

Negotiation often occurs in a 'selling' context and can involve several distinct phases:

- Opening the sale
- Identifying customer needs or problems
- Demonstrating or presenting the product or issues
- Handling objections
- Negotiating
- Closing the sale.

Planning to negotiate

Negotiations often require careful planning about the following:

- What are your objectives?
- What are the objectives of the person with whom you are negotiating?
- What do you know about the person and the organisation that you are negotiating with?

Concessions

You should identify:

- What is to be achieved and what can be given up i.e. what is the bare minimum required for a satisfactory outcome? This is sometimes referred to as the fall-back position.
- What should be achieved i.e. what is the optimum outcome?

What can be given up are referred to as variables or concessions. These could include price, discount, delivery, payment terms, documentation, follow-up service, timing, schedules, guarantees, conditions and options.

Managing negotiations

In conducting a negotiation you should:

1. Know your authority – i.e. your negotiation limits and those of the person you are negotiating with.
2. Know your opposite number's needs – i.e. if you know what they really want you are in a better position to negotiate a deal that will satisfy.
3. Be prepared to barter and make concessions that are meaningful to the customer in order to clinch the deal.

Negotiation styles

There are a number of different negotiating styles:

- You can take a pro-active direction – making suggestions, giving information and promoting your position.
- You can take a reactive direction – asking for suggestions and checking you understand the other side's position.
- You can adopt a 'hard' approach – where there is no movement on your position which must be accepted.
- You can adopt a 'soft' position – where you accommodate the other person's position.

Negotiation seeks to narrow the differences between parties in order to achieve a satisfactory result for both sides.

Outcomes

Outcomes to negotiation can vary:

- Lose/lose, which means neither party has achieved its objectives and the negotiation has failed.
- Win/lose, where one party achieves its objectives and the other party does not. The negotiation has failed because both parties do not find the situation acceptable.
- Draw, where both parties achieve some of their objectives but not all.
- Win/win, where both parties achieve their objectives.

Techniques to keep ahead in negotiations

- Use silence.
- Summarise frequently.
- Keep track of complex negotiations, particularly about concessions offered on either side.
- Promote a good feeling.
- Read between the lines about what is really being said.
- Think on your feet but hold your fire when necessary.

Interpersonal behaviour

- Good negotiators listen carefully and do not allow themselves to be distracted.
- Ask questions to keep the negotiations open.
- Ask probing questions where necessary.
- Look for signs of open minded body language, e.g. open hands.
- Look for wariness, e.g. arms across chest.
- Look for signs of confidence, e.g. 'steepling' of hands, or territorial dominance, such as hands behind head and leaning back.
- Look for signs of nervousness, e.g. clearing throat, perspiration, fidgeting, avoiding eye contact.

Activity 6.4

You are the Account Manager at a PR agency and have been asked to renegotiate your firm's contract with a client. Your assistant is interested in the negotiation process and asks you the following questions:

1. What is meant by the term 'negotiation'?
2. How could you use effective body language in a negotiation?

Summary

In this unit you have studied:

- Why and how meetings are used in marketing.
- When documentation is needed and how it is used in meetings.
- How to lead and manage meetings effectively.
- How and why interviews and negotiations are used in marketing.
- How to improve your interview technique.
- How to be a successful negotiator.

Further study and examination preparation

Go to the end of the book and attempt question 5a) from June 2000 examination paper.

Exam hint

You need to know whether a meeting or informal discussion is required in a given situation. If it is the former, you may be asked to explain the steps that need to be taken to plan and hold the meeting. It is therefore important that you are conversant with all aspects of meetings, notably the issuing of a notice, setting the agenda and producing minutes.

You may be given a fictitious scenario and out of this asked to set an agenda and/or issue a suitable notice – all settings will have a marketing context and you may need to rely on your knowledge from other parts of the Certificate course to place suitable details in these documents.

You will be expected to know the general rules and guidelines in the planning of interviews and to explain these in the examination. You need to be aware of the different types of interview that can take place in business and how to plan and contribute effectively to negotiations in marketing. You should be aware of the different types of questions that can help you to solicit the required information. You should also expect to comment on any body language, speech and listening skills as important tools in meetings, interviews and negotiations for successful communication.

Using statistical data and visual information

Objectives

In this unit you will:

- See the relevance of interpreting, analysing and presenting data in marketing.
- Understand how to interpret and summarise data.
- Appreciate the value of using graphs, tables and charts in the visual communication of marketing information.
- Study a range of graphs, tables and charts and understand when they should be used.
- Appreciate how information can be distorted.

By the end of this unit you will be able to:

- Analyse and interpret oral, written and graphical information accurately.
- Be selective with data that you include in reports.
- Produce a range of graphs, tables and charts from raw data.

Study guide

This unit covers indicative content 2.3.5. It will also provide you with the underlying knowledge and understanding to be able to deal with data that occurs in the compulsory question in Part A of the Customer Communications paper.

In this unit you will examine how to analyse and interpret information and look at the ways in which information can be communicated using a variety of visual presentation techniques. This unit will help you when you come to tackle Part A questions because as part of the compulsory question, candidates are regularly asked to read narrative material and examine statistical data or visual data. They are then asked to interpret the data and are often asked to convey the key points in some communication format or other (often a report). In addition they are often then asked to use some part of the information on which to base a chart or graph.

Consequently it is important that you familiarise yourself with the format of the Part A questions asked in previous years (go to the back of the book for the last two papers), and you will see that this unit directly relates to answering these type of questions.

It will take you a minimum of two hours to read through this unit and a further two hours to do the activities.

Study tip

To put this area of the syllabus and this unit into context you need to appreciate why it is an important aspect of your marketing studies.

As a starting point write a list of the types of visual and number or statistical information that you have come across in your personal and working life in the last month.

For instance, you may have watched the news on television and seen a feature about employment figures, crime rates or trends in tourism. If you had, you would probably have noticed that the presenter did not go into great detail, explaining every possible figure and percentage that the report was based on. It is much more likely that the he or she would have given you a 'snapshot' view with some key, pertinent points that summarised the overall situation. Any figures would not have been shown in a long list of numbers but would probably have been presented in a visually appealing and easy to understand format, using graphs, charts, maps and possibly including graphical symbols in a picto-gram format or even moving images to attract your attention.

Similarly in your working life you may have attended a sales and marketing presentation or meeting where market share and sales turnover figures were discussed. The presenter would probably have manipulated the data so that it could be presented in a user-friendly format such as handouts, slides or a Powerpoint presentation.

These are just some examples. Now, using your own experience before you start reading the unit, you should be in the correct 'mindset' to read this unit and appreciate why this is an area of significance when you are studying Customer Communications.

Why is data relevant to marketing?

If you work in marketing you will find that you often have to use information to make decisions and may need to convey it to internal and potential or actual external customers. The information you deal with could range from market size, the number of brands in a range, to pricing and distribution information, or information about promotion activities, media spend, sales levels or market share.

The information can be in one of the following 'formats':

- In a raw 'data' format (facts that are not organised in any particular way), such as market research data or sales figures.
- In an 'information' format, where the information has been selected and sorted or analysed for a purpose, such as showing how sales of one brand compare with those of another.
- In an 'intelligence' format, where the information has been interpreted and analysed, for instance where figures show that sales have increased compared with competitor brands over the period of a special promotion.

Data can be in the form of narrative prose or consist of a series of numbers or percentages. It can be very detailed and there can be too much of it to make sense of in a short time. In situations like this, it is necessary to be able to select the most important data, summarise the key points and where appropriate use visual presentation techniques to make the information user-friendly.

Numerical and statistical information is used in a variety of ways in business:

- For record keeping.
- To provide progress updates on advertising and promotion campaigns.
- For budgeting to compare actual with forecast figures.
- As evidence to support proposals.
- To show trends in sales revenue for different brands or to indicate staff turnover or absenteeism.
- To demonstrate proportion and show market share.

Interpreting, selecting and summarizing information

When you communicate information you rarely convey all the facts and details that you have. For example if you are asked the question, 'What happened in the Manchester United game against Bayern Munich?' your answer would probably be to give the final score but not a detailed account of every pass of the ball and attempt on goal.

Similarly, when dealing with marketing information and communicating with colleagues and customers, you need to be able to select the relevant information given in the circumstances and to make some sense of it. For instance, in the football game example, rather than listing every single attempt on goal and every foul you might want to sort the raw data to make the information easier to digest. For example, you might want to say that there were four fouls and two yellow cards given to Bayern Munich players and five attempts each on goal. You might also want to summarise what happened in the general flow of play, for example, Bayern Munich attacked well although their defending left a lot to be desired but Manchester United played with flair and were unlucky not to score another goal.

Now, look at these survey findings and note the process used for summarising this information for part of a brief market research report.

'300 out of the 500 female customers questioned in a postal survey said they would be interested in the x company home shopping service. Their catalogue was judged to be appealing and to feature the kind of products that shoppers find difficult to track down, especially when parents had young children to accompany them on shopping trips.

Due to the large numbers of people who were interested in the home shopping service, the x company is looking into the possibility of expanding its retail operations to include a home shopping service.'

- Firstly, the original material is read thoroughly to identify the main facts and how the ideas are developed.

- The information in the whole report is grouped into different categories under main headings.

- The main points in each paragraph are selected and this key information is interpreted to give it meaning. If necessary it is expressed differently to give it impact and/or make it more understandable.

- The material should be expressed in the third person, i.e. 'it has been shown' or 'the figures show that'.

- Now look at how the information has been summarised for the report:

  'Sixty per cent of female customers who responded to the survey said they would be interested in a mail order service provided by x company. Because the majority of customers would use such a service, the mail order option will be further investigated.'

- Any summary of information should be checked to ensure the main points are covered and that the key points link together with some continuity.

Activity 7.1

You have recently joined Robinsons's, a grocery chain with 96 outlets in the north of England. Following a survey which was carried out by the magazine *'Food Retailer'*, you are required to analyse the information given below and to deliver a presentation to senior management.

Prepare a brief report on the main findings from the perspective of the senior management at the Robinson's grocery chain. (For more information on report formats go to Unit 8). You should be selective with the information you use and summarise the main findings. Ensure that you interpret the statistical data where you can.

Table 1 How often do you shop for groceries not including the times when you have forgotten something?

	%
More than twice a week	7
Twice a week	17
Once a week	60
Every two weeks	11
Every three weeks	1
Less often	2
Miscellaneous	1
No response	1

Table 2 On what day(s) of the week do you usually do most of your grocery shopping?

* results add up to more than 100% because respondents could choose more than one day.

	%
Monday	12
Tuesday	4
Wednesday	8
Thursday	24
Friday	40
Saturday	31
Sunday	6

Table 3 What is the main reason you do most of your grocery shopping on that day?

	%
Most convenient time	45
Fits in with pay day	30
God day for special offers	26
Habit	19
Not crowded	8
Stock up for the weekend	7
Leaves weekend free	6
Run out of food on that day	6
Better selection of groceries	3
Miscellaneous	13

Table 4 At which one store do you shop for groceries most often?

Top UK Retailers	%
Sainsbury	11.2
Tesco	10.4
Co-op	6.9
Asda	5.7
Safeway	4.7
Robinsons	4.5
Fine Fare	4.5
Gateway	4.4
Spar	4.2
Kwiksave	3.2
Others	40.3

Table 5 What are your reasons for shopping at (name of shop) most often?

	%
Convenient location	42
Special offers/low prices	38
Good meat	25
Carry all brands	22
Friendly assistants	20
Quality of fresh produce	17
Good display	14
Adequate parking	12
From habit/miscellaneous	47

Table 6 What are your reasons for not shopping at the other stores?

	%
Prices too high	45
Too far to travel	27
Slow check-out	22
Prefer the shop I go to	17
Very few special offers	17
Poor selection	15
Unattractive store	7
Too small	7
Too overcrowded	5
No particular reason	3
Miscellaneous	28

Table 7 On your major grocery shopping trips, how often do you buy advertised special offers?

	%
Frequently	35
Occasionally	15
Seldom	10
Never	38
No response	2

Table 8 Which of the following are your best source of special offers? Which second and which third?

	Source		
	First	Second	Third
Newspapers	40%	10%	21%
Store leaflets	25%	24%	15%
Leaflet drops	15%	31%	19%

Table 9 Please look at these advertisements and tell me the reference number of the one you like best.

	%
Safeway	20
Fine Fare	16
Asda	14
Gateway	13
Kwiksave	10
Tesco	9
Sainsbury	8
Co-op	6
Robinsons	2
Aldi	1
No response	1

Table 10 Why do you like the advertisement you picked?

	%
Special offers are easy to find	42
Eye catching	38
Easy to read/large print	27
Easy to find specific brands	19
More bargains	17
Good variety of items	15
Other replies, none more than 8%	45
No response	3

Why use visual information?

Visual presentations including pictures, diagrams, icons, logos, charts and graphs can be quickly assimilated and can make information much easier to comprehend. People are adept at speed-reading visual messages and find it easier to interpret figures shown pictorially.

You can use graphics to explain relationships and actions that would be difficult to convey concisely in words. For example, you could use a pie chart to show market share more effectively than a list of percentages or you could use a bar chart to show rising sales figures over a five-year period rather than explaining the year-on-year increases.

You can use visual messages to create impact and attract the attention of an audience. If you present information visually it is also more likely to be retained in your target audience's memory.

You can choose from a variety of ways to display data visually:

- Tables can be used for recording and displaying a wide range of numerical data.
- Bar charts help to compare changes in relative quantity.
- Line graphs help to show trends and moving averages over time, so are useful for planning and forecasting.
- Pie charts help you see proportions of a whole.
- Pictograms show pictorial symbols of statistics to simplify messages.
- Organograms show reporting relationships between people in organisations.
- Gantt charts help with project planning.

How to present visual information

Nowadays it is much easier to generate graphs and charts with a professional appearance on a computer using a spreadsheet or database software. (See Figure 7.1 for an example of how computers can produce three dimensional and other techniques to represent data.) You should be aware of how each of the main display options can be used and be able to produce them without the aid of a computer.

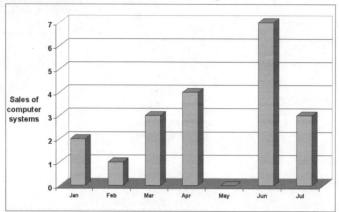

Figure 7.1

As a general rule it is best to keep charts and graphs simple. Visually it is better if the chart takes up the full axis space available. Use of colour or a three-dimensional aspect can create impact. All graphs and charts should have a title indicating the content – for example, 'marketing spend for product x' – and sometimes this is used to indicate the values being shown, for instance, whether it is £000 or %. There should be two axes on each graph, a horizontal axis (the x axis) and a vertical axis (the y axis). It is best to orient the data so that values on the horizontal axis are those where there are has been a choice, such as, when to measure or where to measure (this is known as the independent variable). Values on the vertical will depend upon the corresponding position on the horizontal axis (they are therefore known as the dependent variable). For example, when showing the change in sales revenue over the course of a year, the independent variable is time since we can choose when to measure sales revenue. The dependent variable is sales revenue since it will change according to the time at which it was measured

The key or the legend relates the shading or pattern used on a chart to what it represents. In addition to or in place of a legend, labels can be used to mark what each bar, segment or line represents. All bars and charts should display the source of information. It is also advisable to cross reference all graphs and charts within the text, such as 'see figure x' or 'see attached appendix y'.

Tables

Tables can be useful for presentation purposes to sort complex data. However, the information presented in this way can often be used as the basis for further analysis because while the information is in this format it is often difficult to read or follow trends.

	Product line sales turnover (£000s) 2000–2001					
Salesperson	A	B	C	D	E	Total (£)
Helen Jenkins	13	15	8	12	10	58
Jane Atkinson	8	10	9	6	5	38
Andrew Salter	16	12	10	12	14	64
Luigi Romero	23	26	13	28	22	112
Karen Mann	33	34	24	22	30	143
Sunil Singh	12	16	11	17	15	71
George Vassiliades	4	7	3	8	11	33
Alan Bennet	11	12	12	12	11	58
Tony Taylor	15	7	7	9	8	46
Christine James	22	13	21	10	15	81
Total	157	152	118	136	141	704

Figure 7.2 A table showing product line sales per representative

Bar charts

Column/bar charts demonstrate relationships and differences in variables by the respective heights of the columns/bars, which can be displayed vertically or horizontally, with the data on or near the bars. They are particularly useful when you want to:

1. Compare the size of several variables in one presentation.
2. Demonstrate important differences between the variables.
3. Demonstrate changes over a period of time.
4. Demonstrate the composition of variables.

There are three types of column/bar chart that can be presented:

1. Simple column/bar charts.
2. Multiple column/bar charts.
3. Component (stacked) column/bar charts.

Guidelines for producing simple column/bar charts

Simple column/bar charts demonstrate the value of one piece of data by the respective length of the column/bar(s) on the chart. Where the horizontal axis cannot have values midway between each measurement (bar), such as between two brands or between two countries, then a bar chart should be used. Where the horizontal axis has values which can gradually change, then a line graph is best, since it shows the possible points midway between each measurement.

1. The chart must be titled and each axis of the graph must be labelled.
2. There must be a scale to indicate values on each axis (see Figure 7.3 where market share percentages are shown on the y axis)
3. The vertical axis must always start at 0, so that the relative values can be accurately demonstrated, or indicate with a staggered line that the data does not begin at 0.
4. If possible, the data should be presented in some order of value, i.e. lowest to highest or vice versa; this is usually not possible if time comparisons are made.
5. Use spaces between columns/bars for ease of interpretation.
6. Use shading to highlight the columns/bars, making them easier to view. Figure 7.4 demonstrates how to draw a simple column/bar chart based on the data below.

1995	1996	1997	1998	1999	2000	2001
0.4%	0.7%	1.9%	2.6%	3.0%	3.0%	2.8%

Figure 7.3 *Market share for Brand 'A' for the years 1995 -2001*

Multiple column/bar charts

Multiple column/bar charts use several columns/bars for each variable, each column/bar demonstrating a particular aspect of the overall data.

Guidelines for producing multiple column/bar charts

1. Two or more columns/bars are used to present aspects/divisions of the data.

2. Shading must be used to distinguish the columns/bars representing different data.

3. Use spaces appropriately to draw attention to similarities, differences or trends, either in the columns/bars separately or groups of data.

4. Columns/bars can be drawn horizontally or vertically.

	1999 (000s)	2000 (000s)	2001 (000s)
B1	150	180	225
B2	230	245	205
B3	340	560	480

Table 7.1

The multiple column bar chart example shown in Figure 7.4 has been based on the information in Table 7.1.

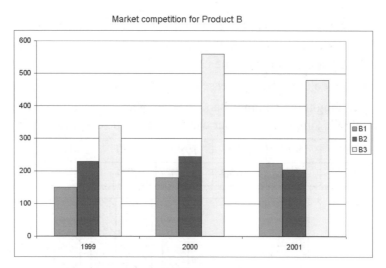

Figure 7.4 A multiple column/bar chart of market competition for Brand A

Component (stacked) column/bar charts

Component (stacked) column/bar charts can be segmented or broken lengthwise to show the relative size of components of an overall total. An example is presented in Figure 7.5.

Guidelines for producing component column/bar charts

1. The components can be ordered in any way on the column/bar, but must remain consistent if more than one column/bar is demonstrated.

2. The relative values should be kept in order, with either the highest or lowest at the top, and then presented in ascending or descending order.

3. Use shading and/or a key if the components cannot be labelled directly.

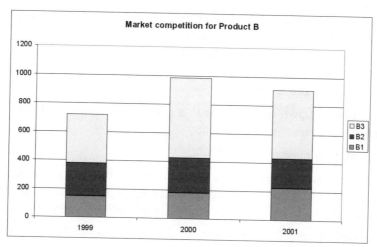

Figure 7.6 *A component bar chart*

Histograms

Histograms should not be confused with bar charts. Bar charts are used for discrete or non-continuous data and so are best drawn using a separate bar for each item that is being represented. Histograms are used to display continuous data such as earnings, mileage, examination marks, heights of people, etc. and as such there is usually no gap between the bars to indicate the continuous nature of the data.

If you were to show the monthly salaries of the marketing staff at Switzells (listed below), in a histogram, you would first group the information together to produce a frequency table.

Monthly salaries of marketing staff at Switzells Limited: £1150, £690, £1270, £1450, £1350, £880, £750, £970, £1080, £1290, £1600, £1700, £680, £1090, £950, £1400, £550, £1180, £1250.

From this you can see that there are three staff whose monthly salaries are in the £500-£700 category.

Monthly earnings (£)	500-700	701-900	901-1100	1101-1300	1301-1500	1501-1700	1701-1900
Number of employees	3	2	4	5	3	1	1

Having organised the information into the frequency table it is much easier to plot it on a histogram. Histograms can show the distribution of information. In the example in Figure 7.6, there is a normal 'bell curve' distribution with a few people at the lower and higher ends of the scale and most people in the middle salary range.

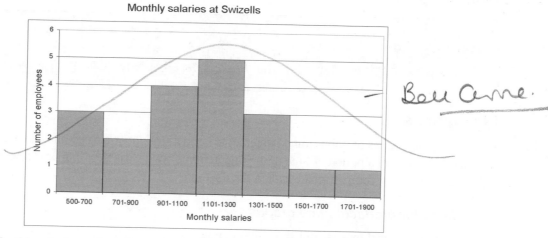

Figure 7.6 *Monthly salaries at Swizells*

Pie charts

Pie charts are circular diagrams that are particularly useful for showing the composition of all the data, with the segments demonstrating the relative values of the data. They are used to show the relative size of different items making up a total, and are useful to show proportions of a whole.

Ideally there should be no more than eight sections with the largest segment usually shown running clockwise from the top of the pie. Each segment should be labelled, sometimes including a value and a percentage share. The overall total is usually stated.

Guidelines for producing pie charts

1. Pie charts should be drawn accurately with a compass to represent the 360° of a circle and divided up into segments.

2. The component parts must represent 100%.

3. To draw the segment sizes accurately, use a protractor by putting the base line across the middle of the circle and marking off degrees to represent percentages (which must be worked out, based on numerical values). For example, 180° represents 50%, 90ø 25%, etc.

4. Keep the maximum number of segments to seven, otherwise the chart will look too congested and be more difficult to interpret.

5. Place the most important (largest) segment at the 12 o'clock position and the others relative to it in some logical order.

6. Use shading to draw attention to salient features, usually largest and/or smallest segments.

7. Label all the segments and show their relative values either on the segments or beside the chart. A key will be necessary for this.

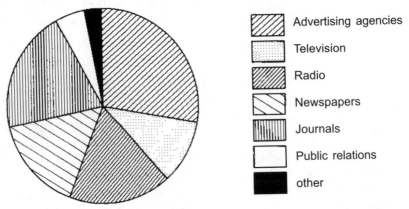

Employment for graduates in Media Studies (2001)

Figure 7.7 A pie chart

Activity 7.3
Draw a pie chart based Table 2 in the 'Food Retailer' survey featured in Activity 7.1.

Line graphs

Line graphs are a series of points joined together to form a straight or curved line and are usually used to reflect a trend over a period of time or the interaction of two variables. In many cases several lines will be used to show comparisons between the data.

Guidelines for producing line graphs

1. The horizontal axis should show the time period (years, months, hours, etc.).

2. The vertical axis should show the amount or value being measured.

3. Both scales should begin at 0 and increase in equal amounts, or indicate with a staggered line that the data does not begin at 0.

4. Both negative and positive values can be shown on line graphs.

5. Use different colours for more than one line on the same graph, to distinguish between them.

6. Use solid lines or broken lines to distinguish between different data or to draw attention to significant features of the data.

7. In order to avoid clutter and to make observation of the chart easier, a maximum of three lines on any graph should be used, especially if they are likely to cross over.

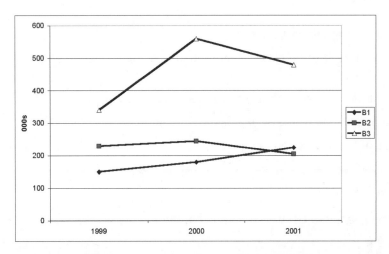

Figure 7.8 *A simple line graph*

Activity 7.4

Draw a line graph based Table 4 in the *'Food Retailer'* survey featured in Activity 7.1.

Gantt charts

Gantt charts are a type of column/bar chart which show dimensions of a variable over a period of time and can be used to measure a number of different aspects of business activity in terms of actual, planned and cumulative. They are often found in marketing plans to show how the plan will be 'phased in' over a period of time.

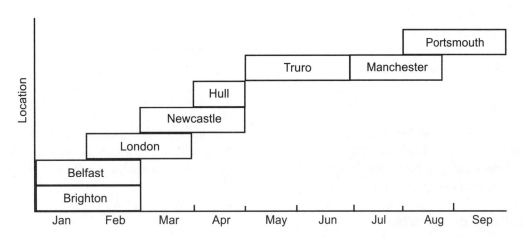

Figure 7.9 *Gantt chart. Rolling national launch of Brand Q in different regional cities in the UK from January to September 200X*

Pictograms

Pictograms are charts in which the data is represented by a line of symbols or pictures. They are usually used for presenting information in a novel format and are often used in the transmission of simple messages. They can give impact to data as it can be represented by a striking image or picture. For instance numbers of employees or customers can be represented by matchstick people; aeroplane sales can be shown as drawings of aeroplanes.

An increase in quantity can be shown by more images (where the image is given a value) or the size of the image might increase to represent the quantity change. However, the problems with doing this are that quantities can be misrepresented because the scaling is unclear.

In addition, although pictograms can make a visual impact, certain audiences could perceive them as frivolous or patronising.

Guidelines for producing pictograms

1. Use a symbol which will be clearly representative of the subject matter, eye-catching and appealing.
2. The number of pictures or symbols must reflect the values they represent.
3. Use a key to indicate the value of one picture or symbol.
4. Keep the size of the pictures and graph consistent with the overall presentation.

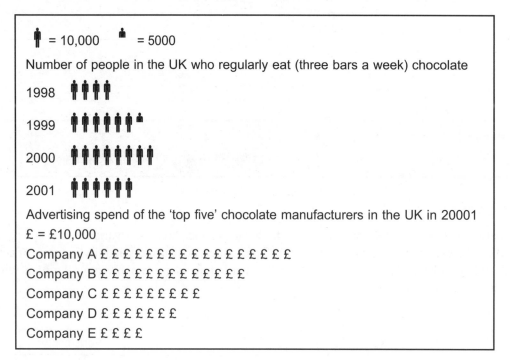

Figure 7.10 Examples of pictograms

Flow charts

Flow charts are useful for demonstrating conceptual relationships, processes and procedures and business activities, where numerical values are not important. The relationships between various parts of the activity being demonstrated are shown in sequence from beginning to end and geometric shapes are used to distinguish between various aspects. (See Figure 7.11.)

Organization charts

Organization charts are frequently used in business organizations to show the hierarchical positions and relationships of employees, which also represent the main formal channels of communication. (See Figure 7.12.)

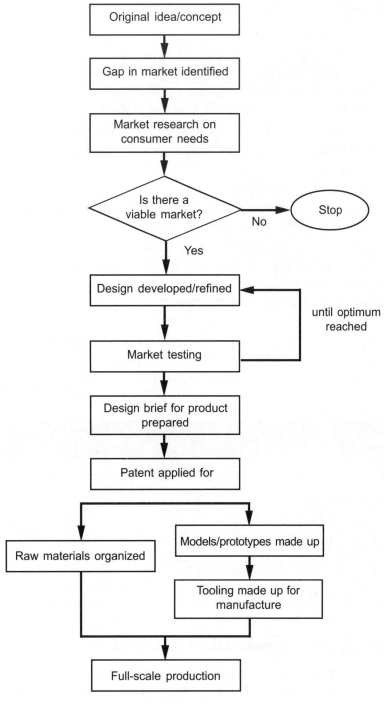

Figure 7.11 *A flow chart for the stages involved in the introduction of a new product*

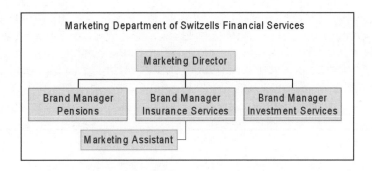

Figure 7.12 *An organization chart for the Marketing Department of Switzells Financial Services*

Problems with distorting information

You should avoid using value-loaded expressions to alter how a statistic sounds as this could distort the information. For example, 47 per cent sounds different when described as 'nearly half the population, which sounds different again from 'barely half' or 'not even half those questioned'. Similarly you should remember that if 'nearly one in ten of the population has a problem with x, y or z' it means that over 90 per cent of people don't have that problem.

Graphs and charts can be very effective communication media, but it is easy to confuse an audience or be confused yourself if the wrong medium is used to communicate data or if it is constructed incorrectly.

Be aware that you can distort the information you are presenting if the axis on graphs and charts does not start from zero. Trends in the top part of a chart will be more exaggerated than if you see the whole picture with zero at the bottom left-hand corner.

Similarly, if you use a set of line charts but use a different scale on each of them you could distort the information. For example if you expanded or compressed the y axis (vertical axis) you could make a curve showing sales steeper or flatter which could effect the way that sales performance is perceived. Spreading out or compressing the distance between values on the x-axis (horizontal axis) could cause the same effect.

Computer packages offer you the facility of producing graphs and charts that have a three-dimensional appearance. However, sometimes the cosmetic benefits of blocking out areas of graphs and charts can be outweighed by the problems of readability. The problem is that it is difficult to see the how the 3-D lines and bars line up against the relevant scale so data values are difficult to determine.

Summary

In this unit you have studied:

- Why data is relevant to marketing.
- How to interpret and summarise data.
- Why visual data is an effective communication tool.
- How to present a range of visual data, including charts, graphs and diagrams.
- How to avoid distorting data.

Further study and examination preparation

Go to the end of the book and attempt question 1a) and b) as well as question 3a) from the June 2000 examination paper and do question 1b) and c) from the December 2000 paper.

Exam hint

Candidates studying for the examination should be aware that this unit is particularly relevant to the compulsory Part A question. Ensure that you can interpret written and/or visual data in order undertake a number of tasks, such as, writing a report (see unit 'The communication process' for information about report writing) and producing graphs and charts. Ensure that you can analyse, interpret, summarise and present information in a concise and accurate manner.

Objectives

In this unit you will:

- Examine the variety of written communication formats.
- Look at when and why you would use a particular written communication format.
- Develop your writing skills for each of the formats included here.

By the end of this unit you should be able to:

- Use the correct layout and presentation format for different types of written communication.
- Communicate effectively using each of the formats included here.

Study guide

This unit covers 2.4.1 of the syllabus. It provides you with the knowledge and understanding necessary to enable you to use a variety of written formats to communicate with internal and external customers. These formats are letters, memos, e-mails, notices, reports and articles. It will take you two hours to read through this unit and a further hour to work through the activities.

Study tip

Spend some time evaluating the written communications that you are exposed to in your personal and working life. Select a good and bad example of each of the following:

- Letters
- Memos
- Notices
- Reports
- E-mails

For each example note down why it is effective or not.

Why study communication formats?

Written communication is still important in marketing even in these days of sophisticated information communications technology.

You may use your writing skills in letters, memos, e-mails and reports regularly, in which case you may wish to proceed directly to the activities and past examination questions to check how well prepared you are to be tested in this area. On the other hand, you may find that, because of your role or the type of organization you work in, all letters and memos are produced by someone else (such as a secretary). Or it may be that you are not yet in a position that requires you to use all the communication formats tested in the exam (such as reports). Whatever the case, you should be aware of how to use the various communication formats, and you may need to spend some time looking at how you could develop your writing skills.

If you work in an organization where there is a 'house style' for reports and letters, then this style can be used in the examination situation, but if this is not the case, then you may find you can use and adapt the templates and examples provided in this unit.

Written communication skills in marketing

For any situation, whether you are writing a letter, memo or report the following structure should be adopted:

- A beginning – where you get to the point of why you are writing whatever you are writing.

- The middle – where you communicate your message.

- The end – if appropriate, where you summarise the main points (especially for reports) or where you state any action required (more for memos and letters).

The PASS (purpose, audience, structure, style) mnemonic can prove to be a useful guide when you are writing (see Unit 5 for more details) or be a useful way to cross-check when you review your writing.

In addition, the AIDA principle (see Unit 4) is relevant to most written communications:

A	Gain **attention** of the recipients by putting the essence of your message at the beginning.
I D	Stimulate **interest** and create **desire** by writing positively, for example, referring to benefits or writing from the perspective of the audience and/or taking a personal approach when appropriate (using the word 'you' but not in reports).
A	Generate **action** by motivating the recipient to undertake the desired course of action, for example, 'please confirm/reply by ...' or just getting the reader to read your message.

Most business documents should be clear and concise. To keep letters, memos and reports brief it is best to keep to short sentences, simple expressions (avoid analogies) and words that people can understand. In other words, try not to use words that your audience may be unfamiliar with and avoid jargon. Abbreviations should be explained by giving their meaning in full the first time they are used.

Start new paragraphs when you move on to new ideas. Arrange your thoughts in a logical sequence so that ideas and information flow from one paragraph to another in a clear and easy to understand way.

Use terms that are unambiguous. For instance, the words 'quickly', 'as soon as possible' and 'large' could be interpreted in different ways by different people. Generally it is better to be specific, giving an amount or a date instead of using words that could be misinterpreted.

For letters in particular, you should avoid the kind of official and cliché-sounding terms that can lead to readers not understanding exactly what you are trying to say. For instance, instead of 'Re your correspondence dated...'. You could say, 'Thank you for your letter of ...' And the phrase 'The contract should be submitted to the undersigned upon completion' could be more simply written as 'Please return the contract when you have completed it.'

In general you should avoid passive phrases, such as 'should be sent to'. Use the active form, 'please send to...'

You should try to avoid negative terms when writing to customers. For example, 'I am unable to make a booking until you pay a 25 per cent deposit' could be phrased in a positive way as 'When you pay a 25 per cent deposit, your booking will be completed and confirmation sent to you within 3 days.'

You will get a better response to the letters and memos you send if you use a courteous 'please', 'thank you' or 'I would be grateful if you could...' instead of using a brusque or directive tone.

If you are writing a memo which does not require a specific action, then you should include the phrase 'for information only'.

If you are writing a report, you should avoid sexual bias in your writing. By using 'he' or the masculine form of a noun, you could cause offence. Either use non-gender specific terms such as 'staff', 'employees', 'individuals' or 'people', or change the sentence round. For example, the sentence, 'The number of air stewardesses will have to be increased on each flight...' could be changed to 'The number of air crew will have to be increased on each flight...'

When to use letters

Whatever type of organization that you work in, if you are in an office, you are likely to write and receive letters. However, if you work in marketing then communication is likely to be a vital part of your job and therefore letter writing will be too.

Although letter writing is not the quickest way to communicate there are many different types of letters and many occasions when letters are a suitable format for communication.

Letters provide a permanent record of a message, which could be useful if you are confirming details of an exhibition stand booking or enquiring about late payment and need proof at a later date that a letter has indeed been sent.

Letters are also quite formal, which means they are an excellent way of sending important information. For example, you would want to send a formal letter if you were informing someone that they were successful in a job interview, if you were giving someone notice about a disciplinary matter or if you needed to send a covering letter with a cheque payment.

Letters are suitable for long, complex messages that can be read and re-read over a period of time. Consequently they are often used for direct marketing purposes (mailshots) where the 'offer' has a number of benefits that need to be read in detail. They are often used where the product is quite complex as they can be read again when the person has had more time to think about the offer.

Letters are suitable for communicating personal information directly to the individual concerned. The use of computers in even the smallest firms means that professionally presented letters can be produced easily by most staff, not just trained secretaries.

The use of mail-merge facilities means that standard letters can be produced, saving time and money. This means an organization can decide to communicate with some or even all of its customers by linking letter production to an updated customer database.

And if a letter is necessary and speed is important, then it could be sent by facsimile machine or as an e-mail attachment.

Letters are generally sent to external customers although in very formal situations (such as confirmation of terms and conditions, requests for leave or with disciplinary matters) letters may be sent internally within an organization.

The layout of a business letter

Undoubtedly you will already have been involved in writing business letters as millions are composed, produced and delivered daily. Every organization has its own style (which is important in reflecting image and efficiency) but there are a set of basic rules of layout that all will follow:

1. A blocked layout with all entries starting from the left-hand margin or an indented style where the main body of the letter is set to the left-hand margin and all other parts are centred; either method may be used but should be consistent throughout the organization or department (Figure 8.1).

2. Business letters are made up of the following parts:
   - Letterhead and/or logo – communicates the corporate image through its graphic style and usually also contains address, telephone, telex, fax and e-mail details.
   - Letter references – initials of the typist and author.
   - Date – usually the month is first, fully written (not numerals), followed by the day.
   - Recipient's title, name and address.
   - Salutation – for example, Dear Sir, Dear Madam or Dear Mrs Jones.
   - Subject heading – this is usually indented and underlined, for example, Conference on Marketing Communication, September 25 20XX, Queen Elizabeth's Hall, London.
   - Body of the letter – short paragraphs centred on the page.
   - Complimentary close – 'Yours sincerely' for named recipients, (i.e. Dear Mr Brown); 'Yours faithfully' for formally addressed recipients (i.e. Dear Sir(s), Dear Madam)

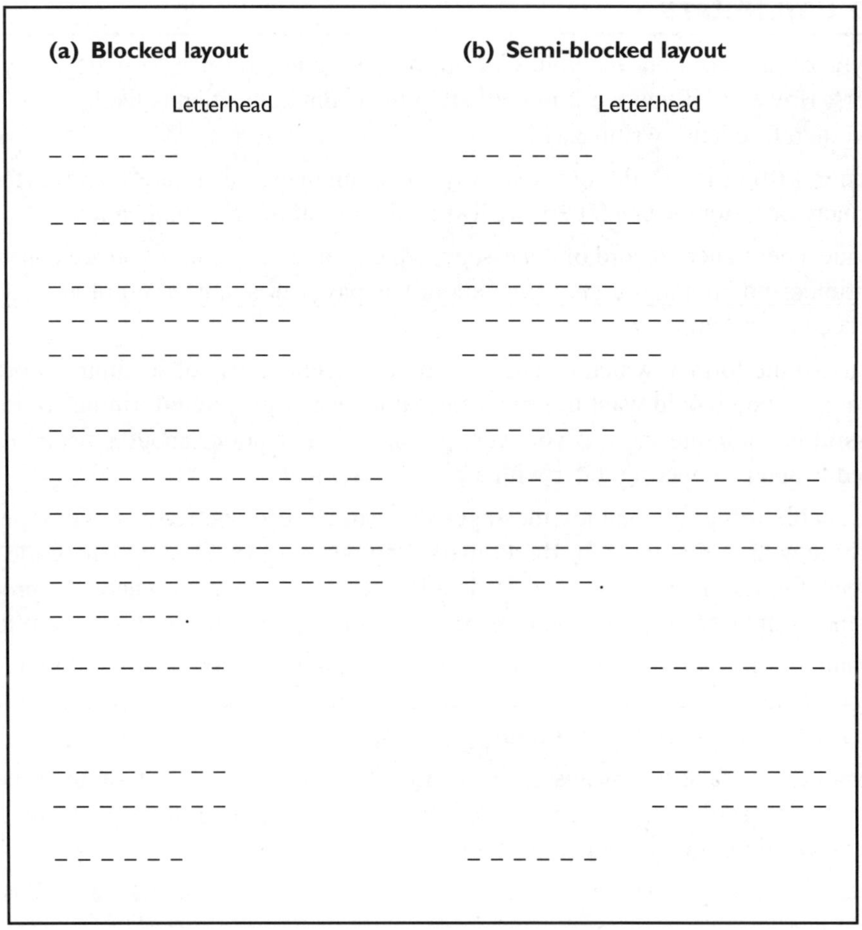

(a) Blocked layout

Letterhead

(b) Semi-blocked layout

Letterhead

Figure 8.1 Layouts for business letters: (a) blocked; (b) semi-blocked

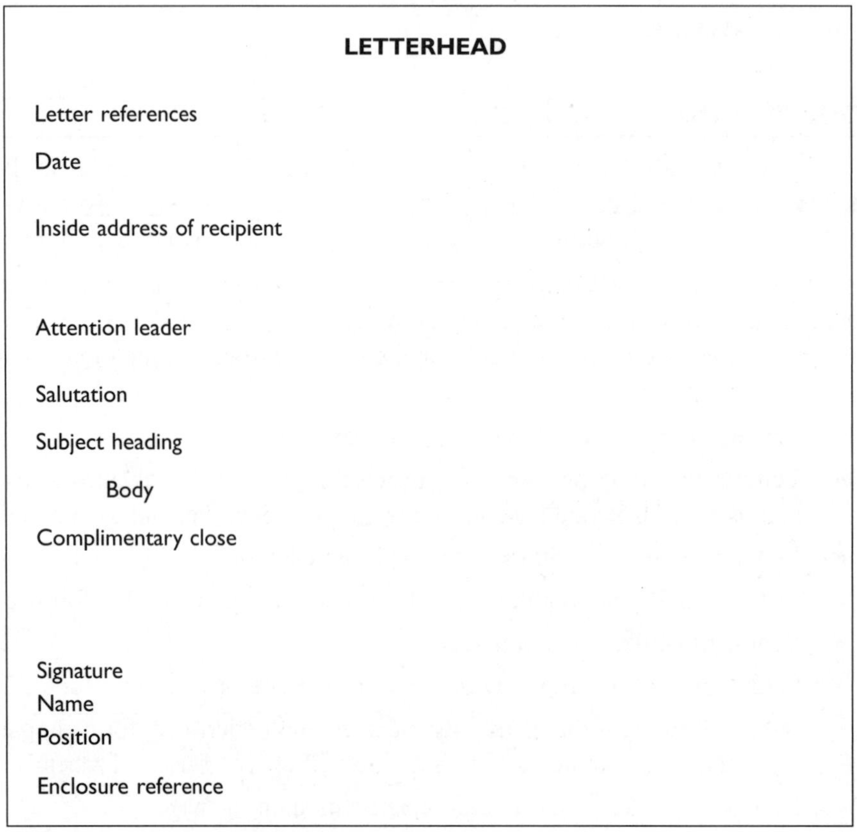

LETTERHEAD

Letter references

Date

Inside address of recipient

Attention leader

Salutation

Subject heading

     Body

Complimentary close

Signature
Name
Position

Enclosure reference

Figure 8.2 A template for a business letter

- Signature – usually in the sender's own handwriting.
- Position/title of sender.
- References to enclosure and copies.

Types of letters

Letters in marketing can be about any topic. Here are some examples of different types of letters:

- Letters giving information to customers.
- Letters confirming negotiations or a booking.
- Sales letters.
- Letters requesting information.
- Letters requesting a meeting or an appointment.
- Complaint letters.
- Letters of adjustment.
- Letters requesting payment.
- Covering letters to go with payment, maps or leaflets.
- Letters querying an invoice.

Midshire Bank Plc

High Street

Assington

Berkshire AS1 6EL

Mr Joe Davies
17 Goldthorpe Way
Assbury
Berkshire AS2 4WQ

12 April 200X

Dear Mr Davies

At Midshire Bank we try to provide banking facilities of the highest quality in order to accurately meet our customers' needs. To do this it is essential that we listen to what our customers have to say. We would like you to help us by giving us your opinion of Midshire Bank's services.

We are asking an independent market research company, TMI Limited to interview a number of customers over the next few weeks. TMI Limited is a reputable company and your individual responses will be completely confidential to them, according to the Market Research Society's Code of Conduct.

They will be conducting the interviews by telephone and so an interviewer may telephone you at some point over the next few weeks.

Because TMI Limited will choose who to interview, you might not be contacted in this instance. If you are, we would value your contribution and hope you will be able to help us if asked.

Yours sincerely

CGowers

Charles Gowers
Branch Manager

Figure 8.3 A sample customer letter

Writing customer letters

These can deal with any topic and you have to be clear about the message you are trying to convey as well as what you want the customer to do.

Writing order letters

Letters are rarely used for placing orders because pre-printed order forms are usually more convenient and efficient. However, if you need to write an order letter, state your needs clearly by presenting the information in column form, with double-spacing and totalling the balance of prices at the end, explaining to which account the balance should be charged. State the delivery address (it may be different from the address on the letterhead) and the mode of transport which should be used.

MAKE-IT BUILDING SUPPLIERS
Churchyard Grove
Pickwick
Lancashire LU1 5TF
Tel: 0123 668791

Our ref: HBJ/abc

October 1st 20XX

The Timber Merchants Ltd
Station Road
Ripon
Yorkshire YU8 TR3

For the attention of Deborah Jones

Dear Ms Jones,

Account Number: 5690   Special order under invoice 123

Further to our last order, would you supply the following additional items:

1	20 metres of extra hard-wearing timber for fencing.	£5.95 per metre excl. VAT =	£119
2	5 litres of creosote liquid in natural colour.	£2.75 per litres excl. VAT =	£ 13.75
3	24 litres of indoor wood varnish in antique pine.	£1.44 per litre excl. VAT =	£ 34.56
		Balance	£167.31
		VAT on items	£ 29.28
		Total balance	**£196.59**

The balance should be stated on the above invoice and charged to our existing account. I would appreciate delivery by November 15th, latest.

Yours sincerely,

Harold Jenkins
Purchasing Manager

Figure 8.4 *An order letter*

Letters of enquiry or request

These can deal with a variety of questions, such as asking readers to supply certain information or make a presentation or inviting them to attend a function. Such letters almost always require a reply and some action to be taken, therefore they should be sent out in advance of the action date and be well-written and tactful.

The opening paragraph should state the nature of the enquiry or request clearly and simply, with a personal tone that will make the reader want to respond.

If further explanation or justification is needed, explain the importance of the information required and the situation which prompted the inquiry or request and, if appropriate, the benefits to the reader. Next, specify the desired action in a positive manner.

Close the letter with a courteous statement and explain the type of action needed, the deadline by which a reply should be made and assure the reader that the information will be treated as confidential (if appropriate).

ULTIMATE COMPUTER COMPANY Ltd
3 The Gateway
Hounslow
Middlesex TW15 6TU
Tel: 0181 967 6345

TRJ/abc

October 1st 20XX

Mr Andrew Collins
Marketing Communications Consultants
'The Nook'
Twinkle Lane
Beaconsfield
BUCKS DU18 74R

Dear Mr Collins

Ref: 'Computers of the World' Exhibition, London, 20XX

I had the pleasure of using your professional services in helping us to prepare and present at the above last year.

We are now in the process of planning to exhibit our new product range again this year and would like to know whether you would offer us your services. I am pleased to enclose our latest catalogue.

Please contact me at the end of next week to arrange for a meeting at our offices.

I look forward to hearing from you.

Yours sincerely,

Timothy R. Jones
Marketing Manager

Enc. Catalogue of product range X.

Figure 8.5 *A letter of enquiry*

Writing sales or persuasive letters

(Also see the section on Direct Marketing in Unit 9)

You could use the AIDA formula:

Grab the reader's **attention** by putting the focus on the reader and their situation.

- Know who you are writing to. One way to grab the reader's attention is to use their name and to personalise the letter by using 'you', 'your' and 'yours'.
- Ensure you know what need your 'offer' is fulfilling. You must write from the reader's viewpoint in relation to their needs and wants.
- Know all the benefits, particularly the most important one.
- Attract the reader's attention with a headline, picture and colour.

Create **interest** in your product or service by stating how the reader may benefit.

- Convert features into advantages and benefits for the reader. Keep sentences short and simple.
- Use subheadings, white space, double spacing, underlining, italics, emboldening, and graphics to keep the reader's eye moving.
- Use the word 'you' often.
- Use facts.

Stimulate **desire** by using persuasive language where possible.

- Make the reader desire your product/service by telling them how it will improve their life.
- Make it sound easy to obtain.
- Repeat your offer/best benefit using new wording.
- Be credible.
- Use the present tense as if the reader already owns the product/service.
- Use testimonials with signatures and pictures of people.

Engender **action** by explaining what the reader needs to do next.

- Put a close date on your offer.
- Offer a bonus for quick reply.
- Use reply paid envelope or freephone number.
- Make it easy to reply, e.g. using a coupon or order form which is easy to complete and cut out.
- Show the telephone number prominently.

Writing complaint letters

In marketing, complaint letters are likely to deal with faulty, mishandled or lost merchandise and other types of customer complaint.

If you are writing a letter of complaint, your motive for communicating is to have the claim sorted out and therefore written documentation is better than verbal communication as there is evidence of action you have taken.

In writing a complaint letter, you should include the following:

1. Opening paragraph with a clear statement of the problem.
2. Further information that will verify the claim or adjustment needed.

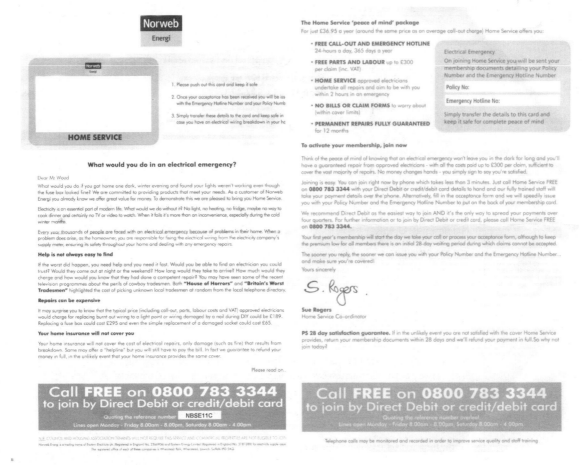

Figure 8.6 A sales letter

3. Closing statement with a polite, non-threatening request for action, emphasizing that the business relationship need not be affected if the matter is resolved satisfactorily.

Answering complaint letters (letters of adjustment)

If you are replying to a complaint letter you should not delay your response, even if all you do is confirm receipt of the letter and explain that you need to investigate the matter, if it is a serious complaint. You should show empathy and concern for the customer and if you can make an adjustment, you should apologise and do so.

If the matter is not a legitimate complaint then you should explain your reasons why there will be no compensation or adjustment. In this situation, the following layout should be used:

1. An opening statement with reference to the claim or adjustment but with a notable point on which both parties might be agreed.

2. An explanation which is tactful and maintains the goodwill of the organization, whilst ensuring that the claimant accepts (some) responsibility for the nature of the claim.

3. The refusal, possibly with the suggestion of an alternative course of action.

4. A pleasant close.

Activity 8.2

You are the manger of a restaurant and receive a letter from a customer complaining about the quality of service and the rudeness of a member of staff. You have investigated the complaint and have found it to be genuine. Write a letter in reply to the complaint.

BEAUTY POTIONS LTD
2–6 Staines Road
Windsor
Berkshire BK7 9LE
Tel: 01753 576423

JK/abc

October 1st 20XX

Variety Fragrances
10 Harrow Road
Wembley
Middlesex 8TU 65R

For the attention of Mr Gardiner

Dear Mr Gardiner,

On September 5th 20XX, we received your order 1112, together with the invoice, 2224.

You will note that the first item on the invoice is listed as 50 · Fragrance 'Irresistible', but unfortunately we received 50 · Fragrance 'Uncontrollable'. A copy of the invoice is attached.

Please be kind enough to collect the wrong items and have them replaced by 50 · Fragrance 'Irresistible' at the same time.

I look forward to receiving the correct order by November 1st 20XX.

Sincerely,

Joanna Kemp
Sales and Purchasing Manager

Enc. Copy of invoice 2224

Figure 8.7 *A letter of complaint*

Writing letters of credit

In most organizations today, the process of buying and selling goods and services is facilitated by credit. The credit manager has responsibility for accepting or rejecting an application for credit, which is based on an assessment regarding the person or organization's financial viability and outstanding debts, in relation to the type and value of credit required.

Approving credit

1. A pleasant opening paragraph which grants the credit request.
2. Details of the terms and conditions under which credit is granted, addressing any specific points that may not be in line with company policy, but which have been raised.
3. A courteous close.

Refusing credit

1. An opening statement appreciating the request for credit. Make the refusal, but with a notable point that both parties may agree.
2. Details for the refusal in positive terms which are specific to the reader, whilst maintaining a tactful tone to ensure goodwill.
3. A courteous close, with a sales pitch in relation to the correspondence, if appropriate.

```
                    CATERING WHOLESALERS LTD
                          35 Redruth Avenue
                              Tunbridge
                           Kent TN15 UC1
                          Tel: 01932 57311

HB/abc

October 1st 20XX

Mr R. Anderson
The Manager
'The Restaurant'
76 Sevenoaks Road
Sevenoaks
KENT


Dear Mr Anderson,

Thank you very much for your recent application for credit. I am pleased to
inform you that this has been approved.

Our terms and conditions are as follows:

1   A credit limit of £2000 is available for your establishment.
2   Invoices must be settled within 15 days of the date of issue, after which an
    interest charge of 5% will be levied on outstanding balances.

Yours sincerely,



Harry Bains
Credit Manager
```

Figure 8.8 A letter approving credit

Writing letters of recommendation

Letters of recommendation convey information about people, their characteristics and suitability for the position. Figure 8.9 gives an example of a letter of recommendation. These are usually confidential and must contain the following:

1. The name of the person.

2. The position that the candidate is seeking.

3. The nature of the relationship between you and the candidate.

4. Relevant details to the position being sought by the candidate.

5. Evaluation of the candidate by the correspondent.

If you feel unable to provide a letter of recommendation, be brief and factual in your reasons.

Memoranda

Memoranda (or memos) are widely and routinely used by organizations, mainly for internal correspondence to convey short specific information. They could be written for any of the following reasons:

- To arrange a meeting.
- To give the results of research.
- To book a meeting room.
- To organise training.

```
┌────────────────────────────────────────────────────────┐
│                    FINANCE and INSURANCE Co              │
│                         The Causeway                     │
│                  Newcastle upon Tyne NN4 65T             │
│                      Tel: 0191 35202                     │
│                                                          │
│                                                          │
│   SB/abc                                                 │
│                                                          │
│   October 1st 20XX                                       │
│                                                          │
│                                                          │
│                                                          │
│   The Membership Secretary                               │
│   Chartered Institute of Marketing                       │
│   Moor Hall                                              │
│   Cookham                                                │
│   Berks                                                  │
│                                                          │
│                                                          │
│   Dear Sir/Madam,                                        │
│                                                          │
│   **Re: Caroline Taylor**                                │
│                                                          │
│   I am pleased to support Ms Taylor's application for    │
│   membership of the Chartered Institute of Marketing.    │
│                                                          │
│   Ms Taylor has been in our employment for 6 years       │
│   working in the area of Direct Marketing.               │
│                                                          │
│   I understand that she has passed all her CIM           │
│   examinations and will be pleased to receive further    │
│   benefit as a member of the CIM.                        │
│                                                          │
│   Yours faithfully,                                      │
│                                                          │
│                                                          │
│                                                          │
│   Sheila Brown                                           │
│   Marketing Director                                     │
│                                                          │
└────────────────────────────────────────────────────────┘
```

Figure 8.9 *Letter of recommendation*

- To organize attendance at an exhibition.
- To ask for staff cover.

Of course this list is not comprehensive as the reasons for sending a memo are almost unlimited. What can be stated is that memos can be stored for future reference and follow composition principles similar to that for writing business letters.

```
┌────────────────────────────────────────────────────────┐
│                          MEMO                            │
│                    Medical Software Ltd                  │
│                                                          │
│   To:        Carole Francis (Sales and Marketing         │
│              Director)                                   │
│   From:      Clare White (Marketing Manager)             │
│   Copy to:   Hannah Craven (Secretary)                   │
│   Subject:   Software 20XX Exhibition, Amsterdam,        │
│              December 1st–3rd                            │
│   Date:      October 1st 20XX                            │
│                                                          │
│   We have 8 weeks before the exhibition takes place and  │
│   need to finalize the details of the follow-up          │
│   campaign, particularly the role of our sales force.    │
│                                                          │
│   Further to our meeting last week, we also need to      │
│   discuss the sales promotion initiatives to push our    │
│   products following the exhibition.                     │
│                                                          │
│   Please confirm that a meeting on October 5th at 3 pm   │
│   in my office will be convenient.                       │
│                                                          │
└────────────────────────────────────────────────────────┘
```

Figure 8.10 *A memo*

Memo paper is often preprinted on A4 or A5, in the following format:

MEMO To: From: Date: Subject:

The sender and recipient of the memo are usually addressed by job title (e.g. sales manager), but their full name may also be included. It may be necessary to circulate the memo to other interested parties, and this should be indicated on the memo.

The subject title should be clear and concise and tell the recipient exactly what the memo is about.

The body of the memorandum should be in short paragraphs, with summary headings if appropriate.

E-mail

E-mail is a quick and simple way to communicate internally and with external contacts who are connected to the Internet. There are no rules about layout and the medium is usually used to send short messages though longer documents, such as letters and reports, are attached by selecting the Insert, File Attachment option.

The best way to experiment with e-mail is to send and receive some and you will soon become adept at recognizing when e-mail is appropriate and when it is better to telephone someone, write a formal letter or send a memorandum.

As a rule of thumb, if you need an urgent reply, the telephone is the best way to actually check details with a colleague or an external contact. This is because you will know if you have got through to the person or not by telephone whereas you cannot be sure that your e-mail message has been read, which can lead to uncertainty when you want an instant response.

For more formal communications it is better to send a letter to external customers or a memorandum to colleagues.

How to write effective e-mail

Some people do not use normal punctuation, such as capital letters and full stops, but this can lead to confusing messages and is best avoided.

Figure 8.11 *An example of an e-mail message*

Because of the speed, e-mail is like a cross between a telephone conversation and a letter. Consequently, it is often too easy to send an e-mail which is like an unstructured written conversation.

Before you send a message you should consider what you expect to happen as a result of sending your message. If it is purely to provide information or an update you should say so. If you require a certain action then you should make sure your message is focused on achieving it.

It is better to avoid sending a message that attempts to fulfil many different purposes at once as you risk causing confusion.

You should ensure that you are sending your message to the right recipients and if appropriate use the Bcc (blind carbon copy) line to send the message to other recipients without others knowing.

If you expect anyone on the Cc list to take specific action as a result of receiving your message, then you should make it clear in the message. Otherwise recipients in the Cc list might assume that the message is 'for information only'.

Your message will be one of many that a recipient might receive in a day. Therefore your subject line should be concise but give an indication of the context of the message.

There is no set rule about using a salutation, such as Dear John or Dear Sir. If you are unsure of what to do, it is better to err on the side of caution and include a greeting as the absence of one could make you appear rude. Generally though, e-mails do not require formal greetings in the way that letters do. Similarly you do not need to use a formal close such as 'Yours sincerely' or 'Yours faithfully' unless you have opted for a formal greeting. Most people sign off with a closing term such as 'regards' followed by their first and last name if they do not know the person even though it is usually clear who is the sender of an e-mail message. If you do include a formal greeting you may want to include your job title and company web site details.

Although you do not really need to think about layout in conjunction with an e-mail it is better to avoid sending e-mails that are one long block of text. They are much easier to read if you use spaces between paragraphs.

If you are sending attachments you should say so in the main body of the e-mail. If you are worried about other people being able to access the document you can password protect the document so that it can only be opened using the password. You could then contact the recipient by another method and provide them with the password so they can open the document.

As running costs are often related to the time online, problems could occur with being too brief. It is much better to work off-line and send a message that you have planned out and considered rather than rushing off a message and sending it without adequate forethought.

A good e-mail message should:

- Have a definite purpose
- Be properly addressed
- Be well structured
- Be written clearly
- Use attachments wisely
- Be protected appropriately.

Activity 8.3

S & G Construction Group has relocated its head office to Hong Kong and has been forced to undertake a restructuring exercise, which has resulted in the company reducing its international sales operation. As Sales Director, you will move to Hong Kong. Offices in Nairobi, Singapore, Dar-es-Salaam, New York and London will be retained.

Write a memo to the sales managers at each of the offices advising them of the importance of keeping open the lines of communication with their colleagues in each of the regions. Outline the disadvantages of relying on writing letters and explain the advantages of using IT and telecommunications facilities such as e-mail, fax and voice mail.

Notices

Notices can play an important role in disseminating information to a large number of people who share a common interest. Effective notices should follow these rules:

1. The size of the paper should correspond to the amount of information to be conveyed and its effect when displayed on the noticeboard and possibly viewed from several feet away.

2. The AIDA principle can again be used with a large, bold heading to capture attention, detail which holds the reader's interest and creates desire, and clear instructions as to the action which should be taken.

3. The message should be simple and concise.

SAFETY FIRST!

A Special First-Aid Course designed to give you basic introduction will be available free to all employees on the following dates:

October 1st 5–6 pm
November 1st 5–6 pm
December 1st 5–6 pm

The number of places is limited to 20 per class so early booking is advisable.

Contact: Jane Slater, ext. 123

Figure 8.12 A notice

Reports

Reports can be used internally and externally in a range of contexts either to give information or to make proposals with justifications.

Progress reports may be of a routine nature to provide an update on a particular job or project. Special one-off reports can be requested or prepared voluntarily to interpret data, inform and/or influence recipients – for example, to analyse market research data, give information about sales trends or to propose a change of company policy.

Reports are used for a variety of purposes and can be short (such as progress reports) or long (such as investigative reports or the annual report), formal or informal, routine, occasional or specially commissioned. Before any report can be prepared, decisions about the exact nature and purpose of the report, the recipient, distribution and likely reaction all need to be addressed because these factors will determine the structure, length and style (i.e. the degree of formality) of the report.

In marketing, a formal report could be written on the current state of the market in a particular sector, or a short memorandum report could provide a range of quotes from printers for a new catalogue. Somewhere between these two extremes, an informal report could be written, proposing the use of videoconferencing in a firm for example, or outlining sponsorship opportunities or reporting back from training or the success of a exhibition stand.

How to write reports

A report should not be written in a personal style highlighting the report writer's personal view if it has been commissioned to uncover facts and /or highlight the views of several people. A report should therefore be factual and written in an unbiased style. If necessary, it should show a range of opinions and conclude with the majority or most accurate viewpoint.

The report will sound more objective and professional if impersonal constructions are used, such as:
- 'It was found that...'
- 'It was evident that...'
- 'The statistics revealed that...'
- 'The investigations showed that ...'
- 'It appears that...'

Your report will be more balanced and objective if you avoid emotional sounding phrases, such as '....a desperate situation' or 'This must be done at all costs'.

How to structure a report

The guidance given earlier also applies to reports – they should have a beginning, middle and an end. However, you can also organize the material schematically, using a system of numbers and/or letters. This not only makes the material easier to read and follow but is also useful for referencing purposes.

Using a combination of numbers and letters, your report could appear as follows:
1. Terms of reference
2. Procedure
3. Findings
   a.. Main point
      i. Sub-point

Or you could use a decimal numbering system:

1 Main heading
   1.1 Sub-section
   1.2 Same sub-section but dealing with another area.
      1.2.1 Subordinate point.

In addition to using a numbering system to organize a report's contents, you could use different types of headings. These are used with the three main different types of reports: formal reports, informal reports and memorandum reports.

Formal reports

Formal reports are designed to achieve a number of goals but mainly to provide information and arguments based on investigating a problem or opportunity.

For a formal report it is usual to have the following headings/sections and structure:
- *Report title* which should be brief, specific and informative.
- *Recipient's name.*
- *Author's name.*
- *Date.*
- *Contents table* including headings and page numbers if the report size warrants this.
- *Terms of reference* should outline the scope of the report and the reason why it is being written.
- *Procedure or research method/methodology* should identify how the information in the report was obtained.
- *Findings* relevant facts and findings in order of importance, chronological order or just grouped to together in relevant categories.
- *Conclusion* should summarise the main findings and should not introduce new findings.
- *Recommendations* not always required and used only if there are solutions to a problem which has been identified and if these have emerged from a detailed analysis in the report.
- *Appendices* where there is a large amount of factual data, tables and diagrams that could interrupt the flow of the document and cause confusion. They appear at the end of the report and their presence should be highlighted in the report. Each appendix should be numbered.

REPORT

TO: Denise Wood, Marketing Manager

FROM: Amy Mills, Marketing Assistant

DATE: 6 December 200X

GO EASY – THE CASE FOR A WEBSITE & ON-LINE BOOKING SERVICE

1. Introduction The aim of this report is to identify reasons why our company, Go Easy, should invest in a web site and on-line booking service. This will be demonstrated by looking at the current state of the Internet market, predicted trends and competitor Internet activity.

2. Findings

a. The On-line Market Recent studies by Business Research (December 2000) have looked at the US and UK on-line markets. Their information shows that in the US a third of all households with the Internet have shopped on-line in the past six months. Similarly, the figures for the UK are high, with 22% of Internet users making a purchase on-line within the past three months.

   Their data indicates that in the UK, travel is the third most popular on-line purchase after PC's and books, with 15% of on-line expenditure being spent on travel.

   In the US, expenditure for on-line travel is set to grow from 0.5$ billion to over 7$ billion.

b. Competitor Activity

   EasyJet, one of our competitors, has made significant headway in this area since launching their web site and booking service in October of last year.

   A recent report by 'Promotions and Incentives' magazine shows that 4% of all their bookings are currently made on-line. EasyJet's aims to increase this to 30%, equating to £60 million worth of revenue.

   EasyJet have linked up with the *Times* to offer discounted flights to customers who book on-line.

c. Benefits of on-line booking

   The information given in the Promotion and Incentives report shows that EasyJet can handle up to 200 bookings at a time over the Internet, but only 90 at a time by telephone. Thus Internet booking gives a more efficient service to their customers.

   Benefits to EasyJet itself are that they do not have to pay 80p commission to the telephonists, who would normally handle the incoming calls.

3. Conclusions

   On-line sales are continually growing, with huge numbers of individuals potentially purchasing from the travel sector. Go Easy flights should have access to this market.

   Our competition are establishing a firm foothold in this valuable market, using huge promotion and above-the-line advertising activity to do so.

   On-line purchasing has advantages for both the consumer and the company.

4. Recommendations In order not to miss out on the ever-growing on-line market, Go Easy must introduce a web site with a suitable and efficient on-line purchasing capability.

Figure 8.13 *An example of a formal report*

Informal reports

For an *informal* report it is usual to use the following headings:

- Introduction
- Findings
- Conclusion

or

- Purpose and scope of report
- Background information
- Findings
- Conclusions and recommendations

PRINTMAN PRINTING COMPANY

Report on Office Telecommunications Facilities

To: Mark Scrivens, Managing Director

From: Jo Goodwin, Sales and Marketing Manager

Date: 2 December 200X

Introduction

As a small printing company trying to succeed in a competitive market, we need to be able to use various office equipment to improve our efficiency and effectiveness when communicating with customers and internally. This report sets out to identify where we could upgrade our current systems and equipment to improve how sales representatives and account managers operate.

Findings

Voice Mail

During busy periods customers often have problems getting through to the switchboard with our current telephone system. With a voice mail system connected to a computer, customers could use an interactive menu system which would mean they could ring up and choose to be connected to any one of a number of our account managers without having to go through the switchboard. Customers could also leave messages when a person is not at their desk, which saves colleagues spending time taking down messages.

Networked Laptop Computers

Laptop computers could be used by our account managers and sales team while they are out visiting clients. It means they could access information here at the office and give clients quotes on print jobs immediately. In addition they could show clients examples of relevant jobs we have done on their laptops rather than carrying round a large portfolio or briefcase of printed material. Also when it is not worth staff coming back to the office because their last client visit was near to their home, it makes sense to give them the means to finish off work, such as, quotes, reports and design briefs, in their own time at home.

An Extranet

As we have now got a computer system with Internet access, it would be good to upgrade the system to incorporate an extranet so that customers can access their accounts and check the progress on their various print jobs with us. This would reduce the number of 'checking' calls that account managers deal with and free them up to develop new business and cross-sell our services to clients more effectively.

Conclusions

These are the three main systems and pieces of equipment that we could use at the moment to improve how we operate in sales and marketing. If these proposals are of interest, then it would be a simple task to collate various information about different systems and do a price check against different products in the market.

Figure 8.14 An example of an informal report.

Memorandum

To: Bob Bloggs, Sales Manager

From: Marcia Merchant, Sales and Marketing Assistant

Subject: Report on Negotiation Skills Course

This memorandum report outlines the value and effectiveness of the recent Negotiation Skills course attended on 4 December 200X run by Total Training at the Willow Bank Hotel.

Course Details

It was a one-day course and cost £150 per delegate. Delegates who attended were from a variety of sectors but all were working in sales and marketing jobs.

Course Content

The course was delivered with a mixture of input, case studies and interaction with the audience. The course was well organised and the trainer was well organised and interesting.

Topics covered included preparing for negotiations, building rapport, trading concessions, maintaining advantage and controlling interpersonal behaviour.

The course was delivered from a 'buying and selling' perspective and provided comprehensive coverage of theory, practical suggestions and skills testing.

Conclusion

The course runs again early next year and I recommend that others in the department attend it.

Figure 8.15 An example of a memorandum report

Memorandum report

For memorandum reports, it is usual to use a memo format and to group relevant information together under different headings and categories.

Articles

If you work in the marketing department of a firm that produces a staff newsletter with the aim of improving internal communication, you could occasionally be asked to contribute – or you might even be responsible for all aspects of it, such as writing, designing and arranging the printing. However, you might never be asked to write an article or an advertorial (like a press release but in the form of a newspaper or magazine article) because it is not part of your job. Nevertheless an article is a communication format that is occasionally tested on the examination paper.

The way to approach writing an article is to use the writing skills you have honed when you have written letters and reports and to combine that with your skill in producing press releases. When you are writing an article for an advertorial or for a company newsletter, you must try to adopt an independent, unbiased tone – in other words, the 'sell' should be very subtle.

Design Works

Labelling and Signage Designs know that good design is essential for firms that need to communicate with their staff, customers and suppliers.

Essential safety notices in the workplace need to stand out so people take notice of them – in a way that words alone cannot manage. Graphical symbols can show hazards and directional symbols can indicate specific areas, e.g. toilets, disabled access, fire exits, litter bins, etc. At Labelling and Signage Designs these can be tailor-made for any individual work environment. Just visualise the 'Keep Britain Tidy' logo or the Olympic Games symbol or even a 'No smoking' symbol to understand the power of images in communicating with people.

To communicate instantly with members of the public who are unfamiliar with an area or environment, it is important to use signs which indicate where dressing rooms, pay points and exit doors are located.

However, all imagery in the corporate environment should be consistent with the image and identity the company wants to communicate to its staff and public.

Consequently, handwritten, poorly designed signs and images would portray an amateur, uncaring and unprofessional image. A professional signage company knows how important the right typeface, shape and colour is to presenting the correct image and conveying the message effectively.

Corporate Identity

The corporate image that is communicated in a company's logo is seen on its letterheads, business cards, lorries, shop or office front, sales promotion literature and packaging or carrier bags, depending on the firm's type of business.

The designers at Labelling and Signage can use graphical symbols, visual communication and typefaces to give a company an appropriate image. A particular typeface can convey a certain personality or culture, e.g. formality, long-established or modern and technical. A logo which stands out can create recognition and differentiate the firm from its competitors. The right logo can link the various products and services of one organization into a single, consistent identity. Think about the distinctive type style of the Coca-Cola logo, the use of the black horse symbol that distinguishes Lloyds Bank; Kodak's outstanding black and yellow packaging certainly makes its products stand out. These well-known logos and symbols actually provide customers with reassurance that they are dealing with the best.

The logo can even indicate a firm's field of activity: an international worldwide firm might even include a globe; a people-oriented firm might show linked hands.

It is difficult with a new firm, or a company with a new product, to find a name that has not been used before. But the right acronym such as Esso or Persil could mean a product is easy to pronounce and has a distinctive name. In a similar vein, the right slogan can help customers remember a firm or its products.

Figure 8.16 An advertorial

Figure 8.16 is an example of an advertorial article, written by a partner in a small labelling and sign company for a newspaper, about why logos, letterhead design and graphical symbols are important for companies' internal and external communications.

Summary

In this unit you have studied:

- Why you need to be familiar with a range of communication formats.
- How various communication formats are structured.
- How and when to write effective letters, memos, notices, e-mails, reports and articles.

Further study and examination preparation

Look over the reports you did in Unit 7 in answer to question 1a from the June 2000 examination paper and question 1b from the December 2000 paper.

In addition, go to the end of the book and do Questions 4 and 7 from the June 2000 paper and question 6c from the December 2000 paper.

Exam hint

You need to be familiar with all the communication formats used in this unit as they will be tested throughout the examination paper. You will find that most questions in fact require candidates to write their answer in the format of a letter, report, memo or e-mail. Also question 1 usually includes a report which is often awarded a possible 20 marks so this is obviously an important area for you to study.

Objectives

In this unit you will:

- Extend your knowledge of the communications or promotional mix.
- Examine the differences between above- and below-the-line promotion.
- Appreciate what influences promotional decisions.

By the end of this unit you should be able to:

- Formulate a promotional brief.
- Determine the suitability of various promotional activities.
- Evaluate the appearance of corporate literature.
- Devise a press release.

Study guide

This unit provides you with a basic understanding of the communications or promotion mix and covers indicative content area 2.4.2 of the syllabus. It links with the Marketing Fundamentals syllabus indicative content area 1.2.9 which is covered in unit 7 of the Marketing Fundamentals coursebook. With the Marketing Fundamentals syllabus you are looking at the promotional mix as one element of a total marketing mix; with Customer Communications this topic is key to understanding how organizations communicate with their external customers.

With this syllabus, you not only need to know about the various communication tools but also how to use them. For instance, you need to be able to write a press release, suggest the layout for a press advertisement or write the copy for a mailshot. However, you would not be expected to be able to make a television or radio advertisement because these are very specialised activities that would be difficult to assess in a written examination.

You need to appreciate that although some larger organizations subcontract all their marketing communication activities out to specialised agencies, there are many smaller organizations where working in marketing is synonymous with drafting press advertisements and being able to write a press release or the text for a mailshot.

For further information for how this material in this unit will be examined, read the Exam Hints section at the end of the unit.

The unit will take you one hour to read through the unit and a further two hours to work through the activities.

Study tip

This unit provides an outline of the main advertising media and their main attributes. To provide further examination of this topic you need to spend some time looking at examples of advertising using different media. For each advert you should specify the advertising objectives, identify the target audience and consider why that particular medium has been chosen.

You could undertake a similar activity looking at sales promotions. List how many different types of sales promotion you can see when you next go shopping. Consider the objectives of each promotion.

The communications mix or promotions mix

You have already looked at the various ways that individuals inside an organization use to communicate either with colleagues or others outside their organizations. The communications *or promotions mix* refers to those forms of communication that are used not on behalf of an individual but on behalf of the entire organization to promote either itself or its goods and services.

See Figure 1.3 in Unit 1 for an example of the communications mix and Figure 1.1 for the target audiences that organizations may want to communicate with.

The communications or promotional mix can be categorized as *above-the-line activity and below-the-line activity.* (These definitions will be explained as you work through the unit.) Organizations usually use a mix of above- and below-the-line activity to communicate with their target audience.

These activities include:
- Advertising using main media.
- Direct marketing.
- Sales promotions.
- Sales or corporate literature.
- Sponsorship.
- Point of sale material.
- Public relations.
- Exhibitions.
- Personal selling.
- Branding and corporate image.
- Packaging.
- Internet marketing.

How the communications mix works

Advertising is just one activity in the 'tool box' of promotional activities that marketers can use but it is the most visible of all communication activities because it uses the main media of print, television, radio, cinema and outdoor. (You will look in more detail at the different types of advertising and other types of promotion or communications later in the unit.)

Promoting goods and services came about because as goods and services became mass-produced and supply outstripped demand, organizations realised that advertising and selling could help 'shift' items from shop windows and company shelves.

Initially the main medium for advertising was print (mainly newspapers) and it helped the owners of newspapers and magazines to cover their production costs. Gradually owners of other media appeared, such as, poster sites and cinemas. During the 1950s and 1960s in the UK, commercially owned radio and television stations also gained revenue from advertising.

Now there is a proliferation of media globally which means that people are exposed to a mass of advertising messages.

As a result of this, advertising has had to become more sophisticated to attract people's attention. A single advert placed indiscriminately in a magazine or newspaper without careful planning is unlikely to attract your customers' attention.

Nowadays you would need to consider carefully what your objectives are and who you are trying to reach before deciding which promotional activities you need to use and what approach you need to take. You would need to consider the following factors:
- What is to be achieved? What are your objectives?
- Who do you want to communicate with? Who is your target audience?
- How big is your target audience? How can you reach them? What are their media habits?

- What is your message? How can you express your message?
- When do you need to communicate your message?
- How much money do you have to spend?

Promotional objectives

Here is a selection of promotion objectives:

- To create an image.
- To create awareness.
- To inform about a new feature.
- To change attitudes.
- To correct misconceptions.
- To reassure.
- To remind.
- To generate interest.
- To generate response.
- To encourage trial.
- To prompt purchase.
- To support other promotional activity.

Case histories

Promoting a sports brand in Thailand

In a recent article in *the Nation* (courtesy of Lexis-Nexis) the managing director of Adidas (Thailand), Michael Wellman, said: 'We are the number one sports brand in Thailand in terms of revenue and we would like to maintain the position.'

Wellman said that the company would be working on improving visual merchandising in its retail outlets, as well as promoting in-store activities such as bringing in local athletes to talk with customers to enhance their knowledge of sports.

Adidas has already launched its 'Be Better' campaign in Thailand, which is part of the firm's global strategy to strengthen its leadership as a sports brand.

'All sports fans in Thailand already recognise Adidas as a sports brand that provides genuine sports products. And we want to convey to people the terrific feeling they can get through sports and exercise,' Wellman said.

'It makes you feel good and you want to share the feeling with others and help others be better. That is what this campaign is all about,' he added.

Promoting a film in the UK

The recently released film 'Bridget Jones's Diary' will run at cinemas throughout the UK for a fixed period this year. But before its release and during the period of its release, it has been heavily promoted to ensure that exposure of the film will be maximized in order to attract audiences and revenue.

Around the time of the release of the film, an extensive bus shelter and billboard hoarding campaign was mounted, showing the lead actors or 'stars' of the film. Those sited near cinemas also provided information about when the film would be showing.

To celebrate the first showing of the film in London (its premiere) the 'stars' of the film allowed themselves to be photographed, along with other celebrities invited to see the film, so that national newspapers would print their pictures and a related story to publicise the film.

Around this time, film reviewers/journalists who had been invited to a special screening wrote reviews of the film that appeared in many national newspapers and magazines.

Once the film was on general release the major cinema chains produced material in their 'free' magazines about it, to target regular cinema-goers.

Some of the film stars have been interviewed on television and radio chat shows to publicise their latest movie.

If the film had been targeted at children, a great deal of merchandising material would have been produced as well. (Think about the remake of '101 Dalmations' and the variety of merchandising material that was produced (including toys, books, posters, pencilcases, etc.) not only to generate income but also to indirectly publicise the film.

The role of integrated communications

From the case examples, you can see that organizations are aware that one advertisement on its own would be unlikely to make any real impact on people because of the amount of advertising 'noise' that exists. As a consequence, organizations repeat their message many times and in many ways to achieve 'coverage' of their target audience. These efforts are often referred to as 'integrated communication campaigns'.

Above-the-line promotional activity

'Above the line' is a slightly out-of-date expression that refers to advertising on which a commission fee is paid by the media to the agency that placed the advertising. As the rules and methods for booking advertising and the whole area of remuneration has changed, it has come to refer to the main advertising media of television, radio, cinema, outdoor and the press.

Television advertising

This is the most visual medium, as most people spend at least some time watching television for entertainment. Because it can reach large numbers of people, the cost of one spot or commercial break can be very high. In order that the television commercial does not look out of place with all the other professionally filmed programmes that appear either side of the commercial, television advertising requires production specialists, which adds to the cost of production. The relatively short exposure time (most commercials last for no more than 30 seconds) means that television advertising has to be repeated many times and, as the cost of airtime is very expensive, this means that it tends only to feature in the marketing budgets of the mass-market fmcg (fast moving consumer goods) brands.

Television is a very creative medium that offers:

- Sound, movement, interesting visual effects.
- Entertainment that famous people are happy to appear in.
- Impact – you can see it in action or being demonstrated.
- Credibility to the product or service.

Television is a very transient medium that can easily be missed. This is more so since people with video recorders can fast-forward past commercial breaks in programmes they've recorded (zipping) and people with a remote control can quickly change channels (zapping) to avoid television advertising. There is also no opportunity to sample or smell a product.

Take for example the UK television advertising situation, where it is possible to buy television advertising that appears only in one of the 13 ITV regions and so target a specific area of Britain. However, it is also possible to buy national advertising airtime covering all the television regions, which makes it ideal for mass-market products or services.

Until recently it was a difficult tool to use for targeting specific groups, except in a fairly crude way. For example, media planners could make generalizations that mothers mostly watch daytime television, the evening news is watched by upmarket business people, and teenagers watch late-night television.

With the introduction of more channels via cable and satellite television, there are more opportunities for specialist programmes, for example, about specific sports. With this comes more opportunities to target specific audiences. For example, MUTV is a channel devoted to the interests of Manchester United fans. With greater audience fragmentation comes greater opportunities for niche advertising.

Radio advertising

Radio relies only on sound. It does not therefore have the same creative impact as television and cannot show products. However, it can tap into the listeners' imaginations with the use of evocative sound effects and voices (including famous voices) to make it a very effective advertising medium.

It can reach large audiences as in the UK there are several national commercial radio stations. These stations specialize in particular types of music (from jazz to classical). In addition, most regions have local radio geared to the needs of people in their catchment area. In this way radio advertising campaigns can be targeted geographically and according to lifestyle/tastes.

Cost varies with the size of audiences reached but production costs are not as high as television. However, advertisers usually have to buy a large number of airtime 'spots' because of the transient (and sometimes background listening) nature of the medium.

Cinema advertising

Cinema advertising has the same creative characteristics as television and perhaps even more impact because there are fewer distractions and potential interruptions from zipping and zapping. In addition, media buyers can ensure that advertisements fit the audience profile that applies to particular films. In the UK most cinema advertising is sold on a national basis through various cinema chains and two contractors. There is some opportunity for geographic segmentation, with a small proportion of advertising aimed at purely local audiences.

Outdoor advertising

This type of advertising covers a whole range of different types of media that can be found outdoors and indoors. It includes large roadside billboard hoardings, small poster sites on bus shelters and bus stations, on underground and ground level train stations, the inside and outside of various types of transport, such as buses, trains, tubes and taxis, and even peripheral sites, such as parking meters and street furniture.

Although a poster site can have plenty of impact, it is limited to short messages with bold images. Usually there is a very short exposure time as people are moving past the advertising. (Exceptions here are people waiting at tube or rail stations.) Most outdoor advertising does not incorporate sound or movement in the message. However, there are some moving poster sites where the image changes every few minutes. There are also some well-known three-dimensional sites. For example, an airline has one in the form of an aeroplane at Heathrow and there was a famous one designed to look like a pub that sold Guinness.

Press advertising

Press advertising comprises all printed media. In the UK this covers national newspapers, local newspapers, specialist trade and technical magazines (one for almost every industry sector and job), general-interest magazines (the most popular of which are female interest magazines aimed at different age groups) and specialist magazines that cover almost every hobby and interest area, from fishing to stamp collecting.

Therefore advertising in print media can be carefully targeted at demographic and geographic segments. Quite complex messages can be conveyed because print media can be retained and seen more than once. Advertisements can also benefit from the credibility of the newspaper or magazine.

However, advertising in the print media has limited impact and there is little flexibility for creative messages compared with television advertising. Although magazines can be in full colour and quite glossy, newspapers tend to be in black and white with only spot colour.

Internet advertising

According to Kohl (*Getting @ttention -Leading Edge Lessons for Publicity and Marketing*. Butterworth-Heineman, 2000) spending on Internet advertising will continue to grow despite that fact that some people consider that online advertisements do not work. Kohl cites the Forrester Research which estimates that global spending for online advertising will reach $33 billion by 2004.

The Internet is a global advertising medium which uses web sites, banner advertisements and streaming media as ways to target web users with information about products and services. Although it is a developing industry which is difficult to evaluate in terms of advertising effectiveness, it is still possible to compare the number of click throughs on a web site after a banner advertising campaign has run. Alternatively if a web site can be used for transactions then the amount of business conducted can be measured, say after an e-mail marketing campaign.

See Unit 10 for more information about the way the Internet is used as a promotional tool.

Activity 9.1

Look at the following scenarios and evaluate the proposed advertising media decisions.

1. Calvin Klein are considering using local newspapers to promote their expensive new fragrance, 'y', which is aimed at fashionable young men and women.

2. The manager of a small hotel in Wales would like to use television advertising to attract tourists.

3. Harvey Goldsmith Entertainments sell concert tickets in the U.K. They are considering using radio to advertise a number of outdoor summer concerts featuring the famous Three Tenors.

4. ASH (the anti-smoking lobby group) has identified that there is a massive growth in the number of young female smokers and is considering using cinema and teenage girl magazines like *Jackie* and *19* to target them in a hard-hitting anti-smoking campaign.

Below-the-line promotion

Basically, any promotional activity that does not come under the five main media mentioned above comes under the category of below-the-line promotion.

Corporate literature

Corporate literature, such as stationery, brochures, leaflets and annual reports, is a visual record of an organization's corporate identity in which branding and logos are often featured extensively. An organization's corporate literature has a vital role to play in communicating information about a company, its products/services and its annual performance to its stakeholders.

Production of literature

Unless it is specific to your job role, it is unlikely that you will need to have extensive knowledge of graphic design and print production techniques. However, you should be able to critically evaluate rough drafts that designers supply to you for corporate literature and provide layout information for items to be published in-house and by printers.

Here are some points you should look for.

Consistency

Overall, there should be some consistency in headings, margins, spacing of paragraphs, white space, text justified or ranged left/right, typefaces and typesizes. It is better that a page has unity, which can be created by a dominant headline or illustration or a combination of both, so that the reader is focused and is not confused by too many visual 'tricks' or devices. However, there is often justification for text and images to be arranged in an interesting way to encourage the reader to follow through the text.

Colour

Colour can be used to provide variety, impact, interest and even to communicate a mood. However, too many colours can bombard the reader and convey a cheap and 'tacky' feeling.

Typefaces

Typestyles are a whole area of study on their own. If you look at the various typestyles or typefaces (also known as fonts) on your computer, you will have an idea of the choice and variety available. Different typefaces convey different visual images. Some have an old-fashioned/traditional feel, others appear modern, some give an impression of formality and others appear light-hearted and would be appropriate for a party invitation.

Some typefaces are easier to read than others; others provide more emphasis for headings and sub-headings. You should ensure that there is consistency in the typefaces used in your organization's corporate literature.

Typesize is also an important consideration and you should ensure that all printed material is legible.

Figure 9.1 *Printed material plays an important role in the communications mix*

Activity 9.2

You work in the Marketing Department of the local chamber of commerce. An international conference is planned on e-commerce (business on the Internet). A gala dinner will launch the event. An expert speaker will make a keynote speech on the topic and dignitaries and interested parties will be invited to attend.

Draft an invitation to the gala dinner to be printed on A5-size card. Include layout instructions for the printer.

Corporate image

An organization's image and that of its products/services are a vital way to communicate with target markets.

A corporate identity or image can be communicated by the following:

- An organization's logo.

- The typeface on an organization's letterhead.

- The materials it uses for correspondence (stationery, business cards).

- Corporate literature (brochures, annual reports, internal training material, application forms, internal newsletters, exhibition stand material).

- Its headquarters and offices, including signs inside and outside the building.

- The signs on its vehicles.

- The appearance of personnel (uniforms, badges) and the way they deal with people (they are ambassadors for the organization).

- Its public relations image – how it is reported in the media and public perception in general.

However, Dolphin (2000) says that corporate image is often used as a synonym for reputation, which can be the single most significant point of differentiation between competing companies. However, he states that organizations cannot always control their image. He cites Albert and Whettan (1985) who differentiate between image and identity. 'If identity answers the question "who/what do we believe we are?" then image answers the question "who/what do we want others to think we are?"'

Dolphin makes the distinction between product and corporate advertising in a reference to the Chrysler Corporation when it announced its 'first corporate advertising campaign in years'. The campaign was to concentrate on changing the company's image as a whole – rather than just selling a single car or truck brand. Post-campaign research showed that few consumers associated some of Chrysler's most successful brands with the parent company and that most people thought that JEEP was a company.

Dolphin also makes the point that corporate image is concerned with a mental impression. If a public thinks well of an organization it is more likely to wish to do business with it; and it is more likely to encourage others to do the same. A favourable image is more likely to encourage would-be investors – who are often the lifeblood of an organization.

He adds that an organization that is well regarded by its audiences is likely to do well. It is more likely to have a good foundation on which strategic success can be built and will probably to be one step ahead of the competition – its image being an added value factor.

Case history

British Airways

When British Airways decided to change its corporate image to give itself a more international feel so it could compete more effectively in a global market, it had difficulties in persuading some parts of the British media and public why it needed an image change, particularly one that cost so much. By replacing the Union Flag with bold 'images of the world' on its aeroplanes, it had angered some of its domestic market but the new corporate image was in keeping with its advertising strapline 'the world is closer than you think'.

Brand image

Whereas a corporate image refers to the organization as a whole, the organization may be the umbrella for a number of different brands. For example, Virgin is an organization with a corporate image and there are a number of Virgin brands, such as Virgin Vodka, Virgin One (financial services) and Virgin Trains, each with their own brand image.

A brand can be communicated by any of the following:

- A name.
- A term.
- A design.
- A trademark.
- A symbol.
- A logo.

With brands, consumers can be encouraged to associate certain attributes with a product. These attributes can be used to personify the brand and add value to a commodity. For example, it is much easier to promote Andrex toilet paper using the Andrex puppies than if the manufacturers could only talk about the product and show images of toilet rolls. It allows Andrex to distinguish the product from its competitors and allows the manufacturer to charge a premium price.

Logos

Logos can be just as important as a brand name or brand image in that they can:

- Attract attention.
- Create an impression.
- Create recognition.
- Convey information about a product or organization.
- Provide consistent imagery.
- Differentiate the product/organization from its competitors.

Logos can be applied to a range of products or used in a variety of situations. By using a brand in this way the credibility of the original brand can be transferred. (See Figure 9.3 where CIM's logo can be used by 'accredited colleges' and this enhances a college's credibility in the minds of potential and existing marketing students.)

Figure 9.2 The CIM logo

Figure 9.3 Adapting a logo for different purposes

Activity 9.3

Read the following extract from 'The Power of Brands: How to enhance your brand in Asia' by Paul Temporal. It has been adapted and is used courtesy of Lexis-Nexis. Choose two brands mentioned in the article and explain what feelings they evoke in the minds of consumers.

> The first thing to recognise when we talk about brands is that they are not just names, terms, symbols, designs or combinations of these, although it is true to say that such things can and do differentiate certain products and companies from others.

The additional ingredient that makes a successful brand is personality.

In Asia, Coca Cola, Sean Connery, Nestlé, Sony, Batman, Mercedes and Michael Jackson are equally well known. People tend to relate to brand personalities in the same way as they do to human personalities.

Some brands appeal to the rational part of a person, to the elements of logic and good sense such as toothpaste which prevents decay and cholesterol-free foods.

Some brands attract the emotional part of people, appealing to their feelings such as warmth, affection and belonging. Products such as Harley Davidson motorcycles and companies like Benetton with its global village branding exemplify these.

Then there is the strange phenomenon of intuition. Some companies and products are attractive to people who intuitively feel comfortable with them, because they see these brands as an extension of themselves, a good fit to their personality, lifestyle, aspirations and behaviour – companies like the Body Shop, with its environmental approach.

Brands influence consumer decisions to buy in any of the above ways or through combinations of them.

The Marlboro brand personality is a good example of how a company understands and combines the physical and emotional elements that appeal to certain customers who live or would love to live a certain lifestyle. Products such as gold credit cards, watches or prestige items help people to express themselves to others by demonstrating that they are different and have achieved something. They act as extensions of the personality, so it really is 'all in the mind' and the key to brand management and its development is a clear understanding of what benefits the customer is looking for.

Ask consumers what comes to mind when they hear the name of a big brand such as BMW or Gucci and they will reply with a list of attributes which go far beyond the physical, tangible aspects of product and delivery, but if there is one word which brings all these together in people's minds, it is value.

Brands reduce the perceived risk of purchase and consumers rely on chosen brands to guarantee standards of quality and service.

With product branding, the company gives each product a brand name and there is little or no attachment of the company relationship. Each brand has to compete on its own merit, such as Pizza Hut which normally operates without any endorsement from parent company Pepsico.

With corporate branding the company uses one brand – usually the company name – for all its products and services, as in the case of IBM. If the company uses what is often referred to as house branding, the individual products are separate identifiable brands but the overall company brand is used as an endorsement of origin and quality. This approach is often used by car manufacturers, the hospitality sector and by financial institutions.

Some brands established in the 1930s are still the top brands now. From Coca-Cola to Colgate, Kelloggs to Kodak, many big brands have defended their position in the market and they, along with other famous names, have become synonymous with their industries.

Brands can also assist moves across industries to penetrate new markets. Dunhill is an excellent example of this. Formerly based in the declining-image industry of tobacco, Dunhill is now firmly established internationally in upmarket clothing, toiletries and fashion accessories.

Packaging

Aside from the functional role of packaging, which is to actually provide a container for products, packaging has a role to play in communicating with customers. It communicates the product name and the brand image. Following on from advertising and other promotional activity, this can act as a reminder to consumers at the point of sale to purchase the product in favour of a competing product.

Point of sale display and merchandising

Point of sale display and merchandising refers to the in-store display that can influence consumers to purchase products in shops. It involves the layout and design of the shop and the way the goods or merchandise are presented. Manufacturers can have in-store display material produced to remind customers of their products at the point of purchase. For example, manufacturers of chocolates and confectionery might arrange with shops to display special branded stands, mobiles or life-size cardboard cut-outs of characters used to advertise the chocolate brand. Similarly, cosmetics manufacturers might supply shops with hanging signs or revolving display stands. This is another tool for marketers to communicate brand imagery and act as a reminder at the point of purchase.

Powerful manufacturers that spend vast amounts on advertising tend to have more influence on retailers in terms of where their products are displayed. The most effective display areas are at 'eye level', where products are easy to see and reach for.

Sales promotion

Sales promotion is another communication tool that marketers use. It is often described as 'A short-term tactical marketing tool that gives customers additional reasons or incentives to purchase'.

Sales promotions can offer temporary added value to the customer at the point of purchase (often referred to as a sales pull strategy). Manufacturers can also direct promotions to the trade (often referred to as a sales push strategy).

There are many different versions of sales promotions that are directed at consumers:

- Price reductions.
- Coupons/money-off vouchers.
- Entry to competitions/free prize draws.
- Free goods.
- x per cent free.
- 3 for the price of 2.
- Free samples.
- Free gifts.
- Guarantees
- £x goes to y charity if you purchase.
- Reward points/tokens against a free gift (for example, Air Miles).
- Refunds or free gifts on a mail-in basis.

Sales promotions aimed at the trade include:

- Discount on bulk orders.
- Free supplies.
- Incentives (for example, shopping vouchers for Marks & Spencer or a free alarm clock).
- Free prize draw competitions.
- Deferred invoicing.
- Merchandising and display material.

The objectives of a promotion could be to:

- Encourage trial of product.
- Extend existing customer base.
- Prompt customers to change brand.
- Generate bulk buying.
- Overcome seasonal dips in sales.
- Encourage trade to stock product.

Figure 9.4 A bookmark used as a sales promotion item

Exhibitions

In many business-to-business marketing situations, organizations have a sales force that visits the customer. With exhibitions, road shows, seminars and conferences, customers come to see the supplier. This provides organizations with a valuable opportunity to communicate with their customers and potential customers in a face-to-face situation.

These occasions take many forms.

Conferences

A conference may feature speakers from a number of different organizations who are experts in various fields, and attendees pay for the privilege of attending the conference. For example, a recent conference aimed at top decision-makers in NHS Trusts provided attendees with advice about taking advantage of a government scheme to allow Trusts to extend or improve their buildings. The speakers came from a variety of law firms, construction companies and architects. The conference also provided the speakers with an opportunity to promote their organization's expertise and to network with potential customers from the Trusts as well.

Seminars

Seminars are held by companies to provide customers with advice on developments in their market. At the same time, companies have the opportunity to extend their business relationship with attendees. For example, many of the larger accountancy firms provide breakfast budget briefings to discuss the implications of a new budget or taxation laws. Similarly, pharmaceutical firms arrange seminars for doctors to discuss new drugs that are available on the market.

Mobile road shows

These can be in the form of a mobile unit that goes around the country to promote goods/services. For example, the National Blood Transfusion Service attracts donors when its mobile units are placed at shopping centres or university buildings.

Trade fairs

Although there are some exhibitions that are aimed at the general public, such as The National Homes Exhibition, most exhibitions are directed at business-to-business activity.

Trade fairs are generally held in large exhibition halls where firms book a stand area and either hire a stand or pay for one to be designed. The stand and the corporate literature have to be presented in an eye-catching way to attract visitors to the stand.

Companies also have to cover the cost of staffing stands, pay for staff travel and accommodation costs and hospitality costs incurred when sales staff network with prospects and customers.

Exhibitions combine personal selling with non-personal communication activities and bring potential customers, at their expense, to a location that suits you. Nevertheless, many companies find that they usually need to undertake some pre-exhibition publicity to attract people to their stand.

Staff can make sales at exhibitions but they are usually used to generate leads that have to be followed up once the exhibition has finished.

Sponsorship

Sponsorship is another communications tool that can be used to put an organization's name across to a variety of publics and promote an image. Organizations can sponsor the arts, sporting events, individual sportsmen and women or even television programmes.

Organizations are usually interested in the type of sponsorship that either attracts publicity and media coverage or puts their name in front of their target audience in an interesting and maybe novel way. For sponsorship to work, it should be in keeping with the organization or its brand's image.

Sponsorship can be in the form of goods, for example, free football boots or financial reward to the sport or the individual. It could even be some kind of loss guarantee of the kind that occurs with some tennis events if they are rained off.

Sponsoring individuals can be risky if they attract bad publicity and are involved in some form of scandal. This could result in the organization's name being tainted by association. However, most organizations would withdraw sponsorship in the case of a scandal.

Public relations

The Institute of Public Relations has defined public relations as 'the planned and sustained effort to establish and maintain goodwill and mutual understanding between an organization and its publics'.

The above definition is a very broad one. It comprises a number of general activities, some of which you have already examined in previous units, and a number of specific activities that are devised to raise the profile of an organization or even a person representing an organization.

General PR activities generally relate to communicating with a variety of stakeholders and comprise corporate communications, community relations and customer care activities. In addition, there are a number of specific PR activities that relate to communicating with the media.

Corporate communications

Corporate communications can be defined as communications between an organization and its internal and external audiences, the purpose of which is to create greater understanding for, and perception of, the ideals and purposes of the organization.

The following activities are methods used to convey corporate messages.

- In house journals/newsletters.
- Annual reports.
- Gifts/incentives, for example calendars, key fobs, desk items, etc.
- Christmas cards.
- Business dinners/receptions.
- Corporate entertaining, e.g. golf tournaments.

Community relations

- Scholarships or bursaries.
- Charity support.
- Open days for the public – for example, the fire service often has open days.

Customer care

- Customer service departments.
- Complaints management.

- Customer advice and help lines.
- Ethical and environmental policies.

Specific PR activities

These are activities generally related to communicating with the media.

- Press conferences.
- Photocalls.
- Publicity stunts.
- Supplying feature articles.
- Open days/previews for the press – for example, some theatres have press nights.
- Product launch events.
- Advertorials/advertisement features (articles are written for the press but the space is paid for in the same way that an advertisement is paid for).
- Sending press releases.

Case history

An airline company's corporate communications

Dolphin in his book 'The Fundamentals of Corporate Communications' (2000) refers to the philosophy of American Airlines of working with the news media rather than against them. The company goes out of its way to make its officials available to the press; both on a formal and informal basis; and each year the communication department organizes a visit to a city served by the airline so that key executives can meet the local media.

The company puts effort into helping journalists understand the dynamics of the airline industry. It hosts an annual media day consisting of seminars and discussions on the workings of the airline and the industry as a whole.

The communication department peppers the press with position papers, consultants' reports, newspaper articles and speeches by senior airline executives, all of which reflect the company's thoughts on issues that are important in the industry.

The firm also publishes a quarterly corporate fact book that provides a wealth of statistical and analytical information about the airline's operations. The book also gives guidance to managers allowing them to talk directly with reporters in the event of an emergency.

Activity 9.4

Before you start reading the section on how to prepare a press release, read the following abstract taken from a press release that was sent to a local newspaper in a farming region in England. Ignore the format but explain why the content is not suitable and suggest how it could be improved.

PRESS RELEASE FROM XYZ FARMING LTD

Dear Editor

We believe that we can offer your readers an interesting news story and will be happy to provide fuller details if required. A new concept in dairy cow feeding has been pioneered by XYZ Farming Ltd, which is specifically designed to meet the demand of consumers for milk of higher protein content and reduced fat levels. These requirements are reflected in differential prices paid by most dairies to farmers with greater emphasis on protein content rather than butterfat: high butterfats also act as an effective constraint to the full use by the farmer of his quota allocation. In the new Granary range of compound feeds the high levels of rumen bypass starch derived from rolled wheat, is pelletted in combination with high vegetable proteins . . .

Press releases

Most organizations have a PR policy, which means that press releases go through a rigorous checking and signing-off procedure whether they are produced in-house or by an agency. It is a specialized job, and one that you will not be involved with unless it is specified as part of your job role.

Nevertheless you should be able to produce a draft release to show that you understand how they should be written and presented, as it could become a task that becomes part of your job.

You should be aware that while organizations can pay to obtain advertising space, obtaining editorial space through press releases is subject to the editorial team finding the press release interesting and usable. Even if this is the case, the space that can be given to your press release will probably be limited and they will usually change it so that the angle suits their news purposes.

It is wrong to consider that press releases are 'free' advertising, as the time and effort put into writing a good press release has a cost associated with it.

The format of a press release

A press release format should:

- Feature your organization's logo at the top.
- Be entitled 'Press release'.
- Show the date the release was prepared or indicate when the news can be released (an embargo).
- Have a headline that sums up the story.
- Be typed with double spacing and have wide margins.
- Only use one side of the paper.
- Indicate that more 'copy' or text follows by using the abbreviation m/f at the end of each page.
- Clearly mark the end of the release with the word 'end'.
- Contain contact details for the media to make further enquiries.
- Contain additional notes in the form of 'background notes for the editor'.

The press release content should:

- Answer the questions who, what, when, where and how.
- Encapsulate the nub of the story in the first paragraph.
- Start with the key point at the top and add the 'bones' of the story in each succeeding paragraph.
- Contain interesting quotes that are attributed to a person relevant to the story.
- Be geared to the media, so you may have one version for the trade press and another for the local press.
- Use factual not flowery language.
- Be clear and concise.
- Relate to any accompanying photographs.
- Have a 'pic caption', i.e. a few sentences that explain the contents or name the people in a photograph.
- Usually be written as if the event has just happened (even if the presentation or the contract was won a few days ago), although some releases inform of what will happen in the future.

Activity 9.5

See the question scenario in Activity 9.2.

(a) Assuming the event has taken place, prepare a press release for distribution to the relevant media.

(b) State your objectives in preparing the release.

(c) Suggest which type of media you would send the release to.

Direct marketing

Types of direct marketing activity

- Direct mail (mailshots).
- Door drops (leaflets/coupons/vouchers posted through the door).
- Selling via catalogues/brochures (mail order selling).
- Direct response advertising in the press (off the page selling).
- Direct response advertising on the television (DRTV).
- Telemarketing (using the telephone to contact people to sell direct to them).

The most popular form of direct marketing in the UK for both consumer and business-to-business marketing is direct mail. Direct mail usually comprises a sales letter outlining the offer, a response mechanism and sometimes there is a separate piece which gives details of an incentive offer if you respond by a certain date.

How direct mail can be used

The principle is that organizations build a database of current customers' address details and their previous purchase history. By using this information the organization can target products/services that are tailored to suit the recipient's profile. For example, a bank will have all your financial details and could send you a mailshot promoting a gold status credit card if you fitted the income bracket and financial history for that product.

The same bank could rent a list of people with a gold card customer profile, from another organization, to send them a mailshot in the hope of recruiting additional gold card customers.

Figure 9.5 An example of direct marketing material

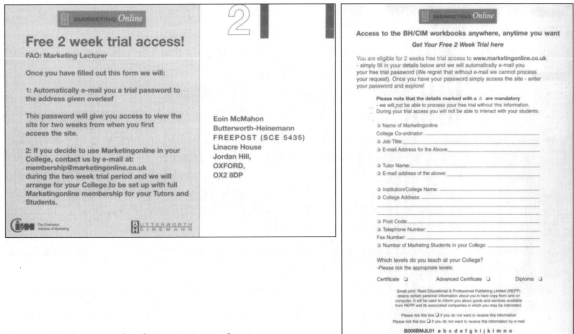

Figure 9.6 An example of a response mechanism

Direct marketing objectives

Direct marketing campaign objectives could be to:

- Generate sales.
- Build up sales leads.
- Invite recipients to visit a store.
- Build the company database.
- Remind people that an offer closes by a certain date.

Dear Mrs Wood,

Wouldn't it be nice if someone else paid for the fun things in life? Air Miles do just that.

Take a look at your 'Spring 2001 offers' booklet and you'll find out how. There are 2 great **NEW OFFERS**: earn miles shopping online with Yahoo! UK & Ireland; and earn 100s of miles when you switch to gas and electricity with Scottish Hydro-Electric or Southern Electric. You could also win 10,000 miles at Sainsbury's.

But what are you going to do with all those miles? Well, for only 80 miles you'll get a cheaper holiday than you can find on the high street with 20 leading companies, or a FREE day out; and there are flights worldwide, with three ways to pay.

And remember, the more miles you collect, the more fun you could be having. So take a look at your statement and 'spring 2001 offers' booklet NOW!

Best wishes

Mary Thomas

Marketing Director

Figure 9.7 An example of a direct marketing letter from Air Miles

Writing direct mail letters

Direct mail can be a powerful communication tool but where it is sent indiscriminately it can irritate people and be judged as 'junk mail'. Wastage can be reduced if the mailshots are targeted at the right people. For example, It is very annoying for existing customers to be sent details of a new 'introductory' offer that they cannot take up because they are not a new customer.

If you want customers to respond, you can make it easier for recipients to respond by using a response mechanism (see Figure 9.6).

Although the style of a letter is personal there are some techniques that you can use when writing direct mail letters:

- Say what you mean clearly – be clear what your key message is.
- Sound enthusiastic – if you are writing with an offer, it should sound worth taking up.
- Write personally – where possible use computer software that enables you to personalise letters with names and even inserting the address or a reference to the customer's current product package in the text of the letter. So for example a breakdown recovery service could write to its existing customers and in the text of the letter say, 'Now Mrs Wood, if your car wouldn't start outside 10 Acacia Avenue, wouldn't it be convenient if you had the 'home start' service added to your current breakdown cover?'
- Questions can be used to good effect when you are trying to get your recipients to desire or want your product/service.
- You can go into detail in a direct mail letter in a way that you cannot in an advertisement.
- You can use additional pieces of materials, such as brochures or flyers to reinforce the message you are trying to convey – so the letter does not have to communicate all your messages.
- In most circumstances you should use a friendly tone – but it does depend on the situation, so if you were writing about critical illness cover, your tone would be more serious.
- If you want a response or some form of action from the recipient, make it very clear what it is, perhaps mentioning it more than once. The p.s. at the end of a direct mail letter can be used to good effect to remind the customer what they need to do and by when. For example, you could say 'P.S. Don't forget that if you want the two free books when you join our book club you need to complete the attached post card and return it before 31 May…'

Advantages of direct mail

- Response is measurable.
- You can test the copy in the letter or the design of mailshot components.
- You can target precisely and therefore it is cheaper than mass-market advertising.
- You can tailor messages to niche groups.
- You can time the campaign precisely.
- There can be short lead times in running a direct marketing campaign.
- Computer technology can mean sophisticated database management.

Disadvantages associated with direct mail

- Can be viewed as junk mail.
- Can be seen as intrusive.
- Investment costs for establishing and maintaining a database are high.

Evaluating the effect of advertising

Research into the advertising process has shown that advertisements on their own do not prompt a sale. Take the example of the 'Chocco chocolate bar'. Consumers do not see an advertisement for 'Chocco' and rush out to buy it: many other factors influence the purchase decision, such as the price, taste and appearance of the product and whether it is actually available in the shop that a consumer visits. What advertising can do is to create awareness about 'Chocco' among its target audience, then convey a particular brand image and communicate the benefits (both rational and emotional) for purchasing it. In other words advertising and promotions work on consumers to lead them through the purchase decision-making process to a sale.

So it is not appropriate to only look at sales when you are measuring the success of an advertisement or a campaign because other factors in the marketing mix or the external environment could affect sales (in either a negative or a positive way). For example, if there was media coverage of research report suggesting that chocolate improved your IQ and reduced stress at the same time as the 'Chocco' advertising campaign then this could be the reason for a sales increase and not the effect of the advertising campaign. Or, perhaps weather conditions could affect cocoa production adversely, which could cause price rises and reduce demand for 'Chocco', no matter how effective the advertising campaign.

One way to evaluate the effectiveness of advertising is to conduct research into customer perception of 'Chocco' and identify levels of awareness or interest in the product to help set the objectives of an advertising campaign. For example, you might find out that only half the target market is aware of the new 'Chocco' bar – in which case if you set the objective of the campaign to increase awareness to 80 per cent, then you could use post-campaign research to identify if this objective had been achieved.

Similarly research can be carried out to assess whether a re-branding project has been successful or to judge whether a PR campaign has changed customer perception (if that was the objective of the campaign).

Another way of evaluating public relations effort is to physically measure the amount of coverage in print and broadcast media. For example, to measure the success of a PR campaign informing consumers about a new type of diet chocolate, you could count how many articles appeared in the national press and specialist press (for example, slimming magazines).

To measure the response to a sales promotion campaign that used a '20p off' coupon for 'Chocco' bars, you could set up a system with retailers to count the number of redeemed vouchers.

To evaluate the success of a business to business exhibition, if the objective was to create leads for sales staff, you could count the number of contact numbers collected by the staff manning the exhibition. You could further refine the evaluation process by measuring how many calls lead to sales appointments and from there, how many appointments were converted to sales. A final sales figure could be checked against the cost of the exhibition to see if the activity was cost-effective.

Similarly the response rates from direct marketing campaigns should be evaluated and, if appropriate, a further check made to calculate how much response actually converts to sales. This way the cost of a campaign can be measured against the monetary gain from sales.

The role of the brief

In the early stages of your career you are unlikely to be developing full-scale campaigns using above- and below-the-line activity. However, one way for your organization and its advertising agency or design consultancy to determine how to communicate with customers is to write down its requirements in the form of a *brief*. A brief can then be used to help designers produce appropriate advertising or promotions or even packaging design.

You should be aware of the components of a brief. Below is an example of the headings that could be used in an advertising brief. However, you should note that a brief could be used to determine any kind of above- or below-the-line activity. In addition, you should be aware that every brief will be individual to the company, the product and the market concerned.

An example of an advertising brief

Client details

In this section you would include the name of the client and the name of the product.

Background information

In this section you would include whatever relevant information you had about the following:

- The company
- The product

- The market
- The competition
- Previous advertising activity that has been undertaken
- Any relevant research data

Objectives

In this section you should outline the objectives of the campaign/project.

Target audience

In this section you should identify who the campaign is aimed at.

Message to be conveyed

In this section you should identify what you want to say and how it should be said. This may include the unique selling proposition (the one key benefit that distinguishes the product/service) and any substantiation for the claims being made. It should also determine the desired tone of voice and brand image that should be communicated.

Media

In this section you should specify where you want to place the message.

Timescale

Here you need to specify when the campaign is to run, its length and duration.

Budget

Here you should specify how much money is available for the campaign.

Miscellaneous information

In this section you should specify if there are any mandatory inclusions – for instance, you may have to mention membership of ABTA in an advertisement for a travel agent. You also need to include contact phone numbers or certain logos.

Case history

The role of the design brief

The design of a new product must start with what we call a 'consumer insight'. Kit Kat is a good example of this – it's based on the insight that people like to sit down with a cup of team and eat something sweet as break from their daily routine. Once a company has found and understood an insight, it will test the market to see if a gap truly exists and if it does it will bring in a designer to help them design it.

At the first meeting with the designers, the company needs to define exactly what it is looking for. The company might have an idea what the product will look like and possibly have a name for it.

From this meeting, the account director in an agency will prepare a detailed brief and present it to the creative team who do the actual designing.

Activity 9.7

You work for a charitable organization that has been established to promote health and safety issues in the workplace. You would like to run a marketing campaign highlighting health and safety hazards in the workplace and the potential financial damages that companies could incur. You also want to send a poster featuring health and safety hazards to a list of companies that are held on your database.

Draft a brief for your Marketing Officer that indicates the objectives of the campaign, target markets and any other details that you consider the Marketing Officer should have.

Summary

In this unit you have studied:

- The communications mix
- The role of various promotional activities
- What to look for when evaluating corporate literature
- How branding works
- How to write a press release
- How to write a direct mail letter
- How to measure the effectiveness of various promotional activities
- The role of the brief

Further study and examination preparation

Go to the end of the book and attempt questions 5bii) and 6a) on the June 2000 examination paper and questions 1a) and 5) on the December 2000 paper.

Exam hint

You will not be asked questions where you have to prepare promotional plans or integrated marketing communications strategy as these areas are examined at Advanced Certificate and Diploma levels.

However, you do need to have a basic understanding of the how organizations communicate with their external customers. You need to have lots of examples of the whole range of promotional activities from your own experience to put into answers where appropriate. So ensure that you do this type of research well in advance of the examination.

Areas that could have questions relate to how logos, branding and corporate image are used to communicate with customers.

Although it is unlikely that you would be asked a question where you just need to regurgitate facts about various media, you could be given a scenario and be asked to suggest relevant promotion activities that could be used in that situation.

Alternatively, you might be asked to write a letter or a memo in a situation relating to exhibitions, sponsorship or whatever, so fundamental to the question might be your understanding of the promotional activity that relates to the context of the question.

You need to have a basic understanding of the importance of layout, typefaces and design so that you could either evaluate the effectiveness or produce a draft of an advertisement, leaflet or some other printed material.

You should be able to write an effective direct mailshot, press release or text for a press advertisement or some other promotional material and know how to monitor or measure the effectiveness of a promotional activity.

Finally, you should be able to draw up a brief that would assist an external supplier, such as, a design, PR ,or Sales Promotion consultancy or advertising agency, to do their job of designing or writing for products or services in a given context.

Although this section cannot comprehensively suggest all the areas that might be examined, it does highlight that you will not have to regurgitate the material in it to answer questions, but will need to be able to apply your knowledge in questions that cover this topic.

Technological developments in communications

Objectives

In this unit you will:

- Examine technological developments in the field of communications.
- Look at the impact of the Internet and e-commerce on customer communications.

By the end of this unit you should be able to:

- Explain how technological developments are affecting customer communications.
- Appreciate the principles of web site design.
- Know how to use e-mail effectively
- Understand how technology can be used to build databases.
- Be aware of the steps involved in an online shopping transaction.
- Know how the Internet can be used to improve customer communications.
- Describe developments in telecommunications and digital technology.

Study guide

This unit covers indicative content areas 2.5.1, 2.5.2 and 2.5.3 of the syllabus. It provides an overview of technological developments and trends in communications. This syllabus area links with 1.5 on the Marketing Fundamentals syllabus which is covered in unit 11 in the Marketing Fundamentals workbook. In Marketing Fundamentals you are looking at how Information Communications Technology (ICT) affects all the elements in the Marketing Mix, whereas with Customer Communications you are looking at how technology specifically affects how you communicate with customers.

It will take you one hour to read this unit and a further hour to undertake the activities.

Study tip

Because the speed of technological change is so fast, you should use this unit as a starting point to think about how Information Communications Technology (ICT) is changing the way you communicate. You need to extend you knowledge by accessing information outside of the workbook, in the quality press, specialist marketing magazines and specialist technical press.

You should also use the Internet to see how it can be used. Look up some web sites that are of particular interest to you and surf the web for more information about technological developments. One of many web sites that you could visit is www.net-profit.co.uk, which is in the form of an online magazine and provides information about technology developments affecting business.

In addition, look at how telecommunications equipment in your workplace has changed the way you and your colleagues do your jobs.

If you cannot access the Internet at home or at work, you could find access at your college or local library or even visit an Internet or cybercafe, where you can pay for access.

How communication with customers is changing

Technological developments in communications are making massive changes to your personal and working lives. They are changing the way you shop, find out information, communicate with others inside and outside your organization; they are affecting the way that organizations promote their products/services and even changing the way organizations do business with suppliers and distributors.

The introduction of computers has transformed the way information is handled and communicated. Data in a digital format means that when a document is typed any mistakes can be quickly corrected before it is printed out and information such as invoices, forms and previous letters can be indexed and retrieved easily.

Electronic point of sale (EPOS) systems allow retailers to record and monitor sales data. Linked to 'smart' card purchases, EPOS data provides organisations with detailed profiles of customer preferences and purchasing habits. Databases can be used to store information about customer purchase history so that mail-merged documents can be sent to customers with offers tailored to their needs.

Even the way you use the telephone has changed. Mobile telephones mean you can be constantly in touch with colleagues and customers even when away from the office. People can leave voice mail and fax messages at any time, without having to rely on others to take the information down correctly. Businesses can deal speedily with massive telephone response through voice mail and automated processes. It is also likely that videophones will gradually be introduced, which will change the way you communicate on the phone, because your body language and facial expressions will be observed.

Even office equipment such as the photocopier has been digitised, so that now you can make multiple copies without ever having to queue at the photocopying machine again.

In addition to mobile telephones, laptop computers mean that you can work away from your desk or while on the move and still access or send information to your colleagues at the office.

The advent of electronic communication has probably had the most impact, and e-mail in particular has become so popular that for many people it is the main way they communicate with others.

The ability to use the Internet has had a massive impact on the speed at which you can communicate either accessing information on web sites or transacting business online.

You can also produce vast quantities of text, sound and picture information and store it on CD ROM or in DVD (Digital Versatile Disks) format which is an extremely versatile and interactive way for customers to access information.

And, finally, you can also use computer software that allows you to use graphics, animation and sound to make a presentation highly polished, impactful and professional.

The evolution of e-business

By 1997 there were 1.55 million Internet account holders and 0.8 million corporate Internet accounts in the UK; by 2000 these figures had grown to 7.49 million Internet accounts and 13.7 million corporate Internet accounts. In other words the business world has taken use of the Internet to its collective heart. The way the Internet is used in business can be described in three ways:

- E-commerce is the trading of goods and services using digital media.
- E-business is the term used to describe applying digital and Internet technologies to business functions.
- E-marketing is the application of the Internet and related digital technologies to achieve marketing objectives.

Global uptake in using the Internet is rising dramatically too. Total commerce over the Internet is over $1trillion (business to consumer). By 2002 it is estimated that over 88 million people between 2 and 22 years of age will be online in the USA and Canada.

In a recent survey conducted by Nielsen//NetRatings, a New York-based Internet rating company (information courtesy of Lexis Nexis), found that South Koreans spent the most time surfing the Web at home (16 hours and 17 minutes per month), followed by Canada (10 hours 48 minutes) and the United States (9 hours and 46 minutes). Other countries emerging as dominant in the Internet market are Hong Kong, Japan and Taiwan and it is predicted that Chinese will become the number one web language by 2007.

Country	% of households with Internet access
Hong Kong	49.5
Singapore	48.4
South Korea	45.5
Taiwan	42.9
Australia	40.0
New Zealand	39.9
Japan	24.1

Table 10.1 Percentage of households with Internet access via a home personal computer: Asia-Pacific, January 2001. Source: Nielsen//NetRatings

Country	Time spent per month (hours:minutes:seconds)	Page views per month per person	Average number of sessions per month per person
South Korea	16:17:16	2008	21
Hong Kong	9:46:20	877	16
Japan	7:56:48	779	16
Australia	7:07:38	446	12
Taiwan	6:57:60	737	12
New Zealand	6:28:05	423	14
Singapore	6:05:17	569	11

Table 10.2 Time spent online at home: Asia-Pacific region, January 2001. Source: Nielsen//NetRatings

Using ICT to improve customer communications

Database marketing involves using computers to capture and store data relating to customers' past purchase history. For instance, if a mail-order company sells clothing in its catalogue, each customer file is computerized so that contact details (name, address, postcode) and purchases (type of item, size, colour preference, price, etc.) are stored. This information can be accessed quickly and cheaply by all the departments in the firm. For example, the accounts department may need to access it to chase payment and the marketing department could use it to target offers to customers. So customers who buy clothes for people under a certain height would only be sent information relating to the 'petite' range of clothing based on their past purchase behaviour.

Loyalty schemes work on a similar principle: the large supermarkets can use their EPOS not only for stock control purposes but also to target offers that are relevant to customers; e.g. a customer who regularly buys dog food would not be sent money off vouchers for cat food as an incentive to stay 'loyal'.

Customer relationship management systems can work on a similar principle. The key idea is that each customer is treated as an individual, and in particular, organizations can use computer software to identify the most profitable customers and 'cherry pick' them because of their customer lifetime value (CLV). For example, basic current account holders are not particularly profitable customers for banks as customers with (or potentially wanting) loans, mortgages, insurance business and pensions are much more profitable. The idea behind CLV is to spend marketing time and effort on those customers who are the most valuable.

Computer software can also be used in call centres where staff are handling high volumes of calls. For example, when credit card customers ring a call centre and quote their postcode or account numbers, customer file details quickly appear on the call handlers' computer screens, enabling them to deal with a query or make a transaction.

Database systems can be used to improve internal communication by creating a 'knowledge management' system. For example, a firm of accountants can have all their customer files in a centralised database so that staff have access to the 'company's shared experience' of how deals and projects have been managed by others in the firm. It also works when the firm want to cross-sell their services to a client. It is much easier if details of the client's dealings with the taxation department are easily accessible by another accountant who might be advising the client on, say, business acquisition.

Data 'mining' is when sophisticated systems are used to track customer/client files in order to identify products/services that could be targeted in the future. They can also be used by managers to monitor sales team performance and help administrative staff improve communications by using them to send e-mails, meeting notes, phone messages and to plan meetings around people's diaries.

The Internet

The Internet allows people from all over the world to communicate with each other via a global network of computers. Since 1991 restrictions that prevented people to use the Internet to make a profit have been removed. This has led to a massive growth in the number of web sites in the world and in the number of people connected to the Internet. Many people use the Internet to communicate with others via e-mail. The Internet can be used by organizations to do the following:

- Promote and sell products/services
- Provide information 24 hours a day to people all over the world
- Enable two-way communication via e-mail
- Capture contact information when people register details on web sites
- Build ongoing relationships (through e-mail marketing or adding services/benefits to customers who use a firm's web site)
- Improve the way businesses do business with each other

Web sites

A browser is required to access the Internet and once you have gained access you can visit an address on the world wide web. A famous web site address is **www.bbc.co.uk** but you will see thousands of others on business cards, on product packaging and in advertising. Any organization or person can set up their own web site. This might contain information about the organization or about a person's interest or hobby. Information can be communicated using a combination of text, image and sound.

Web sites that you may wish to access to help you with your studies are:

- **www.ebusiness.uk.com**
- **www.tbcresearch.com**
- **www.asiasource.org**
- **www.marketresearch.org.uk**
- **www.nielson-netratings.com**
- **www.streamwave.co.uk**
- **www.broadvision.com**

Interesting web sites that you could access to see how the Web can be used are:

- **www.Indya.com** – one of India's top three Internet portals.
- **www.penang.net** – about the island off Malaysia.
- **www.markwarner.co.uk** –easy to use, innovative, well-designed, clear and informative also won a 'best travel site' award in 2000.
- **www.cityorganiser.com** – helps busy business travellers find out about hotels, car hire, restaurants, healthcare and leisure options also with bookable services.

Web site design

In designing a web site you should consider what you are trying to achieve with it and consider who your audiences are, what they will be interested in and what sort of equipment they are likely to have.

Although attractive design with sound and graphics can bring a site to life, you need to consider if your audience will have the latest equipment and a large screen to enable them to benefit from these facilities. One way to deal with this issue is to have an alternative version of your web site so that those not using a conventional desktop computer can still access it without the sound and graphic effects.

It should be easy for visitors to get around or navigate your web site. It also helps if it is easy to access and has a fast response.

The contents need to be designed in a non-linear format because unlike a book, where people start at the beginning, a web site can be accessed from any page. Books are also generally printed in a portrait format but web sites are in a landscape format, where the width of the screen is greater than its height. Consequently web sites should be designed with a landscape format in mind.

Good web design also creates a directory structure for the information and establishes links between every page throughout the web site. Hypertext will allow users to jump to other pieces of related information on the same site or to other sites anywhere in the world. It is also helpful if key words are highlighted and menus of information on the site are listed in bullet points for easy reading.

The content of a web site can start off quite simply with some company and product information. However, it is important that the content and quality is updated. The web site could incorporate an organization's corporate video and music to make it more interesting.

Web sites are developing all the time, so the published word, the animated graphic, the broadcast picture, digital video clips and voice messages can all be presented and interconnected.

Web sites should also be interactive and allow for an organization to build up a database of customers. One way to get people to register with their details is to restrict access to certain pages until details are registered. Another way is to build in some form of response such as a 'freebie' if visitors to the site leave their details. For example, one law firm allowed visitors to their web site to register their details if they wanted to receive an advent calendar highlighting areas of the law that companies could fall foul of. This allowed them to establish a list of firms interested in receiving legal advice that they could target with information.

For many companies it is not just about the number of 'hits' on the site but the way a site can generate leads or actually convert people to business when visiting the site. For example, the Easyjet site is designed to allow people to make online bookings and the company measures the success of its web site by the level of sales.

Web site costs

These can vary from a very simple web site that would cost around £1000 to set up to those costing tens of thousands of pounds which can handle on-line shopping. An average brochure-type site currently costs around £5000 to design and set up.

One aspect that many organizations forget is that once the site is set up it needs to be monitored to measure response and maintained so that its contents are not outdated.

Electronic mail

Electronic mail or e-mail is a method of sending text files from one computer to another which allows you to send messages across the world in seconds. One way to send and receive messages is to set up an e-mail account with an Internet service provider (ISP).

If someone named John Smith set up an e-mail account, his e-mail address could be jsmith@tesco.net.co.uk. To send him an e-mail message, you would connect to the Internet and opt for the 'compose message' facility. You would then complete the various parts of the e-mail and compose your message. Your e-mail message to John Smith would then show who it was from (your e-mail address so that he could reply to you), its subject and the message itself.

A company can have a corporate mailbox, with each employee having private access to their own little part of it. For example, if you worked at Tiger Tours and your name was Mary Smith, your address might be msmith@tigertours.co.uk.

E-mail is like having a postman living inside your telephone who can deliver post anywhere in the world at the speed of lightning. However, it is more than a messaging service because text, graphics, video and sound can be sent and received across the Internet.

The information is stored in the computer until the recipient retrieves it. It is usually cheaper than other forms of communication because it only incurs the cost of connection to the ISP.

Cost comparison of e-mail with other forms of communication

Table 10.3 shows the approximate cost of sending a 10-page document from the UK to the USA.

Cost	Communication method	Time taken to receive message
£1.56	First class post	5-7 days
£2.00	Fax	5 minutes
£30.00	Courier	2 working days
15p (cost of local call)	E-mail	Almost instant

Table 10.3

E-mail etiquette

E-mail can revolutionize the way you communicate because it is so quick, easy and cost-effective. It is also paperless unless you decide to print out the message or the document attached to the message.

Because most e-mail messages are simply text files, the usual conventions connected with letter writing, such as letterheads, typesizes, typestyles, justification, layout, paper quality and signatures, are ignored. This lack of convention encourages people to be less formal than they would be if they were writing a memo or letter on headed paper.

The medium also encourages brevity, which can make you more productive in dealing with and sending messages. However, it can mean that messages sound curt to the extent of rudeness if you are not careful. In addition, because it is easy to copy a message to everyone in your office with the click of a few buttons, it can encourage you and your colleagues to saturate people with more information than they really need.

You should also be aware that your employer owns e-mail messages sent from your workplace and has the right to monitor e-mail you send using their computers.

Legal firms advise companies nowadays that they should guard against e-mail abuse by writing to staff about the perils associated with e-mails:

- Instruct staff not to include any statements or other material that could be held to be abusive, racist, constitute sexual harassment or be threatening or defamatory.

- Point out that someone other than the intended recipient may receive the message and that both individuals and the company could be held liable for anything contained in it.

- Advise them to use password-protected documents for confidential information.

Many firms also attach a legal disclaimer to the bottom of every e-mail sent out from the firm.

Advantages of e-mail

- Local call costs to anywhere in the world.
- Easy distribution to one recipient or many.
- Speedy delivery – almost instantaneous.
- No time zones to worry about – e-mail works while your recipients sleep.
- Can be addressed to a specific person.
- Will be delivered even if the recipient is out.
- No messy paperwork lying around.
- Messages sent and received can be stored for future reference.
- Security passwords restrict access to your mailbox to you.

Intranet

An intranet allows you to communicate on the Internet in a local network that is not publicly accessible. Many organizations use intranets to distribute internal documents.

However, it can be used outside the organization to allow nominated people to share documents, expertise or opinions anywhere in the world. The network would be protected to ensure that only nominated people could access information, thus keeping the network secure.

The most common form of intranet is where corporate information is published on an internal web site, with hypertext links to related documents, enabling enormous amounts of time to be saved searching for information.

For example, a law practice that merged with another firm in a town forty miles away, used the intranet to create an internal 'who's who' of staff, including photographs. It then developed to include internal phone directories, which could be updated without continual reprinting costs, practice guides on word-processing house styles, the staff handbook, and even what was being served in the staff restaurant that week.

Eventually it went on to be used to produce practice-wide know-how material and legal precedents. In other words, it became a giant internal library with easy access to staff from inside the firm.

The benefits of intranets

- Reduced costs in printing and distributing documents.
- Publishing information without delay.
- No physical filing – saving time and space.
- Ability to find information quickly.

Extranet

An extranet is an intranet extended to key players involved in your everyday business processes in order to achieve total collaboration. This may include dealers, suppliers or business partners.

For example, when General Motors started using their extranet to enable purchase orders to be made by their dealers using an electronic form process, the cost of the transaction went down from £35 to less than 10p.

> ### Activity 10.1
> Look at the CIM web site **www.cim.co.uk**. As a student member you can access the private qualifications extranet area and see what information you can obtain there.

E-commerce

Of course, you can visit web sites to do your online shopping for CDs, books and clothes. But for many people who like to shop for clothes and books in the centre of a big city where they can see and be seen, the idea of online shopping is unattractive.

However, those same people may not be so happy to make the same boring weekly shop for routine food items on a busy Saturday morning. So big retailers like Tesco and Sainsbury have grasped the opportunity e-commerce gives them to help their customers save time by enabling them to automate routine purchases (that are only changed by exception) and have the goods delivered as well.

Online shopping transactions

It is very easy to do your shopping on the Internet. The most common way is to access a computer that connects to the Internet through an Internet service provider (ISP). This is usually done through a telephone cable using a modem. You would then access the online store through a web browser, usually by the web site address (URL) of the on-line store. For example, you could connect to the online bookstore www.amazon.co.uk.

If, you wanted to purchase a pair of jeans and you connected to an online clothes shop, you would pull down the menu to choose the style or cut of jeans, the colour and the size of the item you require.

You would then complete an onscreen order form where you would provide payment and address details. You would then need to wait for credit card verification from your bank or credit card company. Once authorization was given you would just need to wait for dispatch of your order from the online store.

E-business

It is a mistake to think of the Internet and e-commerce (doing business on the Internet) as only using web sites to sell goods. E-commerce changes the way you interact with suppliers and organizations and the way they do business with you. For many organizations the key benefit is to use it to provide in-depth customer information. It can also be used to canvass feedback from customers.

Banks are using the Internet to add value to the service they provide to current customers. With some banks you can transfer money from one account to another and find out your bank balance.

Your local doctor may soon be able to improve their service to you by allowing you to order repeat prescriptions via the Internet. This will not only save you time but also free up busy receptionists to deal with people waiting in the surgery.

The Internet is also a fantastic resource for obtaining information and so is an ideal tool to assist distance learning. You can access news and weather sites, and there are many that you can visit just for fun. If you are interested in helping your children find out about space exploration, then you could visit the NASA site.

Utilities and other large organizations with many customers will be able to save time and money by producing automated account and billing information and allowing customers to make online payment.

Some firms are using the Internet to improve communications with potential staff. On-line recruitment information can enable people to have a virtual tour of offices with a 360-degree photograph and 'hot spots' can be clicked on to enable them to go into the still image in more detail.

Electronic data interchange (EDI)

For many organizations the Internet will enable them to source parts, reduce waiting times for stock, cut the storage area they need for stock holding, and will mean cheaper distribution costs.

For example, a network of franchised garages had their purchasing organized centrally using the Internet. This now means that if a franchise operator uses an exhaust from stock, this information is communicated through EDI to the exhaust manufacturer, who can then restock the garage automatically. Business process and business communication is also transformed so that there are fewer telephone calls and less paperwork, which has a great impact on the efficiency of the organization.

EDI is also used to keep track of inventory. For example, FedEx have opened up the 'back room' to business customers so that they can order courier service and track a package. This adds real value to their business relationship with customers. It also means that staff are not tied up with routine queries about the whereabouts of a package but have more time to spend dealing with orders and more complex forms of enquiry.

EDI can therefore improve a company's ability to work with others in terms of sharing documents and other information, which improves strategic partnerships on a worldwide basis.

E-marketing

There are lots of good examples of companies using the Internet as part of their promotional mix. For example, the Adidas web site can be accessed in several different languages and provides information for sports enthusiasts, whatever sport they are interested in. It provides information on athletes, major sporting events, has links to other relevant sites (spotlights on various football clubs) and of course contains extensive product information via a vast online catalogue, more extensive than you could see in one shop. In addition you can buy online.

Banner advertising space can be purchased on portal sites or individual web sites of other companies to promote your firm and its products/services. For example, Virgin's recent banner advertising campaign for personal and stakeholder pensions generated so many e-mail requests for information that the whole sales force was booked up for one month after the campaign ended.

Web sites are a useful means to deliver detailed information before purchase and after-sales support, which is particularly useful for big purchases where people need to look around for information in their own time and at their own pace. For instance, to sell cars, it is very useful to be able to allow potential customers access to detailed information that they request in the comfort of their own home and then have the option to book a test drive. The flip side is that they can also shop around for the best price in an international market.

Brand building through web sites is still in its infancy but it could prove to be highly profitable in youth marketing. It is no coincidence that the soft drink manufacturers and sports goods suppliers have been pioneers in developing high-quality interactive sites.

For web sites to work, it is essential that they are promoted by the following activities:

- Relevant off-line advertising.
- Banner advertising on other relevant web sites.
- Links to other sites.
- Sending details of sites to large search engines.
- Using web site address details on all stationery and advertising.

The best e-marketing web sites are those that really add value by providing information that people want, and are updated regularly. For example, a car breakdown service company could provide an online traffic information service in return for users registering contact details. If they also set up the registration process so that users could opt in to receive further information to be sent from the company, it would be a good way for the company to extend its database. By asking the right kind of questions, registration could enable the firm to tailor future communications such as mailshots or e-mail marketing activity based on where the recipient lived or the type of car that they own.

E-mail marketing

Email has become a useful medium for organizations wanting to market their services. For example, the UK currently has 13 million people with Internet access in the home, of whom 95 per cent use e-mail so it is a viable medium.

'Push' technology means that marketers can post direct electronic mailings to potential customers' online mailboxes rather than paper mail through their front door. This technique has been used by Dell Computers but has been blasted by critics for its intrusive 'junk mail' status. Dell say that they use it to target mail only at people who have requested information and it means that they can use their database to segment targets and send messages that are closely tailored to the recipients' needs.

However, many companies recognize that if they want to win or retain business they must take care of their customers and offer specialised information targeted to individual needs.

One training company started using fax marketing to generate qualified sales leads and then went on to devise an e-mail marketing campaign. They worked with a specialist business-to-business e-mail list broker and rented a specialist list of people who had opted-in to receive information on specific types of training. They combined the e-mail message with an interactive 'how do you measure up in the workplace?' fun-type quiz, which was linked to a competition. To enter and perhaps win a Palm Pilot, web site visitors just had to register their contact details. The web site also included a telephone number that linked visitors to sales staff via an online discussion. This was a very innovative and successful campaign that resulted in 10% of visitors to the web site converting to serious sales leads.

Over 54	11%
45-54	17%
36-44	24%
25-34	25%
Under 25	23%

Table 10.4 *UK e-mail penetration by age*

AB	35%
C1	36%
C2	16%
DE	13%

Table 10.5 *UK e-mail users by socio-economic group*

Advantages of e-mail marketing campaigns:

- Well-targeted, personalised and direct communication method with no gatekeepers (even many relatively senior staff still open their own e-mails)
- Easy to receive and quick to respond to.
- Convenient – waits in mailbox until recipient is ready to open it.
- Can engage rich media content such as colour pictures.
- Quite cheap compared with conventional direct marketing methods.
- Recipients can opt in for further information without going through to sender's web site.
- Can offer more conventional response methods, such as telephone number if recipients want to speak to someone.
- Can be used to send offers to existing customers or new prospects.
- Can be a good way to follow up recent purchases, e.g. to check that customers are satisfied with a recent personal computer purchase and to see if any of them need help/assistance.
- Can be a good way to get customer feedback and research customer opinions (See Unit 3 for more information about this area.)
- Can be used to send conference or seminar invitations to specific markets.
- Ideal for rapid reactive campaigns, for instance where a company has a special offer this month – for example, if a football club wants to sell corporate boxes at the last minute for a rearranged match.
- Can be used to drive click-throughs to sites and generate opt-in requests for more information.

Although people do not want to be 'spammed' (sent unsolicited information), e-mail campaigns where recipients have opted in for information can be very successful as they are a tremendous opportunity to send a message directly through to a relevant decision maker.

Signposts for the future

The way people use the Internet is opening up all kinds of possibilities. You might study for a course using an interactive video tutor. If you are considering moving house, you could see if your current furniture would suit the new house without ever visiting it but by viewing it online. If you are fixing your car, you could access a DIY guide and then change sites to order parts online. If you find that this does not work, you could then access the services of an online mechanic.

Other developments include faster speeds for surfing web sites, improved safety for credit card transactions, improved graphics cards to view web sites and more use of firewalls to protect information from being grabbed by hackers.

Activity 10.2

How is the Internet being used to communicate with existing customers and prospects?

Telecommunications

There have been massive developments in the field of telecommunications.

Automated switchboards are now within the reach of even the smallest firms. This enables customers to leave a message for a person or department through voice mail. It also enables the organization to pre-select the response, so that if customers require information they are put through to department 1, for example, and if they want to order goods, they are put through to department 2 and so on.

Voice mail can enable companies to cope with large volumes of calls and should mean that customers are dealt with more efficiently and effectively. However automated customer-handling systems do not always improve customer communications. Customers become irritated and angry when they have to go through several button-pushing processes and still end up waiting a long time before their call is answered.

The other issue for customers is that if they have a non-standard problem or query, they often find it extremely difficult to speak to a real person who can help them.

ISDN

An ISDN line allows your computer to connect to other computers much more quickly and enables much faster transfer of large documents than a normal telephone line. This technology has been successfully used in teleworking, where homeworkers can source information from the office fast and effectively. ISDN can also be used for:

- Sending information with graphics.
- Video conferencing.
- Broadcasting.
- Telemarketing/call centres

Mobile phones and m-commerce

Mobile phones are getting smaller and more powerful. They can be used to access e-mails. The newest Nokia Communicator is not much bigger than a mobile phone but opens up into a keyboard mode. It doubles as a mobile office with Internet access, e-mail and telefax, and can receive pictures from digital cameras.

Communication methods are now converging so that text messages, telephone calls and video images can all be sent on the Internet. WAP (Wireless Application Protocol) mobile phones can be used to access the Internet on a limited scale. This technology has encouraged m-commerce which means that people can shop online on their mobile telephones or access their bank accounts.

The introduction of 3G (third generation) mobile telephone technology means that equipment will be even more powerful and will be able to download pictures. These mobile telephones are likely to have bigger screens and will be used for videophone calls, to send e-mails with photographs attached, play online games with much better picture quality and conduct shopping and banking transactions more easily.

More organizations are likely to be sending e-mails and text marketing messages straight to consumers' handsets. Mobile network operators, such as BT Cellnet and Orange already use text messages to send customers information about new tariffs, services and promotions. So, for example, an airline operating from a regional airport could send text messages to people in that region saying there were 50 seats left on a flight to a holiday destination at a certain price.

However, mobile phone marketing could result in a consumer backlash if telephones ring at inconvenient times. At the moment an EU directive forbids companies operating automated calling systems to target customers without their consent. In addition a new industry body has been set up in the UK – the Wireless Marketing Association, supported by Orange, Vodaphone and BT Cellnet – which has established a set of self-regulatory rules to govern use of marketing by mobile phone companies.

Although it could offer marketers the ultimate, personalised time- and location-sensitive method of communicating with customers, it could be seen as an unwelcome intruder. It is one thing leaving relevant messages on a business mobile telephone during a working day, but if the recipient was relaxing on holiday that could be seen as something entirely different.

However, in a fragmenting media marketplace, companies are keen to find new ways to get their message across, particularly to a youth market (the most avid users of text messaging) and particularly using a medium that is measurable.

Companies, including Coca-Cola, are pulling back from TV advertising and ploughing resources into marketing which 'adds value' to consumers' lives: music, sport and entertainment sponsorships and initiatives which allow the consumer to interact with the brand.

Mobile marketing is predicted to be huge but marketers have to learn how to create concise mobile ad campaigns with only 160 characters to play with. The main issue for marketers appears to be not to inundate people with messages but to get them to give their permission and provide interesting and relevant advertising that requires a response such as ringing a telephone line or looking at a web site.

Text messaging

Text messaging, which involves sending text messages to other mobile phone users, is becoming more popular than e-mail, particularly with the youth market. A new informal language is developing with no punctuation and abbreviated spelling. Although it is not particularly suited to business situations, here are some examples:

- B = Be
- C = See
- Cu = See you
- Cu18R = See you later
- B4 = Before
- NE = Any
- NE1 =Anyone
- RU = Are you
- 2day = Today
- F2T = Free to talk

- Ic%d mEt U @7 = I could meet you at 7
- tb = Text back
- 1t = Want
- y = Why
- msg = Message
- 1t2 = Want to
- :C = What
- :) = Smiling
- ;-/ =Confused
- :-(= Sad face

Digital technology

Increased bandwidth for electronic communications is a general trend and has resulted in the introduction of digital radio and digital television.

Digital radio

The main benefits of digital radio will be improved sound quality and the ability to send additional data with radio signals. This means that text messages and even pictures could be sent as you listen to the radio. While the idea of having pictures on a radio might seem inherently daft, it could be simply used to have the name of the artist visible as a record is being played. Digital radio will probably be interactive, with 'tell me more' buttons that can be used for people to find out more information if they want it. This will mean it can still retain the benefit of being a background medium (when required), so people can listen to it at the same time as doing other things.

Digital television

Digital television will allow for more channels and two-way communication. It means that information can be sent in the background and be accessed by choice. The implication is that you can find out more about an advert if it interests you. This will lead to television advertising becoming more direct response driven.

The technology involved in digital television will mean that people can view programmes in real time or not, as they prefer. If they do not view in real time, they will be able to filter out things they do not want to see, such as advertising. This may lead to more programme sponsorship.

The knock-on effect of the technology will be that viewers can programme the technology to tailor viewing to suit their TV habits, which will result in a 'Channel You' type of programming. The impact of more channels will lead to audience fragmentation, with more segmented channels. The implication will be that sports goods manufacturers like Adidas will advertise more on channels like MUTV than on traditional television channels.

The threat of e-commerce on traditional high street retailers and the effect on television companies of declining viewing share and advertising revenue will see changes in the way advertisers communicate with customers.

In addition, digital television technology has dramatically reduced entry costs for new broadcasters. Broadcast technology is also converging with the Internet, which is creating new hybrids between companies operating on both platforms. These issues, combined with the fact that existing television audiences and revenue streams are fragmenting, mean that a number of retailer and TV companies are becoming involved in alliances as a means to maintain market share and appeal to specific target markets. For example, the Wellbeing Network was recently launched in the UK. It is a joint-venture web site and television channel from Granada and Boots the Chemist which will air programmes on digital satellite, terrestrial and cable channels. It will mainly feature discussions of health problems, parenting forums, medical phone-ins, interviews and live product-testing. It is this kind of medium that many marketers will want to use as traditional broadcast media changes. However, the kind of direct-response television advertising that is emerging will cause problems for many advertisers because often they do not plan for the peaks and troughs in handling large scale audience response.

Activity 10.3

Explain how developments in ICT have changed the way that people communicate with internal and external customers. Provide examples of how the Internet is being used to add value, improve customer service or change the way business is being carried out.

Summary

In this unit you have studied:

- How communication with customers is changing.
- How e-business is evolving.
- How ICT can be used to improve customer communications.
- What makes a successful web site.
- How to use e-mail and e-mail marketing.
- How intranets and extranets can improve customer communications.
- The role of e-commerce, e-business and e-marketing.
- How telecommunications and digital media are changing customer communications.

Further study and examination preparation

Attempt question 6b on the June 2000 paper and questions 3 and 7 on the December 2000 paper.

Exam hint

You will not be asked questions on how computers work, the history of the Internet or about jargon connected with technological developments. However, you should be prepared to explain how technological changes are affecting the way that people and organizations do business and communicate.

Be prepared to answer questions that are set in a context of new media and technology but test you on other areas of the syllabus.

Objectives

In this unit you will:

- Be introduced to a structure that will help you put together a Continuous Assessment Portfolio.

- Consider all issues that may arise as you work through the module.

- Consider aspects of team working that might apply to this module.

By the end of this unit you will be able to:

- Put together a well-structured portfolio for assessment.

- Manage your time effectively in preparing for assessment.

- Work productively in a team and as an individual to achieve results.

Study guide

In this unit you will be introduced to all you need to know and do to achieve a good result in the assessment of this module. There are no 'Activities' in this unit, as all the work it suggests relates to the assembling of your portfolio. In the first unit of the book, we suggested that you read this unit before you progress too far into your course of study, as much of the work can be done on an ongoing basis. If it is your first read through this, you will find that it makes more sense as you start to work on your assignments. You should return to this section as a final check before your folder is submitted for assessment.

Introduction

The Chartered Institute of Marketing has traditionally used professional externally set examinations as the means of assessment for the Certificate, Advanced Certificate and Postgraduate Diploma in Marketing. In 1995, at the request of industry, students and tutors, it introduced a continuously assessed route to two modules, one at Certificate level, and one at Advanced Certificate.

With the revision of the syllabus for 1999/2000, the decision was taken to offer this route to assessment on four modules, two at each level.

Customer Communications is highly suited to assessment through Projects and Assignments, and this unit is written to assist students whose tuition centres are running this means of assessment.

Carrying out a skills self-assessment

Students studying for the CIM Advanced Certificate in Marketing come from diverse backgrounds; some work in marketing, some are looking to move into marketing, some work in large organizations and carry out very focused roles, and some work in small organizations and carry out a wide range of activities. Some students are not currently working and are looking to acquire a new range of skills to help them find work in the future.

Completing your Personal Development Portfolio (PDP)

The Personal Development Plan Assignment, which may be referred to as a 'Learning Log', gives you the opportunity to develop skills covered by the syllabus that are very relevant to your personal situation. The first Task set in your PDP Assignment involves conducting an audit of your existing skills using the analysis grid (Figure A1.1); copies of supporting material such as your CV, job description, job appraisal/performance review and a personal SWOT analysis may also be useful.

The next step is to identify two areas from your analysis for development, and write a rationale for your choice: this should clearly describe what you want to develop (e.g. a specific part of a large topic

INSERT INTO PORTFOLIO — DEVELOPMENT AREAS:	Syllabus Ref (2 CC)	Current Skill Level (None 0 – High)	Importance to Current Role (Low – Vital)	Likely Future Importance (Low – Vital)	YOUR COMMENTS
Write business letters and memos	4.1	0 – 1 – 2 – 3	[ ][ ][ ][ ]	[ ][ ][ ][ ]	
Write informal business reports	4.1	0 – 1 – 2 – 3	[ ][ ][ ][ ]	[ ][ ][ ][ ]	
Write formal business reports	4.1	0 – 1 – 2 – 3	[ ][ ][ ][ ]	[ ][ ][ ][ ]	
Write direct mail letters and material	4.1	0 – 1 – 2 – 3	[ ][ ][ ][ ]	[ ][ ][ ][ ]	
Write press releases and articles	4.1	0 – 1 – 2 – 3	[ ][ ][ ][ ]	[ ][ ][ ][ ]	
Write sales proposals and quotations	4.1	0 – 1 – 2 – 3	[ ][ ][ ][ ]	[ ][ ][ ][ ]	
Write copy for information sheets	4.1	0 – 1 – 2 – 3	[ ][ ][ ][ ]	[ ][ ][ ][ ]	
Write management briefings and notes	4.1	0 – 1 – 2 – 3	[ ][ ][ ][ ]	[ ][ ][ ][ ]	
Conduct one to one/group interviews	3.6	0 – 1 – 2 – 3	[ ][ ][ ][ ]	[ ][ ][ ][ ]	
Plan and lead group discussions/meetings	3.6	0 – 1 – 2 – 3	[ ][ ][ ][ ]	[ ][ ][ ][ ]	
Plan and conduct sales meetings/visits	3.6/7	0 – 1 – 2 – 3	[ ][ ][ ][ ]	[ ][ ][ ][ ]	
Negotiate sales, price and terms	3.6/7	0 – 1 – 2 – 3	[ ][ ][ ][ ]	[ ][ ][ ][ ]	
'Phone to gather market/sales information	3.7	0 – 1 – 2 – 3	[ ][ ][ ][ ]	[ ][ ][ ][ ]	
..... to make appointments/liaise with clients	3.7	0 – 1 – 2 – 3	[ ][ ][ ][ ]	[ ][ ][ ][ ]	
Plan presentations/briefings/talks	3.5	0 – 1 – 2 – 3	[ ][ ][ ][ ]	[ ][ ][ ][ ]	
Prepare speaking notes/scripts for others	3.5	0 – 1 – 2 – 3	[ ][ ][ ][ ]	[ ][ ][ ][ ]	
Prepare presentations using IT (eg P Point)	3.5	0 – 1 – 2 – 3	[ ][ ][ ][ ]	[ ][ ][ ][ ]	
Make presentations to groups	3.5-7	0 – 1 – 2 – 3	[ ][ ][ ][ ]	[ ][ ][ ][ ]	
Visually present statistical data/information	3.5	0 – 1 – 2 – 3	[ ][ ][ ][ ]	[ ][ ][ ][ ]	
Create visual aids/images	3.5	0 – 1 – 2 – 3	[ ][ ][ ][ ]	[ ][ ][ ][ ]	
Specify layout for promotional material	4.1	0 – 1 – 2 – 3	[ ][ ][ ][ ]	[ ][ ][ ][ ]	
Specify layout for printed advertising	4.1	0 – 1 – 2 – 3	[ ][ ][ ][ ]	[ ][ ][ ][ ]	
Use IT for word processing/DTP	5.1/2	0 – 1 – 2 – 3	[ ][ ][ ][ ]	[ ][ ][ ][ ]	
Use IT to maintain information databases	5.1/2	0 – 1 – 2 – 3	[ ][ ][ ][ ]	[ ][ ][ ][ ]	
Use IT to maintain financial information	5.1/2	0 – 1 – 2 – 3	[ ][ ][ ][ ]	[ ][ ][ ][ ]	
Use IT/Internet to communicate	5.3	0 – 1 – 2 – 3	[ ][ ][ ][ ]	[ ][ ][ ][ ]	
Plan and build a simple web site	5.3	0 – 1 – 2 – 3	[ ][ ][ ][ ]	[ ][ ][ ][ ]	
Identify role/motivation of DMU members	1.1/3	0 – 1 – 2 – 3	[ ][ ][ ][ ]	[ ][ ][ ][ ]	
Articulate FAB statements for key targets	1.1/3	0 – 1 – 2 – 3	[ ][ ][ ][ ]	[ ][ ][ ][ ]	
Identify and use secondary research data	2.2	0 – 1 – 2 – 3	[ ][ ][ ][ ]	[ ][ ][ ][ ]	Please ensure that you note the syllabus reference.
YOUR OWN CHOICE (discuss with tutor)		0 – 1 – 2 – 3	[ ][ ][ ][ ]	[ ][ ][ ][ ]	
		0 – 1 – 2 – 3	[ ][ ][ ][ ]	[ ][ ][ ][ ]	

Figure A1.1 Self-assessment checklist

or using a skill in a particular context – do not feel that you have to develop *all* of the topic) and explain how and why this is important to your current or future work and career. It will be most beneficial if you identify topics relevant to your current or future work; your tutor will provide guidance but you may wish to discuss your choice with your manager, colleagues or fellow students.

Once you have made your selection you need to formulate an action plan. This should clearly state what improvements you are aiming for in relation to each topic. It is important to aim for what is achievable in the time-scale available and to recognize that an incremental gain is sufficient. Your action plan should clearly identify success criteria (SMART objectives if possible) and should map out the strategies you intend to take to achieve them.

ACTION PLAN a)   See also review of PDP process

STEP 1: DEFINE THE DEVELOPMENT AREA AND STATE YOUR RATIONALE

Writing a Press Release

I chose this area as I felt it was not only one that would be very useful when I found a job in marketing, but also one that I could learn and practise doing without being in the job.

STEP 2: Define your success criteria	STEP 5: Conduct a review against your success criteria
1. Produce a series of press releases that show improvements	My press releases are referenced in this folder (Ref 3 - 6). The feedback from the marketing department was positive, but also picked up a few points to help me (Ref 7)
2. Get some feedback from someone in the marketing department on the releases I produce	
3. If possible, produce a press release for my local Drama group and have it published in the local paper	I have produced a press release for the Drama Group, but, as yet, it is still too early to send, as their production does not run until December (Ref 8). This experience has made me even more determined to move into marketing!

Tutor review	Comment/Date	Comment/Date	Comment/Date

STEP 3: Describe the actions to be taken	By date	STEP 4: Regularly review success and set next steps
1. Read the notes on Press Releases in the Workbook.	30.9.01	There is more to this than I initially thought - the style, layout and structure are all very different to letter writing, which is all I have been used to.
2. Write a release on the opening of the new site, and ask Gina in marketing for feedback	30.9.01	The feedback from Gina was also good. She gave me some examples of what she had sent to the press, and what had subsequently been published. This helped me to understand how to structure the writing.
3. Write an improved version, taking the feedback into account	30.9.01	
1. Write a press release about the local Drama Group's Christmas production. Aim to get it published in the local press at an appropriate time.	31.10.01	(See Section 5 on first page)

Figure A1.2 Example action plan

An example of an entry has been provided on the Action Plan pro-forma shown in Figure A1.2. Don't forget that there will be a wide range of resources available to you. These may include advice from your tutor, managers, colleagues and fellow students as well as books, distance learning material, CDs and videos, the Internet, etc. Remember it is important to review your progress against any plan that you make. Set interim review dates.

You will then need to carry out your plan. Don't forget that it may not quite work as you had hoped so be prepared to review and revise it in the light of experience. Discuss any major problems or revisions with your tutor.

LEARNING DIARY a)   Record key learning events

Date	Activity or experience... include comment/reflections on the learning	Next steps/actions	By Date
25/9	I read all the notes on putting together press releases from both the lecture in College, a book I borrowed from the library, and my Workbook. This gave me an initial picture of how to put together the first draft (which I decided to write about the opening of our new plant in Derby)	1. Make notes from my reading. 2. Write my first attempt	1/10
3/10	Ask Gina in the Marketing Department to look at what I have written and give some feedback. Re-write the same release, taking Gina's comments into account.		

Figure A1.3 Example learning diary

As part of this stage you should maintain a learning diary (Figure A1.3) to record your actions and review progress, and add details of any resources you find useful to your resource log (Figure A1.4).

Collect physical evidence of your progress. This might include examples of before and after work feedback from your line manager, information from performance reviews, course certificates, etc.

Towards the end of the module you are asked to review the self-development process that you have gone through in terms of what you achieved. That is, achievements against your stated success criteria; what went well, what went badly, what things you would do differently; how you will use the PDP process in the future to further enhance your skills and career. This should be added in Section 5 of your Action Plan.

RESOURCE LOG a) Record books, magazine articles, Internet articles, TV/radio, CDs, videos, courses etc

No	Resource (title, author, page, date etc)	Syllabus	Outline of subject matter and key learning points	Comments... recommendation to others
1	Copywriting' - Moi Ali, Chapter 14, News Releases, pgs 149 - 156	2.4.2	This chapter was easy to read, and covered all the essential ingredients of a News Release, listing them and then expanding on them.. They are - · A gripping first paragraph · A strong news angle · The 5 Ws · A quote from a named person · Contact name · Phone No · Date	Easy to read and put concisely. Useful basic notes on how to put together a release. It was very useful to me as I had not written one before.

Tutor reviews	No/Date	No/Date	No/Date	No/Date

Figure A1.4 Example resource log

Outputs for your portfolio

When you have finished, this Assignment should consist of the following outputs for your portfolio:

- A completed skills audit, as well as additional background information such as CV, performance appraisal or review forms, notes from meetings with your line-manager, etc.

- A written rationale for your choice of topics (around 200-400 words for each of the two topics selected).

- An action plan (for personal development)

and for each of the two areas:

- A learning diary

- Evidence of the improvements made.

plus

- A resource log of background reading and learning

- A written review of the personal development process

  - this should be around 700-1000 words in length, and so will not fit into the box of the action plan. It should therefore be completed on a separate sheet of paper. This review consists of your own reflective statement of what you have achieved and what you still need to work on. What was the most difficult part? How did you feel at the start of the exercise and how do you feel at the end? Did you achieve your objectives? If not, why not? Your final reflection should conclude your portfolio and 'look forward'. Look back at your 'introductory page'. What were your expectations at that point? Have they been met? Did the strengths you identified then turn out to be real strengths as you worked through your assignments? What have you learned about yourself as you have worked through the module? Did you dread having to make recommendations about a marketing issue, but, on the day, things went really well and you no longer fear being put into the situation at work? How much of your learning have you been able to apply at work? Have you been able to solve any real work problems through work you have done in your assignments? How much has your manager been involved? What does he/she think?

This statement will be personal to you, and should look forward to points you have identified as needing work in the future. We never stop learning – keep up this process of continuous professional development as you go through your studies and you will have acquired the habit by the time you need to employ it to achieve Chartered Marketer status!

Table A1.1 shows how the marks for this Assignment are allocated. You will see from this how much emphasis you should put into each section.

	%
Skills Audit	15
Action Plan	25
Learning Diary entries and evidence of improvements	30
Record of background reading & learning	10
PDP Review process	20

Table A1.1

Working as a team on assignments

Working within a team on assignments can be an area of concern for many students who are being assessed in this way for the first time. However, many students who have gone through the process, state that this has been the most useful area of learning for them. It is very relevant to today's workplace, as many of us now work in a team, or in more than one team on a variety of projects. Areas of concern include – what if I can't keep up with the rest of the team? What if I let the others down? What if one of the others lets us all down? Will it affect my marks if someone else does badly? In fact, most assignments are structured so that some of the marks are awarded for an individual's contribution and some awarded for the work of the team. Also, only one or two of the assignments are 'team' based – you will undertake other assignments as an individual, and so the majority of marks you achieve are on your efforts alone.

An important part of teamwork is working together to ensure that all are able to contribute on an equal basis – you will learn a lot about yourself and others through working closely on a piece of work which is to be assessed.

Dr Meredith Belbin, a British researcher, studied hundreds of managers working to solve exercises in teams.

He establishes that, in order to achieve their goals, individuals in teams have to recognize their differences. Imagine a football team made up of eleven strikers, or eleven goalkeepers! Many organizations think that by putting all their brightest people together, the team will consistently outperform other teams. This is not always the case, and Belbin realized that a successful team needed to be made up of a number of different 'roles' that related to different processes. For example, while there is a need for someone to take a strategic view, who is stable and controlled – there is equally a need for someone to pay attention to the detail of completing the task, and these people tend to be more anxious and introverted.

Belbin devised a questionnaire that identifies the role(s) which individuals are most comfortable in when working in a team. The roles are described as follows:

- **Implementer** – is stable and controlled and perceived by other team members as a practical organizer. They turn concepts and plans into practical working processes systematically. They can be thrown easily by sudden changes or too much uncertainty, and function through knowledge and expertise.

- **Coordinator** – controls the way in which a team moves towards the objectives using the team resources. They are intelligent without being intellectual, disciplined and have natural authority. They recognize the team's strengths and weaknesses and are good at setting priorities.

- **Shaper** – gets things done, is outgoing but can become anxious. They seek to impose some shape or pattern to group discussions. They have a high control need and can become impatient, impulsive and easily frustrated. Their outward confidence often conceals self-doubt.

- **Plant** – brings new ideas and strategies to the group through bright intellect. These ideas can inspire but a plant can sulk if these ideas are not accepted. The plant stays detached when team members get bogged down with problems and can then give a spark to move forwards.

- **Resource investigator** – is popular with team members and wonderful at networking outside the team. They build useful external contacts and resources for the team. They communicate, collect ideas, and adapt to find solutions from an outside view, preventing the team from stagnating.

- **Monitor evaluator** – analyses problems using their intellect. They can be perceived as cold, but their objectivity can prevent the team from making a mistake. They can be negative to change but their judgement is worth listening to.

- **Team worker** – cares about the team members as people and fosters team spirit. They are sensitive and loyal and don't like confrontation. The team worker likes harmony and works to develop this in team members.

- **Completer finisher** – is an anxious introvert who is particular about getting things done properly. They have personal discipline and give tasks more than the usual degree of attention. This can be perceived either as compulsive perfectionism or paying attention to detail. They also have a sense of urgency.

- **Specialist** – is someone who has a particular knowledge or skill. This individual is often more comfortable working alone than in a team. However, their contribution of specialist knowledge can often overcome a problem that is delaying progress.

You may not have the opportunity to identify your own team role, or those of others in your team. However, the key point to remember is that we are all different, and all have various strengths and weaknesses that can be used to best effect when working with others. It is up to everyone within a team to 'manage' the situation so that all are able to contribute, and that one person's strength is used to overcome another's weakness. Perhaps those of us who are most impatient with others when looking to make progress towards a goal have the most learning to do – it is part of everyone's role in a team to encourage, help and support the less experienced and less confident so that all achieve together.

There are a variety of issues that may arise when you are working with a team from your tuition centre. For example, most of you will be in demanding full-time employment that may involve working away from home from time to time. A member of your team may be ill, or have family commitments that make it difficult to attend meetings outside tuition sessions. Again, it is part of team working to use the individual parts of the team to overcome such difficulties. Perhaps there are parts of the work that can be shared out and undertaken between meetings to minimize the time taken working as a group. How are you going to communicate? Is everyone on e-mail at work or home? Will contact be made by phone or fax?

Team working can be very rewarding, and can forge strong bonds. Teams formed at Certificate level for continuous assessment work often stay together when they move on to the Advanced Certificate, and are still supporting each other when they tackle the Case Study at Diploma level.

Managing your time

What is time management? It's wisely using one of your most precious resources – TIME – to achieve your key goals. You need to be aware of how you spend your time each day, set priorities so you know what's important to you, and what isn't. You need to establish goals for your study, work and family life and plan to meet those goals. Through developing these habits you will be better able to achieve the things you want to achieve. When study becomes one of your key goals you may find that, temporarily, something has to be sacrificed in favour of time needed for reading, writing notes, writing up Assignments, preparing for group assessment, etc. It will help to 'get people on your side'. Tell people that you are studying and ask for their support – these include direct family, close friends and colleagues at work.

Time can just slip through your fingers if you don't manage it – and that's wasteful! When you are trying to balance the needs of family, social life, working life and study there is a temptation to leave Assignments until the deadline is near. Don't give in to this temptation! Many students have been heard to complain about the heavy workload towards the end of the course, when, in fact, they have had several months to work on assignments and they have created this heavy workload themselves.

By knowing how to manage your time wisely you can:

- Reduce pressure when you're faced with deadlines or a heavy schedule.
- Be more in control of your life by making better decisions about how to use your time.
- Feel better about yourself because you're using your full potential to achieve.
- Have more energy for things you want or need to accomplish.
- Succeed more easily because you'll know what you want to do and what you need to do to achieve it.

Putting together your portfolio for assessment

At last – you have finished all your assignments and your folder needs to be prepared for submission! A question often posed by students is 'How much should be in my portfolio?' There is no simple answer to this and it will depend on many things. Your tutor will have given you a 'Portfolio Front Sheet' that is shown in Figure A2.5.

This should be used as a checklist of your folder's contents and guide you through the process of putting it together. The first question you should ask yourself is 'Will this make sense to someone

Candidate name: _____	CIM reg. no: _____

Centre: _____

Section 1 (to be completed by the student)

Item	✓
CV and job description (if appropriate)	
Introductory pageLearning Log	
Assignment 1	
Assignment 2	
Assignment 3 (if appropriate)	
Other relevant paperwork (not course notes)	
Final reflection	

This section to be removed before portfolio is returned to student

Section 2 (to be completed by tutor)

Item	Mark
Learning Log	
Assignment 1	
Assignment 2	
Assignment 3	
Total mark	
Tutor comments	

_____

_____

_____

_____

Figure A2.5 *Portfolio checklist*

who has not met me?'. The folder contents will be looked at by an 'Internal Moderator' – someone who works in your tuition centre, but has not taught you during this module, and may be looked at by one or more 'External Moderators' – people whose job it is to ensure that all students on Chartered Institute of Marketing continuously assessed modules are marked fairly and consistently. This overview is taken as part of a quality control process that looks at the consistency of assessment within tuition centres and across the network of tuition centres.

So, when your folder is chosen, will the Moderator get a true picture of who you are and all the hard work you have undertaken within this module? The first way you can help this process along is by including your CV and a brief description of your current work role. This will help the Moderator put your work 'in context'.

The next thing that is asked for is an 'Introductory Page'. This again helps the Moderator make sense of your Portfolio. It does not have to be more than one page, and will consider your 'starting point' in terms of the skills covered within this module.

For example, you might say:

When I started this module I was looking to move into my first marketing role. I was still uncertain of all that I would be expected to do within such a role, and this is why I decided to study for my CIM Certificate. When I looked at the Skills Audit it was quite easy for me to identify my strengths and weaknesses. I had done a few presentations when I worked in Sales, and had also worked in telemarketing for a while, so was confident on the telephone. I had never been involved with writing Press Releases before, and also was keen to learn about the Internet and e-mail – so much so, that I had recently started to study for a European Computer Driving Licence (ECDL), which included learning these aspects.

Once I had looked at this exercise I actually felt better about taking the module – but realised that I still had some way to go. Our Tutor encouraged us to select topics from the list that would provide us with a challenge as well as being useful in our current and future work role, and this helped me pick the areas to work on in my PDP.

Your folder should now contain all the work you have done within your assignments. Again, it may be necessary to put a few introductory comments to each assignment, and a note of what your main learning points were from going through the exercise. If you have undertaken research for an assignment, then it may be appropriate to include this in the back of your folder as an Appendix. Your course notes should not be in this file.

Summary

In this Unit we have looked at all the issues involved in tackling this module by 'Continuous Assessment'. Like life, you will get out of this process what you are prepared to put in. It is possible to achieve high grades, but you need to balance the work you are putting in to your examined modules with the work you are putting in here. Do not be tempted to neglect one in favour of the other as this will only lead to disappointment. One of the advantages of 'Continuous Assessment' is the feedback you are given on an ongoing basis to help you improve your practice. Remember however that your final 'Grade' will be issued with your other examination results. Your Tutor will be able to give an indication of how it may be graded, but final grades are awarded at 'Moderation' and can be adjusted at this point.

Tips for completion of a Learning Log

- Ensure that the learning log is put together logically and will make sense to anyone who needs to look at it in the assessment process.
- Start with an Introductory Statement, which summarises where you were at the beginning of the course and why you selected the particular areas for development.
- Include a CV, a job description, and anything else you think will help the assessor.
- Undertake your 'Skills Audit' or similar self-assessment exercise.
- Talk to your manager at work, as well as your Tutor and colleagues to help you identify areas for development.
- If you have an appraisal at work, this may help you look at your objectives.
- Select areas that will challenge you in your learning and that are relevant to your work role.
- Complete a Personal Development Action Plan that sets your objectives for improvement and strategies for achieving these objectives.
- Write up your learning on a regular basis – this requires a high level of self-discipline, but is easier to do than trying to remember situations at a later date.
- Ask for early feedback to build your confidence that you are 'on the right track'.
- Attend tutorial sessions that are arranged for you.
- Put all the work that you have done within your Assignments in your folder, together with a few introductory comments and a note on your main learning points.
- If you have done any research for Assignments, put this in as an appendix.
- Your Course Notes should not be in this file, but do include your 'Resource Log'.

Finally, remember to continue to apply your new skills within your job – study and learning that is not applied is wasted time, effort and money! Well done and keep it up.

Preparing for your examination

You are now nearing the final phase of your studies and it is time to start the hard work of exam preparation.

During your period of study you have been used to absorbing massive loads of information, trying to understand and apply aspects of knowledge that are very new to you, while information provided may be more familiar. You may even have undertaken many of the activities that are positioned frequently throughout your text, which have enabled you to apply your learning in practical situations. Whatever the position is of your knowledge and understanding and level of knowledge application, do not allow yourself to fall into the trap of thinking you know enough, you understand enough or even worse, thinking you can wing in on the day.

Never underestimate the pressure of the CIM examination, getting into the examination hall, and wishing it had all been different, that indeed you had revised and prepared for this big moment, where all of a sudden the Senior Examiner becomes an unrelenting question master!

The whole point of preparing this unit for you is to ensure that you never take the examination for granted, and that you do not go into the exam completely unprepared for what you find what might come your way for three hours at a time.

One thing for sure, is that there is no quick fix, no easy route, no waving a magic wand and finding you know it all.

Whether you have studied alone, in a CIM study centre, or through distance learning, you now need to ensure that this final phase of your learning process is tightly managed, highly structured and objective.

As a candidate in the examination, your role will be to convince the Senior Examiner for this subject that you have credibility. You need to demonstrate to the examiner that you can be trusted to undertake a range of challenges in the context of marketing, that you are able to capitalize on opportunities and manage your way through threats.

You should prove to the Senior Examiner, that you able to apply knowledge, make decisions, respond to situations and solve problems. The list of solutions you will need to provide to prove your credibility could be endless.

Very shortly we are going to look at a range of particular revision and exam preparation techniques, methods, time management issues and encourage you towards developing and implementing your own revision plan, but before that, lets look a little bit a the role of the Senior Examiner.

A bit about the Senior Examiners!

You might be quite shocked to read this, or even find it hard to understand, but while it might appear that the examiners are 'relentless question masters', but they actually you to be able to answer the questions and pass the exams. In fact they would derive no satisfaction or benefits from failing candidates, quite the contrary, they develop the syllabus and exam papers in order that you can learn and utilize that learning effectively in order to pass your examinations. Many of the examiners have said in the past that it is indeed psychologically more difficult to fail students than pass them.

Many of the hints and tips you find within this unit have been suggested by the Senior Examiners and authors of the workbook series, therefore you should consider them carefully and resolve to undertake as many of the elements suggested where possible.

The Chartered Institute of Marketing has a range of processes and systems in place within the Examinations Division to help to ensure that fairness and consistency prevail across the team of examiners, and to ensure that the academic and vocational standards that are set and defined are indeed maintained. In doing this, CIM ensures that those who gain the CIM Certificate, Advanced Certificate and Postgraduate Diploma, are worthy of the qualification and perceived as such in the view of employers, actual and potential.

Part of what you will need to do within the examination is be 'examiner friendly' and you will need to ensure that they get what they ask for, doing this will make life easier for you and for them.

Hints and tips for 'examiner friendly' actions are as follows:

- Show them that you understand the basis of the question, by answering precisely the question asked, and not including just about everything you can remember about the subject area.

- Read their needs – how many points is the question asking you to address?

- Is the question asking you to take on a role? If so, take on the role and answer the question in respect of the role. If you are asked to be a Marketing Manager, then respond in that way. For example, you could be positioned as follows:

  'You are working as a Marketing Assistant at Nike UK' or 'You are a Marketing Manager for an Engineering Company' or 'As Marketing Manager write a report to the Managing Partner'.

  These are actually taken from questions in past papers, so ensure you take on board role-play requirements.

- Deliver the answer in the format requested. If the examiner asks for a memo, then provide a memo, likewise if the examiner asks for a report, then provide a report. If you do not do this, in some instances you will fail to gain the necessary marks required to pass.

- Take a business-like approach to your answers. This enhances your credibility. Badly-ordered work, untidy work, lack of structure, headings and subheadings can be offputting. This would be unacceptable in work, likewise it would be unacceptable in the eyes of the Senior Examiners and their marking teams.

- Ensure the examiner has something to mark, give them substance, relevance, definitions, illustration and demonstration of your knowledge and understanding of the subject area.

- See the examiner as your potential employer, or ultimate consumer/customer. The whole purpose and culture of marketing is about meeting customers' needs. Try doing this, it works wonders.

- Provide a strong sense of enthusiasm and professionalism in your answers, support them with relevant up-to-date examples and apply them where appropriate.

- Try to differentiate your exam paper, make it stand out in the crowd.

All of these points might seem quite logical to you, but often in the panic of the examination they 'go out of the window', indeed out of our minds, therefore it is beneficial to remind ourselves of the importance of the examiner. They are the 'ultimate customer' – and we all know customers hate to be disappointed.

As we move on some of these points will be revisited, and developed further.

About the examination

In all examinations, with the exception of Marketing in Practice at Certificate Level and Analysis and Decision at Diploma level, the paper is divided into two parts.

- Part A – the Mini-case study = 40 per cent of the marks
- Part B – Option choice questions – choice of three questions from seven = 60 per cent of the marks.

Let's look at the basis of each element.

The mini-case study

This is based on a mini-case or scenario with one question possibly subdivided into between two and four points, but totalling 40 per cent overall.

In essence, you, the candidate, are placed in a problem-solving role through the medium of a short scenario. On occasions, the scenario may consist of an article from a journal in relation to a well-known organization, for example in the past, Interflora, EasyJet, Philips, among others, have been used as the basis of the mini-case. Alternatively they will be based upon a fictional company, which the examiner has prepared in order that the right balance of knowledge; understanding, applications and skills are used.

Look at the examination papers at the end of this book and see the mini-case.

Approaches to the mini-case study

When undertaking the mini-case study there are a number of key areas you should consider.

Structure/content

The mini-case that you will be presented with will vary slightly from paper to paper and of course from one examination to the next. Normally the scenario presented will be between 400-500 words long and sometimes will centre on a particular organization and its problems or may even specifically relate to a particular industry.

The length of the mini-case study means that usually only a brief outline is provided of the situation and the organization and its marketing problems, and you must therefore learn to cope with analysis information and preparing your answer on the basis of very limited amounts of information.

Time management

Your paper is designed in order that you are assessed over a three-hour period. With 40 per cent of the marks being allocated to the mini-case, it means that you should dedicate somewhere around 70-75 minutes of your time to write up the answer, on this mini-case, plus allowing yourself approximately 20 minutes reading and analysis time. This takes you to around 95 minutes, which is almost half of your time in the exam room.

Do not forget that while there is only one question within the mini-case it can have a number of components. You must answer all the components in that question, which is where the balance of times comes in to play.

Knowledge/skills tested

Throughout all the CIM papers, your knowledge, skills and ability to apply those skills will be tested. However, the mini-cases are used particularly to test application, i.e. your ability to take you knowledge and apply it in a structured way to a given scenario. The examiners will be looking at your decision-making ability, your analytical and communication skills and depending on the level, your ability as a manager to solve particular marketing problems.

When the examiner is marking your paper, he/she will be looking to see how you really differentiate yourself, looking at your own individual 'unique selling points' and to see if you can personally apply the knowledge or whether you are only able to repeat the textbook materials.

Format of answers

On many occasions, and within all examinations, you will most likely be given a particular communication method to use. If this is the case please ensure that you adhere to the requirements of the examiner. This is all part of meeting customer needs.

The likely communication tools you will be expected to use are as follows:

- A memorandum
- A memorandum/report
- A report
- Briefing notes

- Presentation
- Press release
- Advertisement
- Plan

Make sure that you familiarize yourself with these particular communication tools and practise using them to ensure that on the day you will be able to respond confidently to the communication requests of the examiner. You may look back at the Customer Communications Text at Certificate level to familiarize yourself with the potential requirements of these methods.

By the same token, while communication methods are important, so is the meeting the specific requirements of the question. **Note the following carefully.**

- **Identify** – select key issues, point out key learning points, establish clearly what the examiner expects you to identify
- **Illustrate** – this means the examiner expects you to provide examples, scenarios, and key concepts that illustrate your learning.
- **Compare and contrast** – look at the range of similarities between the two situations, contexts or organizations. Then compare them, i.e. ascertain and list how activities, features, etc. agree or disagree. Contrasting means highlighting the differences between the two.
- **Discuss** – questions that have 'discuss' in them offer a tremendous opportunity for you to debate, argue, justify your approach or understanding of the subject area- *caution* it is not an opportunity to waffle.
- **Briefly explain** – This means being succinct, structured and concise in your explanation, within the answer. Make your points clear and transparent and relevant.
- **State** – present in a clear, brief format
- **Interpret** – expound the meaning of, make clear and explicit what it is you see and understand within the data provided
- **Outline** – provide the examiner with the main concepts and features being asked for and avoid minor technical details. A structure will be critical here; or else you could find it difficult to contain your answer.
- **Relate** – show how different aspects of the syllabus connect together.
- **Evaluate** – This means review and reflect upon an area of the syllabus, a particular practice, an article, etc, and consider its overall worth in respect of its use as a tool or a model and its overall effectiveness in the role it plays.

Your approach to mini-cases

There is no one right way to approach and tackle a mini-case study, indeed it will be down to each individual to use their own creative minds and approaches to the tasks which are presented. What you will have to do is use your initiative and discretion about how to best approach the mini-case. However having said this, there are some basic steps you can take.

- Ensure that you read through the case study at least twice before making any judgements, starting to analyse the information provided, or indeed writing the answers.
- On the third occasion read through the mini-case and, using a highlighter, start marking the essential and relevant information critical to the content and context. Then turn your attention to the question again, this time reading slowly and to carefully assess what it is you are expected to do. Note any instructions that the examiner gives you, and then start to plan how you might answer the question. Whatever the question ensure there is a structure: a beginning, structured central part of the answer and finally, always closing with a conclusion.
- Always keep in mind the specifics of the case and the role which you might be performing, and keep these contexts continually in mind.

- Because there is limited materials available, you will sometimes need to make assumptions. Don't be afraid to do this, it will show initiative on your part. Assumptions are an important part of dealing with case studies and it can help you to be quite creative with your answer. However, if you do use assumptions, please explain the basis of them within your answer so that the examiner understands the nature of them, and why you have arrived at your particular outcome. **Always ensure that those assumptions are realistic.**

- Now you are approaching the stage where it is time to answer the question, tackling the problems, making decisions and recommendations on the case scenario set before you. As mentioned previously, these will often be best set out in a report or memo type format, particular if the examiner does not specify a communication method.

- Ensure that your writing is succinct, avoids waffle and responds directly to the questions asked.

Part B

Again, with the exception of the Analysis and Decision case study, each Part B is comprised of six or seven, more traditional questions, each worth 20 per cent. You will be expected to choose three of those questions, to make up the remainder of the 100 per cent of available marks.

Realistically, the same principles apply for these questions, as in the case study. Communication formats, reading through the questions, structure, role-play, context, etc. everything is the same.

Part B will cover a number of broader issues from within the syllabus and will be taken from any element of it, the examiner makes the choice, and no prior direction is given to students or tutors on what that might be.

As regards time management in this area, you should have approximately one and a half hours left, i.e. 90 minutes. If you do have, this means you should give yourself 7 minutes to read the question and plan your answers, with 22 minutes to write and review what you have put within your answer.

Keep practising – use a cooker timer, alarm clock or mobile phone alarm as your timer and work hard at answering questions within the timeframe given.

Specimen examination papers and answers

To help you prepare and understand the nature of the paper, you will find that the last two CIM examination papers and specimen answers are included at the end of this unit. During your study, the author of your book may have on occasions asked you to refer to these papers and answer the questions, providing you with a specimen answer for guidance. Please utilize every opportunity to undertake and meet their requirements.

These are vital tools to your learning. The specimen answers are not always perfect, as they are answers written by students and annotated by the Senior Examiners, but they will give you a good indication of the approaches you could take, and the examiners provide annotation to suggest how these answers might be improved in the future. Please use them. You can also access this type of information through the Virtual Institute on the CIM web site using your student registration number as an access code.

Other sources of information to support your learning through the Virtual Institute are 'Hot Topics'. These give you scope to undertake a range of associated activities related to the syllabus, and study areas, but will also be very useful to you when you are revising.

Key elements of learning

According to one Senior Examiner, there are three elements involve in preparing for your examination.

- Learning
- Memory
- Revision

We are going to look at what the Senior Examiner suggests, by examining each point in turn.

Learning

Quite often, as students, we can find it difficult to learn. We passively read books, look at some of the materials, perhaps revise a little and regurgitate it in the examination. In the main this is rather an unsatisfactory method of learning. It is meaningless, useless and ultimately leaves us mindless of all that we could have learned had we applied ourselves in our studies.

For learning to be truly effective it must be active and applied. You must involve yourself in the learning process by thinking about what you have read, testing it against your experience by reflecting on how you use particular aspects of marketing, and how you could perhaps improve your own performance by implementing particular aspects of your learning into your everyday life. The old adage goes something like 'learning by doing'. If you do this, you will find that passive learning does not have a place in your study life.

Below are some suggestions that have been prepared to assist you with the learning pathway throughout your revision.

- Always make your own notes, in words you understand and ensure that you combine all the sources of information and activities within them.

- Always try to relate your learning back to your own organization

- Make sure you define key terms concisely, wherever possible

- Do not try to memorize your ideas, but work on the basis of understanding and most important, applying them.

- Think about the relevant and topical questions that might be set – use the questions and answers at the back of each of your workbooks to identify typical questions that might be asked in the future.

- Attempt all of the questions within each of your workbooks since these are vital tests of your active learning and understanding.

Memory

If you are prepared to undertake an active learning programme then your knowledge will very probably be considerably enhanced, as understanding and application of knowledge does tend to stay in your 'long-term' memory. It is likely that passive learning will only stay in your 'short-term' memory.

Do not try to memorize parrot fashion, it is not helpful and even more important, examiners are experienced in identifying various memorizing techniques and therefore, will identify them as such.

Having said this, it is quite useful to memorize various acronyms such as SWOT, PEST, PESTLE, STEEPLE, or indeed various models such as Ansoff, GE Matrix, Shell Directional, etc., as in some of the questions you may be required to use illustrations of these to assist your answer.

Revision

The third and final stage to consider is 'revision', which is what we are now going to concentrate on.

Revision should be an ongoing process rather than a panic measure that you decide to undertake just before the examination. You should be preparing notes throughout your course, with the view to using them as part of your revision process. Therefore ensure that your notes are sufficiently comprehensive that you can reuse them successfully.

For each concept you learn about, you should identify, through your reading and your own personal experience at least two or three examples that you could use; this then gives you some scope to broaden your perspective during the examination. It will of course, help gain you some brownie points with the examiners.

Knowledge is not something you will gain overnight, as we saw earlier, it is not a quick fix; it involves a process of learning that enables you to lay solid foundations upon which to build your long-term understanding and application. This will benefit you significantly in the future, not just in the examination.

In essence you should ensure that you do the following prior to the real intensive revision process commencing.

- Ensure that you keep your study file well organized, updated and full of newspaper and journal cuttings that may assist you formulate examples in your mind for use during the examination.

- Practise defining key terms and acronyms from memory

- Prepare topic outlines and essay answer plans

- Read your concentrated notes the night before the examination.

Revision planning

You are now on a critical path, hopefully not too critical at this time, with somewhere in the region of between four and six weeks to go to the examination. Hopefully the following hints and tips will help you plan out your studies.

- You will, as already explained, need to ensure that you are very organized and therefore before doing anything else, put your files, examples, reading material in good order, so that you are able to work with them in the future and of course, make sense of them.

- Ensure that you have a quiet area within which to work. It is very easy to get distracted when preparing for the examination.

- Give up your social life for a short period of time, as the saying goes 'no pain – no gain'.

- Take out your file along with your syllabus and make a list of key topic areas that you have studied and which you now need to revise. You could use the basis of this book to do that, by taking each unit a step at a time.

- Plan the use of your time carefully. Ideally you should start you revision at least six weeks prior to the exam, so therefore work out how many spare hours you could give to the revision process and then start to allocate time in your diary, and do not double-book with anything else.

- Looking at each of the subject areas in turn, identify which are your strengths and which are your weaknesses. Which areas have you really grasped and understood, and what are the areas that you have really struggled with. Split you page in two and make a list on each side of the page. For example:

  Planning and control

Strengths	*Weaknesses*
Audit – PEST, SWOT, Models	Ratio analysis
Portfolio analysis	Market sensing
	Productivity analysis
	Trend extrapolation
	Forecasting

- However many weeks you have left, break down your list again and divide the points of weaknesses, giving priority in the first instance to your weakest areas and even prioritizing them by giving them a number. This will enable you to master the more difficult areas. Up to 60 per cent of your revision time should be given over to that, as you may find you have to undertake a range of additional reading and also potentially gaining tutor support, if you are studying at a CIM Accredited Study Centre.

- The remaining time should be spent reinforcing your knowledge and understanding of the stronger areas, spending time testing yourself on how much you really know.

- Should you be taking two examinations or more at any one time, then the breakdown of your time and managing of your time will be critical.

- Taking a subject at a time, work through your notes and starts breaking them down in to subsections of learning, and ultimately down into key learning points, items that you can refer to time and time again, that are meaningful and that your mind will absorb. You yourself will know how you best remember key points. Some people try to develop acronyms, or flowcharts or matrices, mind maps, fishbone diagrams, etc. or various connection diagrams that help them recall certain aspects of models. You could also develop processes with that enable you remember approaches to various options.

(But remember what we said earlier about regurgitating stuff, parrot fashion.)

You could use the type of bomb-burst in Figure A2.1 as a way of remembering how the key components of STEEPLE break down in your learning process.

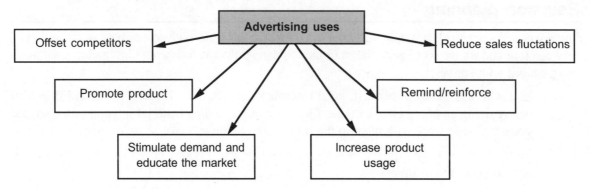

Figure A2.1 *Advertising uses (Source: Adapted from Dibb, Simkin, Pride & Ferrell, Marketing Concepts and Strategies, 4th edition, Houghton Mifflin, 2001)*

Figure A2.1 is just a brief example of how you could use a flow chart diagram which, in this case, highlights the uses of advertising. It could be a very helpful approach to memorizing key elements of learning.

- Eventually you should reduce your key learning to bullet points, from which you can revise. For example: imagine you were looking at the key concepts of Time Management – you could eventually break them down into a bullet list which contains the following key points in relation to 'Effective Prioritization:'

  1. Organize
  2. Take time
  3. Delegate
  4. Review

Each of these headings would then remind you that you need to discuss elements associated with the subject area.

- You should avoid getting involved in reading too many textbooks at this stage, as you may start to find that you are getting a little confused overall.

- Now refer to the end of this book and look at some of the exam questions listed, and start to observe closely the various roles and tasks they expect you to undertake, but more importantly the context in which they are set.

- Without exception, find an associated examination question for the areas that you have studied and revised, and undertake it, more than once if necessary.

- Without referring to notes or books, see if you can draft a answer plan with the key concepts, knowledge, models, information, that are needed for you to successfully complete this answer and list them. Then refer to the specimen answer to see how close you are to the actual outline presented. Planning your answer, and ensuring that key components are included, and that the question has a meaningful structure is one of the most beneficial activities that you can undertake.

- Having done this, now write the answer out in full, time constrained and in hand written not with the use of IT. At this stage, you are still expected to be the scribe for the examination and present your hand-written work. Many of use find this increasingly difficult as we spend more and more time using our computers to present information. Spidery handwriting is often offputting to the examiner.

When you are ready to write your answer in full – ensure you do the following.

- **Identify and use the communication method** requested by the examiner

- **Always have three key parts to the paper** – an introduction, middle section where you will develop your answer in full, and finally a conclusion. Where appropriate ensure that you have an introduction, main section, summary/conclusion and if requested or helpful – recommendations.

- **Never forget to answer your question in the context or role set.** If you answer the question void of either of these, then you will fail to gain marks.

- **Always comply with the nature and terms of the question**

- **White Space** do not overcrowd your page – make sure there is white space. There is always plenty of paper available for you to use. Make sure you leave space between paragraphs, and that your sentences do not merge into one blur.

- **Count** how many actions the question is asking you to undertake and double-check at the end that you have met the full range of demands of the question.

- **Use Examples** – to demonstrate your knowledge and understanding of the particular syllabus area. These can be from journals, the Internet, the press, or your own experience – this really helps you add value to your answer.

- **The Senior Examiner is your customer** – or indeed future employer, as we have previously said. Consider carefully what is wanted to satisfy their needs and do your best to deliver. Impress them and show them how you are a 'cut above the rest'. Let them see your vigour and enthusiasm for marketing.

- **Use the specimen exam papers and specimen answers** to support your learning and see how you could actually improve upon them.

Practical actions

The critical path is becoming even more critical now as the exam looms. The following are vital points.

- Have you registered with CIM?

- Do you know where you are taking you examination – CIM should let you know approximately one month in advance.

- Do you know where your examination centre is? If not find out, take a drive, time it – whatever you do don't be late!

- Make sure you have all the tools of the examination with you. A dictionary, calculator, pens, pencils, ruler, etc. Try not to use multiple shades of pens, but at the same time make your work look professional. *Avoid using red and green as these are the colours that will be used for marking.*

Summary

Many of the hints and tips here are very generic and will work across most of the CIM. However we have tried to select those that are most helpful, in order that you take a sensible planned approach to your study and revision.

The key to your success is being prepared to give it the time and effort required, planning your revision, and equally important, planning and answering your questions in a way that will ensure that you pass your examination on the day.

The hints and tips presented are there to guide you from a practical perspective, the syllabus content guidance and developments associated to your learning will become clear to you while you work through this workbook. Each of the authors have given subject specific guidance on the approach to the examination and how to ensure that you meet the content requirements of the question, in addition to the structuring issues we have been discussing throughout this unit.

Each of the authors and Senior Examiners will guide you on their preferred approach to questions and answers as they go. Therefore where you are presented with an opportunity to be involved in some activity or exam question either during or at the end of your study units, do take it, as it helps you learn in an applied way, but also prepares you for the examination.

Finally as a reminder

- Ensure you make the most of your learning process throughout
- Keep structured and orderly notes from which to revise
- Plan your revision – don't let it just happen
- Provide examples to enhance your answers
- Practise your writing skills in order that you present your work well and your writing is readable
- Take as many opportunities to test you knowledge and measure your progress as possible
- Plan and structure your answers
- Always take on the role and context of the question and answer in that context
- Adhere to the communication method selected by the examiner
- Always do as the question ask you
- **Do not leave it until the last minute!**

The writers and editorial team at Butterworth Heinemann would like to take this opportunity to wish you every continuing success as you endeavour to study, revise and pass your examinations.

Introduction

The secret of success when taking any examination is preparation. With this important thought in mind, The Chartered Institute of Marketing has asked the Senior Examiners to produce these specimen answers to the actual questions set.

The answers are for your guidance and should not be seen as perfect solutions. In marketing, there is never one entirely correct solution. Whatever the style adopted, the format and the content of these answers should be indicative of what the examiners want to see.

It is hoped that you will find these specimen answers, and the examiners' comments, useful and informative. However, it is regretted that no correspondence can be entered into regarding the subject matter. We advise students to practise past questions and to use their tutors for guidance and feedback.

The copyright of all The Chartered Institute of Marketing examination material is held by the Institute. No Case Study or Questions may be reproduced without its prior permission which must be obtained in writing.

Exam material

Cyberspace for Midchester Rangers

Midchester Rangers Football Club's interest in the Internet is growing. Figures show that 11,000 extra adults in the UK are using the Internet each day. In addition 10.6 million adults access the Internet at least once last year, a 48% increase on the previous year's figures. The speed of uptake in the UK exceeds Europe's other big economies, for instance Germany is gaining 9,000 users daily and France 2,000.

In June 1993 there were 130 web sites globally. By June 1994 this had increased to approximately 3,000 and by April 1998 the figure approached 2.2 million. Research also suggests that free Internet access from retailers is attracting older people and the C2DE socio-economic groups. Traditionally, Internet users have been from younger age groups and ABC1 consumers.

The most popular Internet activities are searching for information and reading news. Research shows that 1.3 million people in the UK had shopped online in the second half of last year, spending £570 million Sterling on 5.8 million items.

Midchester Rangers Football Club regularly gets a 45,000 home crowd in its 50,000 capacity stadium. It has a large following through 400 official supporters' clubs worldwide. The club has a turnover of £29 million Sterling and is the UK's tenth largest football club in revenue terms.

The club's first team has had no league or cup success in recent years, and frequent management changes due to this lack of success, have led to disgruntled star players being sold to other clubs.

An increasing number of written enquiries to the manager are not responded to. The club also receives hundreds of telephone complaints and queries from fans about player transfers and team news that often jam the club switchboard.

The current means of communication with fans is via match programmes and a monthly newsletter. Initial research has shown that a web site could be used to communicate with fans.

Large amounts of money have been spent on updating the stadium and facilities at the club. This has left the club cash poor and unable to raise the money to purchase some of the star players the current manager would like to buy. Consequently there is no spare money for developing an elaborate web site.

Two important revenue streams, from corporate hospitality and club merchandise sales, are high and on the increase. Research has shown that a web site could even help boost these activities by putting them onto a worldwide platform.

A web site could enable supporters to look up details of any match in the club's history as well as providing news and updates on match days. Club merchandise could be sold online and eventually tickets for matches could also be sold in this way. The web site could also be used to boost corporate hospitality from companies abroad and there would be opportunities for selling advertising on the web site.

The cost to develop a web site could range from a few thousand pounds for a simple web site to tens of thousands of pounds for one that can be used for online shopping.

To design and develop a good web site requires professional expertise to ensure that the web site is easy to use, has suitable access and also has the potential for data mining and identifying business opportunities.

The estimated timescale for development of such a web site would be a minimum of six months.

PART A

Question 1

You are the Commercial Manager for Midchester Rangers. You are keen to develop a web site to take advantage of new forms of communication and e-commerce. A member of your business development team has provided you with the above information to help you plan a report and presentation to the Board of Directors.

Prepare a formal report for the Board supporting the proposal to develop a web site and recommend the next steps that need to be taken.

(25 marks)

For a presentation connected with the release of the report, prepare the following slides:

1. Draw a bar chart to show the increase over the last two years in the number of adults in the UK accessing the Internet at least once per year.

(5 marks)

2. Draw a pie chart to show the number of additional people using the Internet each day in Germany, France and the UK.

(5 marks)

(10 marks in total)

For both slides, provide production information for your assistant, who will be preparing the presentation slides for you.

(5 marks)

(40 marks in total)

Answer – Question 1a

Proposal to Develop a Web Site for Midchester Rangers FC

Report to the Board

Prepared by: G. Purcell, Commercial Manager

Date: June 2000

1. Terms of Reference

The objective of this report is to set out the case for why a web site needs to be developed for Midchester Rangers. The report will support a presentation to the Board of Directors and has been commissioned by the Club's Chairman.

2. Procedure

Information on Internet use has been researched using press coverage and information from various web sites. In addition, club records and interviews with office staff have been used to identify how the club currently communicates with its fans.

3. Findings

3.1 Popularity of the Internet

- Interest and use of the Internet has grown, so much so that there were 130 web sites in the world in 1993, 3,000 by 1994 and by 1998 there were 2.2 million.
- 11,000 extra people use the Internet each day in the UK.
- 1.3 million people in the UK shopped online last year.
- Free Internet access has attracted older and lower income groups of people.

3.2 Possible Uses for a Web Site

The current form of communication with fans is via match programmes and a monthly newsletter. Research has identified that a web site would lead to better communication in terms of cost and speed of information to those fans with access to the Internet.

Queries to the manager are often not responded to and queries about transfers or team news often jam the switchboard. Fans who have access to the Internet would have access to relevant information which would reduce these communication problems.

Supporters could also look up information on club history and find out information on match days.

Eventually a web site could be used to sell match tickets and club merchandise online.

A web site could be used to boost corporate hospitality business and to generate advertising revenue.

3.3 Development Issues

The cost of developing a web site depends on its capability. One providing information would cost in the region of a few thousand pounds but one used for online shopping would cost much more.

A lead time of around six months is required to devise an appropriate web site. Professional expertise is required to ensure that the web site has the relevant features and is easy to use.

Staff would be needed to maintain the web site and to respond to emails.

4. Conclusion

The demand from club supporters to access information quickly and easily will increase and a web site will enable us to meet this demand. A web site can be used as an effective communication tool and could also be used to obtain feedback from fans.

A web site could be developed to promote corporate hospitality opportunities and club merchandise.

Eventually the web site could be developed so that fans can purchase match tickets and club merchandise online.

Although initial investment in terms of time and money are required, the development of a web site could save money by becoming a cheaper way to communicate with fans and could generate income through other companies advertising on the web site and through the sale of tickets and merchandise.

5. Recommendations

It is recommended that Midchester Rangers FC develop a web site. Initial steps should be as follows:

- To research the opinions of fans to determine the number of fans who would use a club web site and to find out how they would like to use it.
- To look at the content of other football clubs' web sites.
- To contact a number of web site design companies to get quotes for the development of a web site.
- To do a viability study on the revenue potential of a fully functional e-commerce web site.

Examiner's Comments

The sample answer shown here was a good one, written in formal report form. The candidate has selected relevant parts of the case study material to draft a report that supports the proposal to develop a web site. The candidate has also recommended the next steps that need to be taken and gone further than the case material to suggest that research be undertaken to identify if and how club supporters would use a web site. In addition the candidate used his/her judgement to identify the methodology or 'procedure' for compiling the information in the report.

Answer – Question 1b

i) Increase in Internet use

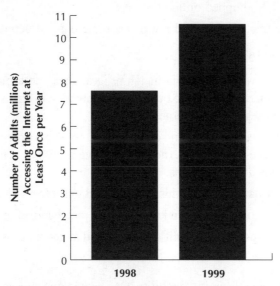

Figure 1 *Increase in Internet use. Source: PricewaterhouseCoopers Internet Report, January 2000*

ii) Number of additional people using the Internet each day

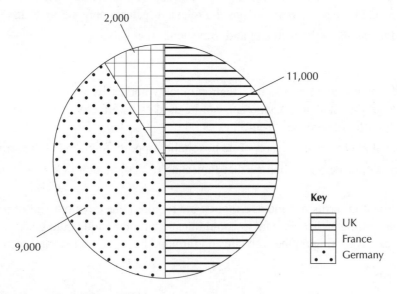

Figure 2 *Number of additional people using the Internet each day. Source: PricewaterhouseCoopers Internet Report, January 2000*

Examiner's Comments

The bar chart and pie chart were awarded high marks for accuracy and layout. They featured a title, labels and the source of the information (the candidate made an assumption about where this kind of information could have been obtained for research purposes.)

Answer – Question 1c

Memorandum

To: Jane Bentley

From: G. Purcell, Commercial Manager

Date: 12th June, 2000

Subject: Production Information for Slide Presentation

Please produce slides showing the information in the two graphs attached.

Please use PowerPoint (Microsoft Office) on a 35mm format. The slides should follow the corporate style, including our logo on the bottom right-hand corner and the club's 'orange' as a background for when I use the digital projector and laptop during my presentation.

I would be grateful if you could 'slice out' the largest segment of the pie chart to highlight the UK's prominence in this area.

I need the slides by the end of this week.

Thanks

Examiner's comments

Although the answer made some good points about house style and the need to highlight some of the information on the pie chart, the answer could have gone further and included information such as type size and font that should be used.

PART B

Answer THREE questions only

Question 2

You are the Customer Services Manager for a large furniture store. Your staff spend a large proportion of their time dealing with customers by telephone. Some of this time is spent answering enquiries and dealing with complaints and the rest of the time is spent contacting customers to arrange furniture delivery times. You have observed that some of this telephone contact could be improved.

Answer only **one** of the following.

Draft a memo to the store's Training Manager requesting that staff training in this area be a priority. Your memo should also explain why good telephone technique is important and suggest guidelines for effective telephone technique that could be included in the staff training.

(20 marks)

Draft notes for a presentation to staff on the importance of customer care, how customer needs have changed in recent years and outline ways in which staff could contribute to the provision of a quality customer care service when dealing with telephone enquiries and complaints.

(20 marks)

Answer – Question 2a

Memorandum

To: Rebecca Daniels, Training Manager

From: S. Markham, Customer Services Manager

Date: 12th June, 2000

Re: Effective Telephone Technique

I have spent some time analysing the work carried out by Customer services staff and have found that, although most of their time is spent dealing with customers by telephone, many staff would benefit from some training in effective telephone technique.

Customer services staff appear to deal with the majority of our customers at one stage or another; this may be to deal with initial enquiries or arrange deliveries. Thus the need for training seems to be a matter of priority. Consequently, I would be grateful if you could tell me how soon the training could be arranged.

I suggest that the training focuses on two areas: first, the importance of good telephone technique and second, how staff could improve their telephone technique.

1. Importance of Good Telephone Technique

- Customer services staff comprise the first line of contact for customers and in the first few minutes of dealing with us on the telephone we can make a lasting impression.

- If customers are dealt with successfully on the telephone, they are more likely to visit the store and we are more likely to retain their custom.

- By using a structured process, we can ensure staff both give and receive the right information, which speeds up the process of dealing with customers and makes our operation efficient.

- Conveying the right information ensures mistakes are not made with orders or deliveries and this makes us more efficient and helpful to customers.

- Tone of voice is very important when dealing with customers on the telephone, as they cannot see your face or body language, so it is important to get this aspect of using the telephone right.

2. Guidelines for Effective Telephone Technique

Dealing with incoming calls:

- Speed of response – the need to answer within 3 to 5 rings.

- Greeting – the need to clearly state the department name and own name after saying 'good morning/afternoon' as appropriate.

- Attitude and tone of voice – the need to convey a helpful attitude with an 'upbeat' tone of voice.

- Getting the detail right – the need for careful attention to product details, customer address and contact information to ensure good customer service.

- Taking responsibility when dealing with complaints – the need to deal with the issue in a helpful manner or get back to the customer later if you say you will.

- Listening – the importance of listening, clarifying details and making notes where appropriate.

- Messages – the need to take down the contact details, a brief summary of the message and the time, date and name of message taker.

Making outgoing calls:

- When contacting customers, be clear about the purpose of your call and have all the information, such as product availability, prices and delivery times to hand.

- It is import to identify yourself and speak clearly.

Examiner's Comments

The answer to Question 2a answered the question well and was awarded high marks. It is written in memo format but the content has been divided by sub-headings to make it easier to read and take the information in. The tone of the memo is good in that it emphasises the necessity for the training but still adopts a polite and respectful tone to a colleague.

Answer – Question 2b

Draft Presentation Notes

The Importance of Customer Care

Introduction

Introduce myself and give overview of why customer care is important, emphasising the following points:

- Customers provide us with our income.
- It is cheaper to retain customers than cultivate new ones.
- Dissatisfied customers quickly spread their dissatisfaction to others.
- Customers need to be valued – examples of other organisations that have had to change their attitude, e.g. banks.
- We face tough competition – customer care is an area where we can add value.
- We can go further and build relationships with our customers.

Main Points of the Presentation

Customer expectations:

- Customers are more demanding than ever before – ask staff about their personal experiences and give examples of what other firms do for their customers.
- Reasons for change – customers are more educated and travel more widely so they have picked up on the high standards elsewhere, e.g. in the USA.
- Difficult environment – more competition and customers are prepared to sue if they are treated badly. Meeting customer expectations will give us a competitive edge.
- We should not focus on reducing complaints but on closing the gap between customer expectation and what they actually experience.
- After-sales service can be an important aspect of the total product.
- The bottom line is that we will not survive if we do not provide a good service to our customers.

Your role in providing excellent customer service when dealing with customers on the telephone:

- The telephone is an important method of communicating with customers – often it is their first means of contact with us.
- Follow telephone guidelines in answering the telephone with the name of department and your name before asking how you can help them.
- Use a helpful tone and speak clearly.
- Not putting customers on hold – arrange to ring them back.
- Not transferring them around the company without listening to the query and either dealing with it or transferring it to the right department or person.
- Keep up to date with product knowledge and prices so you are in a position to help people.
- Familiarize yourself with the order tracking and delivery system so you can answer customer queries.
- When dealing with complaints be ready to encourage feedback, not block it with a defensive attitude.
- Be prepared to apologise on behalf of the company – even if it is to apologise that the customer has been upset about something that is not our fault – this does not stop you going on to explain the reality of the situation.
- Take a positive view in trying to solve problems rather than taking a complaint personally.
- Be diplomatic – use phrases that show empathy, for example, 'This is obviously unsatisfactory…'
- Adopt a helpful attitude.
- Check your details so that you can help solve a problem or track an item.

Conclusion

Customer Services is a vital role. How we deal with customers influences how well we do as a company. Customers have high expectations. We can meet customer expectations – on the telephone we need to communicate clearly and be helpful. We need to be proactive when dealing with queries and complaints.

Examiner's Comments

The answer to Question 2b was also awarded high marks. Not only was the subject matter presented well in note form, using bullet points and relevant headings to show how the presentation would run, but there was also enough detail in the bullet point statements to answer the question and indicate knowledge of the subject matter.

Question 3

You have been appointed to the position of Market Analyst in a company specialising in holiday tours.

Answer only **one** of the following.

Write a memo to your staff explaining the benefits of using visual methods to convey complex data. In addition, provide guidelines on the use of line graphs, histograms and pictograms and how they should be presented in information provided to senior management.

(20 marks)

Write a memo to staff explaining how surveys, focus groups and observation can provide valuable information about the company's current customer communication activities.

(20 marks)

Answer – Question 3a

Memorandum

To: All Staff

From: E. Lannion, Senior Market Analyst

Date: 12th June, 2000

Subject: Visual Information

As a department we are currently being asked to provide a great deal of complex data for special projects, the annual report and the new monthly management reporting system.

We need to convey this complex information using visual methods where possible to save people time, as they can often see trends at a glance.

Visual methods of representing information are not only easier on the eye but are easier for people to compare information about one product against another. In the long term this makes decision making quicker and more effective.

The other benefit is that it often looks more professional and conveys a good image of the company, if we can present information in this way.

However, we need to be sure that graphs and charts are presented in the right way and I have therefore attached some guidelines on the use of line graphs, histograms and pictograms.

Attached Notes

Guidelines for using visual methods for presenting data:

- Graphs and charts should be given a title and labels and keys should be used as appropriate.
- The source of the information should also be included.

- Line graphs are good for presenting sales information, e.g. the latest sales information on holidays to the Seychelles would show how the last five years have seen a dramatic increase in people travelling there.

- Histograms can be used to show groups of data. They look like bar charts but there is no gap between bars to indicate the continuous nature of the data. For example, they are good to show the age range of customers for particular types of holidays. This information is useful for the company when trying to target relevant literature to customers of different ages.

- Pictograms are useful for giving visual impact to information. Relevant images can be used to show the quantity or size of something. For example, if we wanted to present the number of flights we have sold this year, we could use the image of an aeroplane (with one aeroplane equating to 100 flights) to illustrate this information. However, pictograms can mislead if the size of the image is inconsistent and there are problems with trying to present partial images to present an exact number that is not a round 100.

Examiner's Comments

The answer to Question 3a was rather short but gained a pass mark. However, unlike many answers to this question, it did relate to the context of a holiday company. It would have gained more marks if it showed exactly how a line graph, histogram and pictogram should look by providing illustrative examples.

Answer – Question 3b

Holiday Tours Worldwide

Memorandum

To: All Staff

From: M. Wilsden, Market Analyst

Date: 12th June, 2000

Subject: Research Methods

As the department has expanded with additional staff this year, we will be undertaking extensive marketing research to analyse our current customer communication activities.

The emphasis will be on primary research such as surveys, focus groups and observation methods.

Surveys

Surveys can be used effectively to elicit quantitative and qualitative data depending on their structure, question type and contact method used.

By using closed questions, surveys provide number data, which is easy to quantify and analyse. For example, we could ask a question in a survey to find out how many people felt our brochure provided accurate descriptions of their holiday destination and accommodation. We could also use open questions to find out how people heard about our company. We could use rating scales in a survey to rate our literature against the competition and to find out about our customer service levels and how staff deal with customers.

Focus Groups

We will be using focus groups to provide us with more qualitative data. Focus groups explore people's attitudes, beliefs and motives. We could therefore find out what our customer requirements are and see if our current communications are satisfying them or not.

Discussion becomes more wide-ranging as people make comments and either agree or disagree. The moderator runs the group and is useful to bring the discussion back on track.

Areas for discussion include: the company brochure, quality of literature, advertising – recall, message communicated and the effects of public relations strategy.

Observation

This could include looking at the way our competitors communicate with their customers and doing a comparative study. For example, we could look at magazines and newspapers to check competitors' advertising activity.

We could also use mystery shoppers to find out how other tour guides deal with customers and the quality of their communication skills, and use the research to set a benchmark and monitor our standards against this.

Examiner's Comments

The answer to Question 3b was very good and was awarded high marks. The memo adopted a helpful, informative tone rather than talking down to colleagues. It was well structured and contained many relevant and illustrative examples.

Question 4

Write an informal report for your Line Manager about the value and effectiveness of a recent training course you have attended. Include all the details that would be required for company records and any recommendations for its suitability for other staff.

(20 marks)

Answer – Question 4

Introduction

Following my attendance on the 2-day Customer Satisfaction Measurement Course at Wickley Hall, I would like to provide some feedback on the value and effectiveness of the course.

Findings

Course Details:

The cost of the course was £595 for two days and included refreshments, meals and an overnight stay at the conference centre. The cost and facilities compared favourably with other similar training courses that I have been on.

Course Suitability:

The course is aimed at middle and senior managers and therefore is not relevant to everybody on the marketing team but I do believe that the new brand manager for the X product range could benefit from it.

Value and Effectiveness:

The course was run by a marketing professional who had plenty of experience and explained things very well.

The course was structured so that each day contained at least three practical sessions where delegates could put into practice what had been learned.

One afternoon was spent on questionnaire design which was most valuable and will come in useful when we conduct our satisfaction survey at the end of the third quarter.

Another session on strategy was a little too advanced and not very relevant to a company of our size.

The last session which looked at using customer feedback to improve products and services was invaluable and I have attached a copy of my course notes from this session.

Conclusion

Although this was an expensive course it was worth the money as I have brought some very valuable techniques and knowledge back to the company. The course would not be relevant to all staff because of the specialised nature of the topic.

I would certainly be interested in attending further courses run by this company.

Examiner's Comments

This was a good answer that demonstrated the candidate's report writing skill and ability to answer the question. Some candidates did not follow this approach and spent too much time writing extensive notes on a particular course topic, which was not what the question asked.

Question 5

You are the Sales and Marketing Executive for a toy manufacturing company. This year you have decided to take an exhibition stand at an international toy fair.

Draft an agenda for your regular monthly sales meeting. In addition to the usual agenda items, include two additional agenda items relating to the organisation and staffing of the exhibition stand.

(10 marks)

Answer **ONE** of the following questions

1. Write a memo to the staff who will be manning the company's exhibition stand, outlining how they might use appropriate body language to enhance their effectiveness at the trade fair.

(10 marks)

2. Write a memo to staff explaining the importance of exhibitions in achieving company sales objectives and suggest how the value of this type of promotional activity could be measured.

(10 marks)

(20 marks in total)

Answer – Question 5a

Toy World

Monthly Sales Meeting Agenda

Date: 14th June, 2000

Attendees: Sarah Plowmain, Ewan Johnson, Elizabeth Chatwin and Brian Coates

Apologies: Edward Baltram

1. Apologies for absence.
2. Minutes of the last meeting.
3. Matters arising.
4. Sales figures from May.
5. Feedback from each sales team area.
6. Update on sales support material.
7. Frankfurt Toy Fair in October – materials needed, stand design decisions and product decisions.
8. Staffing allocation for exhibition stand.
9. Any other business.
10. Date of next meeting to be decided.

Examiner's Comments

The sample answers to all parts of Question 5. were generally well done and were awarded high marks. The agenda items for Question 5a. were correct but it would have been good to see an answer that included a correctly phrased proposal or motion about the international toy fair.

Answer – Question 5bi)

Memorandum

To: All Sales Staff

From: R. Narayan, Sales and Marketing

Date: 12th June, 2000

Subject: Frankfurt Toy Fair 14-16 October, 2000

At the last sales meeting we discussed how we could maximise our presence at the toy exhibition in Frankfurt.

One area that I thought you would appreciate some helpful guidelines on, is the use of appropriate body language whilst manning the stand.

Here are a few tips that I have picked up from attending previous exhibitions:

- Eye contact – prospective customers are happier talking to sales staff who make positive eye contact, i.e. who don't look away when they are being talked to and look at the person to show their interest in what is being said.

- Facial expression – whatever nationality you are dealing with, a smile is an international greeting and customers do tend to respond to people who have a friendly (but not over-friendly) manner.

- Physical space – most customers get put off if sales staff try to be over-friendly or enthusiastic by standing too near to them. This is seen as 'an invasion of a person's physical space'. However, the extreme is when people sit behind a desk, which creates a kind of physical barrier and creates too formal an atmosphere at an exhibition stand. The best approach is to keep standing so you are ready to greet customers but to have some chairs arranged side by side so you can sit down to talk informally with people.

- Posture – try not to fold your arms because this again can be seen as creating a communication barrier between yourself and your customer.

- Environment – it is best to keep the stand tidy and neat. Used cups and paperwork should be tidied up regularly.

- Image – sales staff will need to wear a formal business suit during the day but smart casual wear will be fine for evening engagements.

Thanks for your views and comments about the forthcoming exhibition and I hope the above information adds to what we have already discussed.

Regards

Answer – Question 5b ii)

Memorandum

To: All Staff

From: Claudia Moore, Sales and Marketing Executive

Date: 12th June, 2000

Subject: Importance of Exhibitions

Some staff were questioning our decision to exhibit at the Frankfurt trade fair for the first time this year. There are several reasons for attending exhibitions and I have outlined these below.

Exhibitions are a valuable way of achieving company sales objectives. They provide us with the opportunity to meet potential customers, look at what our competitors are doing and meet with other suppliers, which could enable us to find alternative, cheaper and better partners.

Exhibitions also enable us to have a 'shop front' abroad and to focus on new target audiences.

Exhibitions enable face-to-face contact with customers so it is possible to get feedback on our range of toys and other invaluable market information.

We can invite current customers to see our latest product range and even meet new ones. We can encourage people to demonstrate our products and can use incentives and competitions to build a database of names for future direct marketing activity.

Exhibitions can also be a good PR and corporate branding exercise if managed properly. They can be used to generate press coverage.

There are several ways of measuring the value of exhibitions and we will use these to evaluate the worth of the decision to exhibit at Frankfurt:

- Counting the number of visitors to the stand.
- Counting the number of actual sales and sales leads.
- Measuring how much the database has been added to.
- Looking at the kind of market information that has been gathered.
- Evaluating the number of contacts and networking opportunities the event provided.
- Measuring the amount of press coverage generated.

Examiner's Comments

The sample answers to all parts of Question 5 were generally well done and were awarded high marks. Question 5b(i) generated many different answers, each looking at different aspects of body language in the context of exhibitions. Although this was a good answer, it could have been improved if it had touched on the issue of international differences in body language with different cultures and people from different parts of the world.

For Question 5b(ii) this was a very good response which answered both parts of the question, including how the value of exhibitions can be measured.

Question 6

You are a Brand Manager for a large Do It Yourself retail chain that has developed a web site.

Answer only **one** of the following.

Write a press release for the consumer press promoting the launch of the web site and encouraging Internet users to log on in order to take advantage of special discounts.

(20 marks)

Write a memo to staff explaining how a web site can be used to increase sales, extend the customer database and improve communication with customers.

(20 marks)

Answer – Question 6a

Press Release

(NB. Press release would be in double spaced type.) Do It Today logo and contact details including web site address.

Date: 12th June, 2000

FOR IMMEDIATE RELEASE

Money off discounts with Do It Today online

Leading retailer Do It Today is giving away 50% discounts to celebrate the launch of its web site.

The MNO web site will be launched on Monday 19th June and the first 50 visitors to the site will enjoy a 50% discount on purchases up to the normal value of £500.

The web site includes a full catalogue of products that can be purchased in your local store or online if that suits you. The web site will be regularly updated to give all the latest store bargains and offers.

Brian Kendal, Managing Director said: 'We are all excited about the idea of extending our service to customers. Not only can they shop online but they can get advice also.'

The launch of the web site will be celebrated at the head office in Durham, where 'Changing Rooms' television star 'Handy Andy' will be joining in the fun and looking at the top projects that people want to undertake.

Andy commented: 'It's great that DIY experts and those who are new to tackling jobs on the house, can visit the site and learn some short cuts and tips on how to do jobs quickly and easily. The web site has a special advice area that shows you how to tackle jobs and tells you what equipment is needed.'

Ends.

Examiner's Comments

The answer was a typical press release as created by candidates under exam conditions. This particular example was good in that it really did make an attempt to motivate readers to log on to the web site with a typical type of discount offer. It was written for both the journalists and readers of consumer magazines and the consumer pages of newspapers. It also featured some quotes and had something of interest in relation to a celebrity that would be likely to be picked up by a journalist. However, the ordering of the material could have been changed to have more newsworthy information at the beginning to give it more impact.

Answer – Question 6b

Memorandum

To: All Staff

From: Xavier Monteux

Date: 12th June, 2000

Subject: Do It Today Web Site

The company web site will be launched with a national advertising campaign at the end of this month and I am writing to staff to give you some idea about how the web site will put Do It Today in a better position to compete in the marketplace.

The web site will be used to increase sales, extend our customer database and generally improve communication with customers.

Increasing Sales

Customers will be able to purchase any item from our product range at any time of day on any day of the week. There will be a small cover charge for delivery. This will not put jobs in our shops at risk but we will be able to extend our customer base to people who do not live within a convenient travelling distance to our stores. It will also be more convenient for customers who cannot visit us during normal opening hours.

Extending the Database

Currently we have a database of regular customers who have Do It Today store cards. We regularly send them mailshots notifying them of special offers and give our regular customers incentives to keep shopping at our stores. Customers who visit our web site will be encouraged to leave their contact details and some information about themselves. This will enable us to send them information at a later stage that is tailored to their lifestyle and purchasing habits. This will also help increase sales and improve our communication with customers.

Improving Communication

Customers will be encouraged to visit the web site to find out handy DIY tips from experts and designers. The first web site feature will be about 'designing a kid's bedroom' and information about how to create a Japanese water garden.

Customers will also be able to e-mail our helpdesk with queries and feedback about products and the information on our web site. This way we will have a better idea of what our customers think and the feedback will help us decide on special promotions. This will gradually take us closer to having two-way communication with customers rather than the situation at present where we tell customers things but get very little information back.

If you have any suggestions or queries about the web site, please contact me on x345 and I will be happy to speak to you. This is a new development for the company and we are keen to get it right, so any feedback from staff will be very much welcomed.

Examiner's Comments

The answer was not a typical answer but one of the better ones marked by examiners. Most candidates in fact forgot that they were communicating with staff for all intents and purposes for the reason of improving internal marketing. This answer also really tackled issues about online sales, database and communication; issues that some candidates did not address.

Question 7

For the company of your choice, assume that you work in the Marketing Department and have responsibility for the staff newsletter. There is a regular feature entitled 'It's our job...' which provides information about various job roles and departments. To improve internal marketing within the firm, you decide to take this opportunity to explain the relevance of marketing to the company and to describe the work undertaken by staff in your department.

Write a 500-word article for the feature to appear in the next issue and provide production and layout information to enable your article to have both visual and verbal impact on the reader.

(20 marks)

Answer – Question 7

'It's our job… The Horse of the Year show needs Marketing'

Working for our organisation you may wonder why we need to market the Horse of the Year show and what I and my colleagues do in marketing.

The event itself is advertised continually throughout the equestrian season although it is an event that everyone (both UK and worldwide) in the sport seems to know about.

Part of our job is to ensure that this continual advertising is successful in keeping up attendance levels at the event and to demonstrate that the show is such a success, so that more riders will want to qualify the following year. It is only by doing this kind of work that we keep the event known by the new riders and the youngsters who become interested in the sport each year.

It takes a great deal of time and money to put together a show of this size and even though it is only held over a period of five days in the year, the marketing has become a year-round job.

Each year we need to ensure that we have enough sponsorship to cover our costs. Coverage in magazines (both general and specialist) and television coverage are very important factors as they enable us to reach new audiences (both those who will attend in the future and/or may take up the sport).

Our job is not only to market this event but to market the sport to many different types of people. This includes ensuring that information about qualifying events is widely publicised.

We have recently developed a web site to promote wider interest including outside the UK. Many children access our site so we need to make sure it is easy to use, informative but at the same time fun so it includes lots of competitions.

People can also purchase tickets for the show online and part of my job is to keep a record of how much this service is used.

My role also includes keeping in touch with television and press contacts and affiliated associations such as the British Horse Society, British Show Jumping Society, the Hack Society and the Pony Club.

Each year we review how the show went and are particularly concerned to make any improvements for our sponsors.

As soon as the show ends our work begins for the next year building up sponsorships, organising the qualifying event during next year's season and keeping our wide range of customers and associates aware of any news and special events happening at the show. If we did not do this the show would not happen, so marketing may seem irrelevant but is in fact crucial to the biggest equestrian event in the UK.

Layout Information

To be printed in newspaper format, i.e. across a narrow column, to show a picture of our web site and to include the logos of our sponsors.

Examiner's Comments

There were very few answers to this question. Most candidates who did attempt it did not produce an answer to this standard. This answer gained high marks because it was clear which type of organisation the marketing staff worked in and clearly communicated the work done by the marketing team. It was a pleasure to mark because it was well structured with facts following a logical order and it adopted a 'sell' tone to others within the organisation. Additional marks could have been gained if more layout information had been included but overall this was a good answer to an unpopular question.

Introduction

The secret of success when taking any examination is preparation. With this important thought in mind, The Chartered Institute of Marketing has asked the Senior Examiners to produce these specimen answers to the actual questions set.

The answers are for your guidance and should not be seen as perfect solutions. In marketing, there is never one entirely correct solution. Whatever the style adopted, the format and the content of these answers should be indicative of what the examiners want to see.

It is hoped that you will find these specimen answers, and the examiners' comments, useful and informative. However, it is regretted that no correspondence can be entered into regarding the subject matter. We advise students to practise past questions and to use their tutors for guidance and feedback.

The copyright of all The Chartered Institute of Marketing examination material is held by the Institute. No Case Study or Questions may be reproduced without its prior permission which must be obtained in writing.

Exam material

Global Online Retailing

Internet retailing grew at extraordinary rates around the world in 1999, according to a report by Ernst & Young. To compile the report, more than 3,000 consumers in six countries (1,200 were US-based), were surveyed online and thirty-eight retailers were interviewed for the company portion of the report.

Table 1 PC and Internet shopping penetration (January 2000)

	US	Canada	Australia	UK	Italy	France
% households with PCs	53	56	47	41	14	26
% households that are online	34	39	22	29	5	14
% households that have shopped online	17	9	5	10	1	2

Table 2 Trends in the number of purchases – purchases in past 12 months (January 2000)

	US	Canada	Australia	UK	Italy	France
1-2	17%	32%	26%	20%	59%	33%
3-4	18%	30%	28%	39%	21%	29%
5-9	26%	24%	26%	26%	13%	23%
10+	39%	14%	20%	15%	7%	15%

Table 3 Shopping volume – Amount spent in past 12 months (January 2000)

	US	Canada	Australia	UK	Italy	France
Light (under $500 US)	52%	70%	60%	63%	66%	53%
Heavy ($500 US or more)	48%	30%	40%	37%	34%	47%
Weighted Average (US $ equivalent)	$1,205	$770	$854	$884	$9,381	$1,120

Table 4 *Future growth of online shopping – Non-buyers purchasing expectations in next 12 months (January 2000)*

	US	Canada	Australia	UK	Italy	France
% intend to purchase in next 12 months	79%	85%	n/a	65%	79%	80%
Average number of intended purchases	4	3	n/a	3	4	4

Consumer Projections

By the year 2002, US online shoppers will spend one-third of their total shopping money via the Internet. American online shoppers who currently spend 15% of their shopping money on the web, will more than double that to 36%. This trend will be mirrored by online consumers in Italy, who will also double their Internet spending, and will increase threefold in Canada, Australia, France and the United Kingdom.

Based on this new consumer data, we see tremendous growth in online retailing in 2000 and beyond. The estimate for online sales is that they will double to $45-50 billion, said Stephanie Stern, Global Director of Retail and Consumer Products for Ernst & Young. We also project significant growth in all categories of products, including apparel, accessories, health and beauty, shoes, sporting goods and toys.

Gender Differences Determine Online Spending Habits

In an online survey of 1,200 US Internet users, men and women had varied responses when identifying their favourite online shopping categories.

Table 5 *Favourite shopping categories ((January 2000)*

Men s Favourite Online Categories	Women s Favourite Online Categories
Computers (76%)	Books (64%)
CDs (60%)	CDs (60%)
Books (59%)	Computers (57%)
Small consumer electronics (44%)	Health & Beauty (42%)
Videos (38%)	Toys (41%)
Air travel (34%)	Clothing (39%)
Magazines (31%)	Children s clothing (31%)
Clothing (29%)	Videos (28%)
Toys (29%)	Magazines (27%)
Hotel reservations (26%)	Small consumer electronics (26%)
Health & Beauty (19%)	Air travel (24%)
Sporting goods (19%)	Flowers (21%)

Shern said: While men and women may differ in the online shopping preferences, the good news is that more consumers are flocking to the Internet than ever before. What retailers can learn from these results, however, is how to adjust and focus their merchandising and marketing efforts according to their audience.

The data also revealed that more men purchased travel-related services online than women. Men made more airline and hotel reservations. In addition, more men (55 per cent) than women (48 per cent) participate in online auctions, and more men (58 per cent) than women (39 per cent) are considered heavy buyers spending over $500 online in the previous year.

Company Findings

Almost every responding company said it is meeting or exceeding its financial goals for online retailing and all have great expectations of the future. However, only 13% of the companies interviewed report being profitable.

The newness of many online businesses has kept them focused in their home country. Fewer than half the respondents are selling outside their home countries.

Table 6 *How new traffic is attracted to Web sites (January 2000)*

Portals/online ads	28%
Media TV/radio	22%
Print ads	22%
Cross-channel marketing	15%
Direct mail	7%
Email	3%
Other	3%

(Material and data extracted from Global Online Retailing Report, January 2000. With grateful thanks to Ernst & Young).

PART A

Question 1

You have been shortlisted for a job in the PR department of leading professional services firm, Ernst & Young, which provides tax, accountancy and management consultancy to firms around the world. As part of the selection process, you have been asked to research into online retailing trends and undertake a number of in-tray exercises.

Based on the information you have extracted above, write a press release for the international business press about how gender differences influence online buying decisions. Use the opportunity to promote Ernst & Young services to business.

(14 marks)

Using the information you have extracted above, write a brief report on the growth of online retailing and the experience of online retailers in the six countries surveyed. The report will be distributed to client companies that have expressed an interest in this topic.

(18 marks)

As an appendix to the report include the following charts:

1. A multiple bar chart to show PC and Internet shopping penetration in the six countries surveyed in the report.

2. A pie chart to show how companies attract new traffic to their web sites.

(4 marks for each chart)

(40 marks in total)

Answer – Question 1a.

Press Release from Ernst & Young

4th December 2000

Gender has Influence on Online Buying

New research released today by leading professional services firm Ernst & Young highlights how differences in gender impact the online retailing experience.

In a survey of 1,200 US Internet users, it was found that men's and women's favourite purchases were different and men were the heaviest spenders when shopping on the Internet.

According to the research, computers, books and CDs were the most frequently bought items. Following these primary categories, however, the sexes diverge. Men lean towards purchasing small consumer electronics, videos and travel-related services, while women prefer to purchase health and beauty items, as well as toys and clothing. Stephanie Shern, Global Director of Consumer Products for Ernst & Young, said: 'While men and women may differ in their online shopping preferences, the good news is that more consumers are flocking to the Internet than ever before.'

Shern, who provides expert business advice to Ernst & Young's retailing clients, said: 'What retailers can learn from these results, however, is how to adjust and focus their merchandising and marketing efforts according to their audience.'

For example, more women than men bought clothing (70%, including children's clothing, versus 29% of men), health and beauty items (42% versus 19%), and toys (41% versus 29%). On the other hand, more men bought computers (76% of men versus 57% of women), small consumer electronics (44% versus 26%), and videos (38% versus 28%).

The data also revealed that more men purchased travel-related services online than women. Men made more airline, hotel and car reservations. In addition, more men (55%) than women (39%) are considered 'heavy buyers', spending over $500 online last year.

This research, carried out by Ernst & Young, is just one example of how the firm can help businesses find out more about their customers to allow them to make better business decisions. This service is provided alongside Ernst and Young's tax, accountancy and management consultancy services, which are available to firms around the world.

Ends

For a full copy of the report or further information about Ernst & Young, contact Jane Hill on 0800 012 101 or visit Ernst and Young's web site at www.globalaccountants.co.uk.

Senior Examiner's Comments

In the answer to Question 1a. the candidate produced a good, well-written press release. The candidate managed to combine the relevant facts with a 'sell' of the company's services, as requested in the question. It was also written in a 'press release' style, i.e. short, sharp and news-like with a newsworthy opening and a title that would catch a busy business press journalist or editor.

Answer – Question 1b

Report on the Growth of Online Retailing

FAO: Client Companies of Ernst & Young

By: Ian Black, PR Department, Ernst & Young

Date: 4th December, 2000

1. Terms of Reference

This report is designed to show the growth of online retailing and the experience of online retailers. It will be distributed to client companies which have expressed an interest in the topic.

2. Methodology

More than 3,000 consumers in the following countries were surveyed online: USA, Canada, Australia, UK, Italy and France. In addition, 38 retailers were interviewed for the company section of the report.

3. Findings

3.1 Growth of the Internet

The USA and Canada were the countries where computers were used the most, with over 50% of households owning one. Australia and the UK had between 40 and 50% of households with computers, with France and Italy lagging behind, with only 26% and 14% of households having computers.

In terms of Internet access, Canada is the leading country, with 39% of households being online, with the USA just behind on 34%. Italy has the least Internet access, with only 5% of households online. The USA is leading the way in the online shopping revolution, with 17% of households reporting that they have shopped online, and with the UK being just behind that figure on 10%. Italian households are the least likely to shop, with only 1% shopping online (see Appendix I for figures).

3.2 Trends in Purchasing

The USA is a clear leader for online buying with 39% of those surveyed purchasing 10 or more items in the last 12 months. Of those who have shopped online, significant numbers have purchased just one or two items, with 59% of those in living in Italy making 1-2 purchases, 32% of those in Canada, 33% in France, 26% in Australia and 20% in the UK.

Of those that purchase more regularly, 39% in the UK and over 20% in Canada, Australia and France, made between 3 and 4 purchases in the last 12 months.

3.3 Projected Growth

Non-buyers in each country were asked what their online purchasing expectations would be in the next 12 months (excluding Australia) and it was found that between 65 and 80% of them intend to make 3-4 purchases on the Internet in the next year.

Online consumers in the USA and Italy are predicted to double their spending on Internet shopping, and spending in Canada, Australia, France and the UK is expected to treble by 2002.

Experts predict that there will be tremendous growth in spending on all categories of products, including clothes, accessories, health and beauty, sports goods and toys.

3.4 Retailer Experience

Most of the companies that responded to the survey said that their financial goal had either been met or exceeded; however, only 13% said that online retailing was profitable.

Their experience has been that most customers are coming to their web sites through adverts and portals on the Internet and others through media advertising, suggesting that other methods are less effective (see Appendix II).

4. Conclusions

More people have computers and Internet access than ever before. The USA has the most people who have shopped online and USA purchasers buy more goods online than those in other countries. Even non-buyers are expecting that they will purchase online in the next 12 months. There is no sign that the growth of online retailing will slow down in the future and online buyers in the USA and Italy are predicted to double their expenditure, while in Canada, Australia, France and the UK it is expected to treble.

It also appears that there will be a tremendous growth in spending on all product categories but although most companies have met their financial targets, only a minority of retailers found online retailing profitable. Companies found that online adverts and portals were the best way to attract customers to their web sites.

Senior Examiner's Comments

In answer to Question 1b the candidate produced a satisfactory report that was well structured with relevant headings. This report provided an overall view with some analysis of the data, not just a mechanical listing. It was not necessary for candidates to regurgitate all the facts and figures from the tables and the information included in the case study. Although some information regarding the amounts spent by consumers was omitted in this specimen answer, overall it achieved high marks because of the analysis and interpretation featured in the answer.

Answer – Question 1c

Appendix I

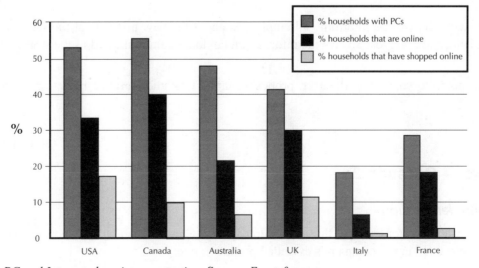

Figure 1 *PC and Internet shopping penetration. Source: Ernst & young*

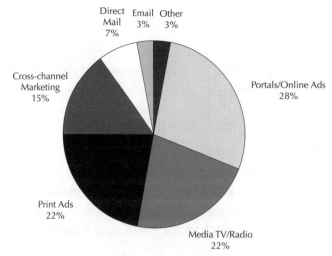

Figure 2 *How new traffic is attracted to web sites (January 2000). Source: Ernst & Young*

Senior Examiner's Comments

The answer to Question 1c was also satisfactory in both presentation and content terms. However, many candidates could not distinguish between a compound and a multiple bar chart and even where they did, a significant number did not put the gaps in the right places between the bars. In this answer the candidate achieved full marks for the pie chart due to the excellent presentation, accurate content and inclusion of relevant information, such as a key and the source of the data.

PART B

Answer THREE questions only

Question 2

You have joined the in-house corporate communications team within a plc that manufactures house-hold cleaning and toiletry products. The company has a head office base in a country of your choice, various factory sites and a number of regional offices. After substantial investment in research and development, the company has developed a new range of extra strong cleaning products which are to be launched this year.

Identify the stakeholder groups that your team will be communicating with in relation to the launch of the new product range, including an example and explanation for each.

(6 marks)

Explain why you will be informing all employees about the new products at the same time as the market launch and suggest 3 ways the information could be communicated to the workforce.

(8 marks)

Write a memo to your Line Manager, proposing that a customer careline be set up. Explain your reasons.

(6 marks)

(20 marks in total)

Answer – Question 2a.

Stakeholder Groups

- Customers; for example those who already buy 'Clever Cleaning' products and who will be interested in the company's extended product range.

- Media; for example it will be appropriate for the company to communicate with contacts at national newspapers and relevant magazines to publicise the new range of products that are to be launched.

- Suppliers; these are important partners for us to work with and communicate our new needs in terms of raw materials if we are to produce the new product range successfully.

- Distributors; for example 'Cash and Carry' warehouses that distribute to smaller retailers will need to be informed about the new products and likely demand as a result of our launch advertising campaign.

- Retailers; for example large supermarket chains that will need to be informed in the same way as distributors.

- Employees; such as factory staff and office staff, who will need to be informed about the new product range, as they are vital to the production process.

Senior Examiner's Comments

In answer to Question 2a the candidate identified and explained the stakeholder groups that the company would need to communicate with. Other candidates cited stakeholders such as shareholders, financial backers and even regulatory bodies because of the safety issues that may need to be considered in relation to extra strong cleaning products. Too many candidates, however, just listed customers and potential customers as the relevant stakeholders in this situation.

Answer – Question2b

All employees need to informed about the new products at the same time as the market launch because knowledge makes employees happier and more motivated. Lack of information and communication leads to dissatisfaction and resentment, particularly if employees have to answer customer queries about something they have not been informed about.

Three ways that employees could be informed are:

- Co-ordinated 'all employee' meetings, all held at the different sites at the same time at 10am on the day of the launch.

- All employees to receive a free sample pack with a covering letter to be distributed at the meetings.

- Information on the new products, the advertising launch campaign and any other relevant information could be put on the company's Intranet so employees could find out more if they wanted to.

Senior Examiner's Comments

The answer to Question 2b was good because it dealt with the internal communication issues well. Other correct answers looked at internal communication methods such as team briefings, the company notice board, a newsletter or an internal memorandum. However, some candidates handled this part of the question from the negative point of 'why we should not tell employees about the product launch until the last minute'. Whilst technically this was a plausible interpretation and so earned marks, the emphasis should have been 'why it is good to keep employees informed and therefore motivated'.

Answer – Question 2c

Memorandum

To: Geoffrey Reed, Communications Director

From: Hannah Pilson, Communications Executive

Date: 4th December, 2000

Subject: Customer Careline Proposal

As part of the work associated with the launch of the Extra Strong Clever Cleaning product range that will take place later this year, I am proposing that we set up a 'customer careline' specific to this product range.

A customer careline would help to ensure that all queries and complaints are dealt with efficiently and effectively. Due to the strength of the chemicals in the products, customers may well wish to seek guidance and a customer careline would allow the company to promote its image as a caring, customer focused business.

The careline would also be a useful tool for collecting customer feedback, which would help us to continue to develop new products in line with customer needs.

The careline could also be used as a means of encouraging potential customers to contact us to obtain a free trial sample.

If you agree that this proposal should go ahead, I would be happy to investigate the logistics and provide a more detailed budget plan for the project.

Senior Examiner's Comments

Question 2c was generally answered quite well and this is a typically good answer. The key point that candidates needed to make was that the careline would improve two-way communications between the organisation and its customers.

Question 3

Write a report for your Line Manager explaining how it is possible to make the best use of databases in order to develop better customer relationships. Give examples of two different types of organisation that use innovative computer software and systems to do this.

(20 marks)

Answer – Question 3

Report

FAO: David Nyman, Operations Manager, Newtown Theatre

From: S. Evans, Promotions Assistant, Newtown Theatre

Subject: Using Databases to Improve Customer Relationships

Introduction

As requested, work was carried out to look at how the best possible use could be made of our database in order to develop better customer relationships. Two organisations, Exhibit Unlimited and Provident Life – neither from our sector but both successfully using innovative software and systems – were investigated with a view to seeing how Newtown Theatre could use its database to improve its customer relationships.

Findings

Exhibit Unlimited designs and manufactures exhibition stands for a wide range of customers, from small firms wanting portable systems to large multi-million pound companies that want a one-off stand for big exhibitions such as the Car Show or the Boat Show.

Using a computer system called Act 2000, it has put all its customer information in one place, such as lists of all new enquiries and information about past and current customers. This means it can quickly analyse its customer portfolio in terms of a customer's value to the company. For example, it can see which companies make the most repeat purchases and the value of the business that each customer gives it.

The system enables it to track which advertising method has been most effective in attracting customers. When staff talk to customers on the telephone, it is easy for them to see the details of past jobs even down to the detail of customer satisfaction and the needs identified. This means the staff are more responsive when talking to customers, even if it is a member of staff who has not personally dealt with the client before.

The system can be used to make direct marketing activities more effective. Consequently unsolicited telephone contact is not made if a customer has previously requested this. Equally though, relevant direct marketing material can be sent to the right people within the organisation based on the information that Exhibit Unlimited keeps.

Provident Life is an insurance company that has a database of information on Independent Financial Advisers (IFAs are the people who act as intermediaries and pass on business to Prudential Life). This information is linked to its 'customer relationship management' software and records every aspect of its dealings with the IFAs, such as every telephone call or visit made to them. Volumes of business done by IFAs are tracked and this can determine how much time to spend on them and what information should be sent to them. In addition, 'soft' personal information is held and is available to staff. Ultimately it brings the client closer to the company because staff know about past situations or problems.

For our own situation, customer information on theatre-goers could be linked to a relational database so that we could store personal details of customers, such as number of tickets purchased, repertoire preferences, seating location preferences and average spend, which could be used to tailor relevant communications to customers.

We would be able to group customers according to their value to us and 'cherry pick'. For example, there are significant differences between occasional attendees and members who are regular visitors, and different communications could be targeted to different parts of our mailing list.

It could help fund-raising and corporate development if customers join our 'membership' scheme and donate to appeals; then their names would get flagged to receive information about special offers and special 'member-only' events.

Based on an analysis of our customer base and where they live, we could use postcode analysis to inform advertising activity.

During each season, it would be possible to get up-to-date ticket sales and this information would determine advertising, poster and point of sales activity as well.

Conclusions

There are a number of different systems that we could test to see exactly how a relational database could work. Overall, this investigation has shown that if one were introduced it would be possible to have a more accurate picture of our customers and it would enable us to communicate with our customers in a more intelligent way, and in so doing enable us to improve our customer relationships.

Senior Examiner's Comments

This was one of the few very good answers to this question. Many candidates attempted the question with very little in the way of subject knowledge. Others had problems in structuring their answer, choosing not to follow the question format, which required that candidates provide two different examples of organisations that use computer systems to achieve customer relationship management solutions. However, while the content of this answer was good, the report structure would have been improved by including sub-headings to group the information in the Findings section.

Question 4

Explain, using business examples, how poor listeners can improve their listening skills.

(10 marks)

Explain how communication barriers could distort an advertising message.

Suggest how this distortion could be avoided.

(10 marks)

(20 marks in total)

Answer – Question 4a

How 'Poor Listeners' can Improve their Listening Skills

Listening skills are an important part of everyday communication, whether the situation is in a meeting with a group of people, or in a one-to-one interview or on the telephone.

For example, 'poor listeners' may improve their listening skills by actively concentrating when dealing with a telephone caller who is making a complaint. Active listening means ignoring what is going on around you while listening to the complaint. In this way superficial listening will be avoided and the real issues will be heard.

In a complex situation, such as a customer complaining about several things that happened over a period of time, poor listeners could improve their listening skills by making selective notes to pick out the key issues or points that the caller is making.

In another situation, such as at a business meeting, poor listeners would be well advised to be open minded when listening to what others say. A barrier to listening can be created if people are prejudiced against others.

At a regular sales meeting, it could be tempting for a poor listener to 'jump to conclusions' about what is going to be said instead of being patient and actually letting the person speaking have their say without interruption.

However, at other times it may be relevant for a poor listener to clarify what has been said to ensure that they have heard correctly.

Being an empathic listener means placing yourself in the communicator's shoes. In a grievance interview, for example, the listener may wish to understand more about what is being said by thinking about the other person's perspective rather than viewing the problem from their own perspective.

Senior Examiner's Comments

The answer to Question 4a was generally well done. In the answer provided here, there were lots of examples of how poor listeners could improve their listening skills. However, what was good about this answer was that it addressed the 'using business examples' aspect of the question and provided plenty of relevant contexts such as meetings, grievance interviews and telephone calls.

Answer – Question 4b

How Communication Barriers could Distort an Advertising Message and How Distortion could be Avoided

Distortion occurs when the recipient misinterprets the message or the meaning of a communication.

The precise intention of the sender of the message may not be translated accurately so that the wrong message is sent if, for instance, jargon words are used in an advertisement for a computer and are misunderstood. This kind of distortion could be avoided by allowing people who are not computer experts to check the advertisement for understanding before it is produced.

The use of words or pictures with more than one meaning could also result in distortion as different recipients of the message may interpret the message differently. If the text of an advertisement for bottled water referred to it as 'mountain stream water' some people could perceive that mountain stream water is pure whereas others may perceive that mountain streams could contain dead animals and so they perceive that mountain streams are impure. The way that this kind of distortion could be avoided would be to use focus groups before the advertisement is produced, to test how others perceive certain words and images.

A lack of credibility could result in a message being distorted. For instance when Virgin, a company that was associated with music shops, started to diversify into other areas, such as airlines and financial services, its message could have been distorted through lack of credibility. One way to get around this distortion was to organise an advertising campaign that stressed the business expertise of the head of the company, Richard Branson.

Senior Examiner's Comments

The answer to Question 4b was not comprehensive but it did adopt the right approach in tackling the issue of 'distortion' rather than providing a list of generic communication barriers, which was the more common but incorrect approach taken. Other useful examples of how distortion could be avoided in advertising were answers that referred to researching the target market appropriately, piloting campaigns and monitoring audience feedback.

Question 5

For a product/service of your choice, explain and provide examples of how the following promotion activities could play an important role in communicating with target audiences.

- Sponsorship.
- Direct marketing.
- Press advertising.
- Public relations.

(5 marks each) (20 marks in total)

Answer – Question 5

I have chosen a new fizzy drink called 'Duncans' that will be in direct competition with products such as Coca-Cola, 7-Up and Tango in the drinks market.

1. Sponsorship

Sponsorship is when a company sponsors or pays to have its name featured at an event or in a publication. The role of sponsorship in relation to fizzy drinks is very important when you consider the media coverage gained for Pepsi when it sponsored the Michael Jackson tour and the Spice Girls world tour. If, for instance, Duncans sponsored a sports event such as the Six Nations rugby competition, it would be a good way to obtain media exposure for the brand name to its target audience; namely young males in the 18-30 age range.

2. Direct Marketing

Direct marketing in the form of mailing vouchers or coupons to rented lists of people in my target group would be a good way of informing people about the product and would even encourage some people to sample the product for the first time. Another way that direct marketing could play an important role in communicating with my target audience is telemarketing. I could call up sections of my database to investigate brand awareness, popularity, compare the product with that of the competition and so gain valuable market knowledge as a result.

3. Press Advertising

Press advertising involves designing an advertisement with copy and images and placing the advertisement in the relevant media to promote a product or service. Advertising in the press would be a fundamental way to promote the benefits of the drink to the target market. To target the right group of people, it would be necessary to select magazines that are about music and sport and are read by the 18-30 age group. A good approach could be to promote the drink as a 'clubbers' drink and link the press advertising to a television campaign that aimed at people who enjoy the clubbing culture.

4. Public Relations

Public relations activities could include sending press releases out to the general press or involving the product being seen to be drunk at parties attended by celebrities that young people aspire to be. Press releases could refer to the Duncans phenomenon that is spreading across the country much in the same way as the 'You've been Tangoed' campaign that established the brand in people's minds.

Senior Examiner's Comments

There were two different approaches taken by candidates answering this question and both were correct. One approach was to use a different product for each form of promotion and the other approach was to use one product and illustrate how each promotional method could be used in relation to that product. The specimen answer here adopted the latter approach. Overall it is a satisfactory answer which could have been slightly improved with better general explanations of what each form of promotion does and how it works. Unfortunately a significant number of students rushed into this question and failed to spot that they should provide product/service examples of how each of the activities could be used.

Question 6

You are the Marketing Manager of a large conference centre that provides training facilities and accommodation to companies from all over the world. You wish to find out about your customers views on how your staff interact with customers.

Provide an example of a question that would elicit relevant qualitative information and one that would elicit quantitative information.

(8 marks)

What factors, other than the questions themselves, would you have to consider in collecting data using a questionnaire?

(7 marks)

Assume the results from the survey show that customers were very satisfied with the way that their telephone queries were handled. Prepare an e-mail for staff to share the good news.

(5 marks)

(20 marks in total)

Answer – Question 6a

Open-ended questions tend to elicit qualitative information. This sort of information is more to do with attitudes, expectations and beliefs but is harder to record and quantify. In the situation where one wishes to find out about customers' views on staff interaction with customers at a conference centre that provides training, such a question might be:

'What could our staff have done to improve your stay at Grenley Grange conference centre?'

Closed questions on the other hand give rise to quantitative information. Examples are where interviewees are given a choice of yes/no answers or a scale on which they choose a rating or a word that describes their opinion. This provides information on the number or quantity of responses to a particular rating or word. An example of a quantitative question would be:

'How satisfied were you with the way your conference booking was dealt with?'

1	2	3	4	5
Very Satisfied		Satisfied		Dissatisfied

Senior Examiner's Comments

Question 6a was generally well answered, although some candidates were obviously confused by the term quantitative and thought that the question had to contain some numbers in it, such as 'How many times have you visited the Grenley Green Conference Centre?'

Answer – Question 6b

Factors other than the questions that need to be considered in collecting data would be as follows:

- Initially it is important to consider what is to be achieved by the questionnaire and to consider if the questionnaire is indeed the best way of gathering the required data.

- The best way of distributing the questionnaire has to be decided; for example, should it be as customers enter the conference centre or as they leave, or should it be left in customers' rooms?

- Consider how you encourage people to take the time to complete the questionnaire, perhaps by including some incentive like free entry into a prize draw.

- The layout of the questionnaire is important because there needs to be enough space to allow respondents to complete the questionnaire but not so much that it appears to be too lengthy.

- Easy questions should be put at the beginning and personal questions, such as, age, income etc. should be placed at the end.

- Questions can be grouped under headings to make them easier to read.

- An introductory paragraph could be included to outline the purpose of the questionnaire and to assure confidentiality if appropriate.

Senior Examiner's Comments

Question 6b caused more problems than question 6a. and many candidates could not come up with a list of factors as included in the above answer. Many people insisted on covering more issues to do with actual questions. While the answer here is good, it does not cover the issues of sample size or sample selection.

Answer – Question 6c

E-mail to: All staff

From: pdonnell@grenleyconference.co.uk

Subject: Congratulations

We have just received the results of the recent customer satisfaction survey. It shows that customers have been very satisfied with the way that telephone queries have been dealt with.

Thanks to all the team for helping us maintain our excellent reputation at Grenley Grange.

Keep up the good work!!

Senior Examiner's Comments

Question 6c was universally well done and there are no specific issues here.

Question 7

For an organisation of your choice, write a brief report on the impact that information communications technology is having on customer communications. Give examples to support the points you make in the report.

(20 marks)

Answer – Question 7

Report on the Impact of Information Communications Technology

Introduction

This report shows the impact information communications technology is having on customer communications in our organisation.

Findings

1. Advances in Telecommunications

- Automated call handling and voice mail facilities have significantly reduced the strain on personnel when dealing with high call volumes and reduced waiting times for customers. This has reduced the number of complaints by customers about this issue.

- ISDN lines have made data exchange with key suppliers much quicker and easier where there are large volumes of data. This has improved the way we can communicate with stakeholders, such as our advertising agencies.

- EDI results in order processing efficiencies with key channels.

- Video conferencing means that staff can have meetings with colleagues or clients without having to travel to a different location. This means meetings can be arranged with less notice and they cost less in terms of money and time. This in turn improves our communication with internal and external customers.

- Mobile telephones have for a long time kept field sales staff in better communication with their internal and external customers. WAP (Wireless Application Protocol) means that it will be possible to send messages to customers about new products or to remind them that they are due to re-order goods/services.

2. Database Technology

- Customer data can be gathered to give detailed profiles of customers. This information can help decide the form of direct mail campaigns and help target customers with particular interests or buying/usage patterns.

- More specific, targeted direct mail campaigns decrease cost and wastage and customers are more likely to respond when we communicate with them.

3. Internet/e-mail

- Customer information is available through the web site. This facility means that it is much easier for customers all over the world to have contact with us at any time that suits them.

- Customers can request specific information, which is better than us sending everyone our full-colour printed brochure. This saves us money and ensures customers get the information they need.

- Customers can be encouraged to register their contact details on the web site and this in turn helps our database and improves customer communications.

- Customers can contact us via email which is usually quicker and more efficient than postal or telephone communication.

- Customers can purchase online when they choose or just use the web site to check prices or availability.

- The web site can be used to conduct online surveys which in turn improve the way we communicate with customers.

- Our Intranet system means that staff have access to information across the firm even if they are not based at the main site.

Conclusion

ICT developments with regard to telecommunications, database capabilities and Internet/email communication mean that it is now easier and cheaper to communicate with both internal and external customers than ever before. Developments in all these fields will improve communications further and the challenge for our organisation is to keep up with and utilise developments or risk being left behind by the competition.

Senior Examiner's Comments

In terms of covering the main ICT developments this was a fairly comprehensive answer. However, the report style is very brief and written in a rather bitty style. The candidate did not specify the context where these developments were taking place and by not stating the organisation, the points raised by the candidate appear to be rote learnt. The question clearly asks for examples to support the points made and marks were lost because the candidate did not give examples of how, for example, direct mail campaigns had become more targeted and effective or how Intranets were assisting with internal communications.

Syllabus

Aims and Objectives

- To provide an overview of the communications process in the context of marketing.
- To enable students to appreciate the importance of the customer when planning communications in marketing.
- To help students understand why effective communication is vital to all organisations.
- To ensure students can select and utilise a range of communication media across a variety of target audiences and business settings.
- To assist students in utilising data to formulate effective customer communications.
- To explore the changing nature of customer dynamics and technological developments and their impact on customer communications.

Learning Outcomes

Students will be able to:

- Utilise marketing research to improve customer communications.
- Analyse and interpret written, visual and graphical data. Formulate a range of communications to suit a variety of media and target audiences.
- Devise appropriate visual and graphical means to present marketing data.
- Select appropriate verbal and non-verbal communication in a variety of contexts.
- Apply customer care principles to create positive relationships with customers.
- Demonstrate an understanding of customer behaviour and use customer information to influence internal and external customer communications.
- Appreciate the changing nature of the communications environment and explain how developments will impact upon organisations and customers.

Indicative Content and Weighting

2.1 Importance of the customer (20%)

2.1.1 Identifying what is meant by the term 'the customer' and appreciating the importance of effective internal and external customer communications.

2.1.2 The changing context of customer needs:

- The impact of customer focus.
- The importance of good customer relations.
- The role of relationship marketing in creating loyalty and customer retention.
- The role of communications in establishing effective customer relationships.

2.1.3 Practical approaches to improving customer care:

- Dealing with complaints and client feedback

2.2 Finding out about the customer (10%)

2.2.1 The role of marketing research in customer communciations.

2.2.2 Basic marketing research methods and sources of information.

2.2.3 Using data to improve customer communications

2.3 The process of effective communication (20%)

2.3.1 The communication process.

2.3.2 The planning process – identifying the purpose, target audience, message, channel and evaluating objectives.

2.3.3 The importance of effective body language, tone, verbal and listening skills in communications.

2.3.4 Identifying and avoiding barriers to communication.

2.3.5 Interpreting, summarising and presenting oral, written and graphical information.

2.3.6 Running effective meetings.

2.3.7 The importance of effective oral communication:

- On the telephone.
- In negotiations and during interviews.
- In presentation delivery.

2.4 Communication formats and media (25%)

2.4.1 Using a variety of formats to communicate with internal and external customers:

- Letters.
- Memoranda.
- Notices.
- Reports.
- E-mails.

2.4.2 The role of promotion in communicating with external customers:

- The use of above and below the line activities, such as, direct response advertising, direct marketing, sales literature, exhibitions, sales promotions, sponsorship, public relations and web sites.
- The role of corporate identity, brand image and logos.
- The appropriate design of media advertising, such as, press adverts.
- Effective news releases.

2.5 Information communications technology (ICT) developments and trends (25%)

2.5.1 The dynamic communications environment:

- How new technologies are changing the way people communicate.
- The growth of The Internet and the different patterns of usage based on organisational size and sector.
- Changing nature of telecommunications.
- Impact of digital technology and the fragmentation of media.
- Mobile e commerce.
- The speed of change.

2.5.2 The impact of e commerce on communications:

- How Web Sites, E-mail, Intranets and Extranets are used.
- On-line shopping.
- Business process re-engineering.
- The Internet as a promotional tool.

2.5.3 The use of ICT in building customer databases and improving customer communications:

- Datamining and creating more personally relevant communications.
- The use of Customer Relationship Management (CRM) software programmes to improve databases.
- The implications of automated customer-handling operations.

Reading list

- P Forsyth, *Communicating with Customers*, Orion, 1999, Essential Reading
- G Wood, *Customer Communications*, CIM/Butterworth-Heinemann, 2001, Workbook
- G Wood, *Customer Communications*, BPP, 2000, Study Text
- Crouch S.& Housden M., *Marketing Research for Managers*, Butterworth-Heinnemann, 1996, Additional reading/resources
- Davis J, *A Guide to Web Marketing – Successful Promotion on the Web*, Kogan Page, 2000, Additional reading/resources
- Dolphin R, *The Fundamentals of Corporate Communication*, Butterworth-Heinnemann, 1999, Additional reading/resources
- Edlington S, *Marketing Your Business on the Internet*, Internet Handbooks, 2000, Additional reading/resources
- Knight A, *Effective Customer Care*, DSE Publishing, 1999, Additional reading/resources
- Payne A, Christopher M, Ballantyne D, *Relationship Marketing*, Butterworth-Heinnemann, 2000, Additional reading/resources
- Varey J R & Lewis B R, *Internal Marketing – Directions for Management*, Routledge, 2000, Additional reading/resources
- Yadin D, *Creative Marketing Communications*, Kogan Page, 2001, Additional reading/resources

Bibliography

1. Barker, A. (1999) *Writing at Work*, Industrial Society
2. Bee, F&R. (1999) *Customer Care*, Chartered Institute of Personnel and Development (CIPD)
3. Berry, L.L,& Parasuraman, A (1992) *Marketing Management*
4. Blundel, R. (1998) *Effective Business Communication*, Pearson Education
5. Carysforth, C. (1998) *Communication for Work*, Heinemann Educational
6. Dolphin, R. (2000) *The Fundamentals of Corporate Communications*, Butterworth-Heinemann
7. Forsyth, P. (1999) *Communicating with Customers*, Texere Publishing
8. Forsyth, P. (2000) *The Negotiator's Pocketbook*, Management Pocketbooks
9. Kohl, S. (2000) *Getting @ttention - Leading edge lessons for Publicity and Marketing*, Butterworth-Heinemann
10. Smith (1997) *Meeting Customer Needs*, Butterworth Heinemann

Websites:

    www.airmiles.co.uk.

    www.lexis.nexis.co.uk

www.adidas.co.uk

Debriefing Activity 1.1

By doing this activity you should be able to see how important communication skills are to your job or daily life and be able to get a measure of areas for self-development where you may want to spend extra time. It may also steer you to take up opportunities for self-development in your workplace.

There is no one answer to the skills audit. You may have identified that, while you do not write business reports at the moment, you may be likely to do so when you take up another position within the firm where you work. Consequently this might be an area of special interest in your studies.

Alternatively you may have identified that you are highly skilled in writing press releases and therefore you may feel this is an area that you want to skim over . You could even go direct to the examination papers at the back of the book and spend some time answering any questions relating to this area.

Debriefing Activity 1.2

Stakeholder	Message	Method	Why
Consumers – broken down into various target groups in the consumer and business to business markets	Information about products, persuasive messages to brand the cars and persuade customers to buy.	All the promotional mix: advertising, branding, sponsorship, sales literature, direct marketing, public relations and a trained sales force.	To raise awareness. To increase sales.
Shareholders	Performance, dividend payout, future developments.	Annual general meeting. Annual report. PR to financial press.	Need shareholder support and need to promote correct image. Legal obligation to set out performance information.
Employees	Company performance. Future plans. Training information. Improvements in staff facilities. Staff news.	Internal newsletter. Memos, meetings, staff notice-board.	To maintain good industrial relations and staff motivation.
Potential employees	What the company does. What job opportunities are available.	Recruitment advertising. Corporate image.	To recruit from the biggest pool of available staff so will have better selection.
Suppliers	Company production plans and requirements.	Meetings. Tender documents. Contracts.	To help firms supply best components at the right time and to ensure that the organization and its suppliers work together in partnership.
Distributors	Product and technical information.	Point of sale material, sales literature and promotional items for branding purposes.	To assist dealerships in selling cars.
Local community – could be residents who live near factories, or local charities	That the firm cares for the local community.	PR activities. Sponsorship.	Good PR which could help, for example, if the firm applies for planning permission to extend factory premises.
The media	Product information and information about company performance.	Press releases. Events.	To raise the company profile. To promote its image.
Government, local, national and international	They are an ethical firm and a good employer.	Via senior management on a personal level.	To establish good relations so can put pressure to bear regarding legislation that might affect the industry.
Pressure groups	They are an ethical firm that cares about the environment.	PR.	To negate effect of conflicting messages from environmental pressure groups.
Competitors	To develop strategic alliances.	Via senior management on a personal level.	To rationalize operations, cutp costs and expand into other markets.

Debriefing Activity 1.3

PRESENTATION NOTES INTERNAL MARKETING AND INTERNAL COMMUNICATIONS

Introduction

I have been asked to deliver a short presentation on the importance of effective internal marketing and internal communications. I will explain what is meant by these terms and how they contribute to the success of a company and then will draw on my experience within other organizations to describe how they have improved their internal communication systems.

Key points

Internal marketing

Internal marketing means creating a culture where staff work together as a team, seeing each other as internal customers, who require good service. With internal marketing the contribution of all staff is recognized and valued as helping to achieve the goals set by the organization.

For example, in my experience at a successful packaging firm where all the staff know what is expected of them and how their individual contribution affects whether a job is completed well and on time, they know this affects whether the client is retained. Contrast this example with that of a building firm where staff have to alter work that has been carried out badly by colleagues and time is wasted because builders are not given the correct information about work that needs to be undertaken.

Benefits of internal marketing culture:

- Shared values.
- Co-operation.
- Efficiency.
- Job satisfaction.
- High-quality work.
- Loyalty.
- Effective communications.

Internal communications

The organization's internal communications system is vital in the creation and maintenance of an effective marketing culture among staff. This approach should transcend all petty differences and encompass both staff within a department and staff in different departments, on different sites and even in different countries.

Improving internal communications

Establish a two-way flow of information so that managers hear staff views and opinions as well as staff hearing about management objectives, views and plans by:

- Regular staff meetings and team briefings to discuss plans, work and how to get around difficulties.
- Meetings with senior managers regarding current performance, future objectives, plans and how they affect staff.
- Empower staff to become involved in improving quality, facilities, systems and procedures.
- Performance reviews to tell staff how they are doing, what could be improved and to identify what training is needed to improve individual performance.
- Feedback to managers on their performance.
- Suggestion schemes.
- Establish a culture where people are not afraid to air their views or grievances.
- Use the staff notice-board effectively to inform of events, training and even to quash rumours.
- Establish an internal newsletter.
- Train managers to run effective team briefings.

- Train staff to hold effective meetings.
- Establish a house style for letters, memos and reports.
- Encourage staff not to resort to sending an e-mail to everyone and anyone.
- Remind staff how to use the internal telephone system effectively.
- Establish effective recording systems, whether for taking messages, informing other staff of your whereabouts, recording sales visits or job instructions.
- Introduce staff manuals and policy documents so that staff are clear about systems and procedures in the firm.

Summary

A culture of internal marketing and an effective internal communications system is vital to the success of an organization. If staff are well informed, empowered and listened to, they are more likely to know and share the aims of the company and work together to play their part in achieving them.

Debriefing Activity 2.1

For this answer the assumption made is that the issue is genetically modified foods and the company is a manufacturer of baby food. The stakeholders might be customers who purchase the products and a pressure group such as the National Childbirth Trust (NCT). Customers might communicate their objection to the use of genetically modified components in baby food by telephoning and writing to the company and boycotting its products. The NCT might undertake a media campaign using print and broadcast media.

The firm could deal with the objections by trying to assure consumers that the genetically modified products are safe via an extensive PR campaign. This would be unlikely to succeed against an intensive lobbying campaign. Ultimately the manufacturer may have to give in to consumer demands to ban genetically modified foods from the production cycle.

If they did give in to public pressure, it would then be advisable to publicize the fact to maintain good relations with stakeholders. The changed stance could be publicized through a PR campaign, changing product labels to announce the change and via advertising. They would also need to set up a customer care line and communicate the news to all concerned callers. They might also get involved in a joint campaign with the pressure group, to promote the banning of genetically modified products in all other baby foods.

Debriefing Activity 2.2

Experiences where customers are delighted will be as varied as the people reading this workbook. You could have gone to the local supermarket, asked for help with packing your bags and been pleasantly surprised when you were also helped to your car with the bags. You may have wanted to buy certain items that were out of stock at the chemist and were surprised that the manager not only arranged to order them but arranged next-day delivery too. You may have asked for the balance of your bank account and been surprised that it was overdrawn. If the bank clerk cancelled the interest charges and arranged for you to have your bank statements sent out more frequently so that you could keep a better check on your account, you would have been delighted. Or you may have been travelling by plane on business and needed something to read but not had time to buy a newspaper. You may have been pleased to find that a free newspaper had been provided and delighted that a selection of all the daily newspapers was available.

In estimating the cost of improving a service, you could, for example, calculate the cost of sending out a bank statement every week to a customer in comparison to the cost of attracting a new customer. A weekly bank statement costing £15 over a year to produce and post, is probably much cheaper than the annual cost of marketing and advertising divided by the number of new customers gained each year.

Debriefing Activity 2.3

Tesco Baby Club Card

Pregnant women are encouraged to apply for a club card and the reward is money-off coupons for baby products. The mother-to-be completes an application form, providing information such as name, address, information about the family and the baby's expected birth date.

The money-off coupons encourage repeat purchase at Tesco's stores. The card means the company can record each customer transaction and establish a customer profile. The company can then target the customer with information about relevant products and services. The organization can also sell this information to other organizations wishing to communicate with customers of a certain age, living in a certain area, who have a particular purchase history.

The baby club card scheme also features a frequent customer contact programme. Mothers are sent magazines with hints and advice to coincide with the various developmental stages that babies go through. So, for example, when the baby is aged four months old, the mother is sent a magazine which gives advice on how to wean babies onto solid food and contains advertising and money-off coupons relating to first-stage baby food products.

In this way both the organization and the customer receive benefits from the relationship that is established between the two parties.

Debriefing Activity 2.4

1. The minimum need is for the customer to be able to obtain the type of petrol wanted without having to wait too long. The additional customer service need that should be met is that the forecourt is clean and tidy with towels available to clean hands. In addition the instructions for obtaining petrol should be clear, concise and friendly, helpful staff should deal with payment. If the service station does not have staff and has automatic credit card payment facilities, then instructions for use should be clear with graphical images to reinforce the message and avoid confusing the customer, who may not have used this method of payment before.

2. The minimum need is to travel from one place to another on time in a clean, comfortably lit and heated or ventilated train. In addition customers should be communicated with if there are timetable problems and all announcements should be spoken in a clear, well-articulated voice that is not distorted by the public address system. Similarly, timetable notices and platform signage should be visible.

Debriefing Activity 2.5

Intelligent telephony services are computer-based applications that fully integrate with a telephone system to provide routing of voice and fax calls to an individual or team regardless of location. Messaging and voice processing are message management and call processing systems that help organizations deal with internal and external calls more effectively, with the potential to increase productivity and reduce call-handling costs.

Personal videoconferencing enables video and data conferencing from any location connected to the ISDN network by using a card that can be slotted into a personal computer.

These flexible office solutions mean that voice, fax and data communication is available to users wherever they are which makes people more accessible. Customers can be automatically routed to the correct department and should get a quicker response.

Debriefing Activity 2.6

You can ensure that personnel in the overseas sales region are kept fully informed by using fax and e-mail communication.

Debriefing Activity 2.7

- Banks have used automatic telling machines (ATMs) or 'hole in the wall' machines where customers can withdraw or deposit money and get account balances, effectively providing 24-hour service.

- Retailers have invested in electronic tills that allow staff to scan goods. This process allows for quicker service, fewer mistakes, itemised bills so customers can check purchases, automatic re-ordering of stock and provides information for retailers to build customer profiles to help target future customer communication.

- Utility organisations use automated telephone systems so that customers can get a quicker response or just leave information without having to speak to an operator.

- Distribution companies use e-mail which enables immediate communication within and between organisations.

Debriefing Activity 2.8

1. Minimum standards for dealing with customer telephone calls:

- Answer the telephone within six rings.
- Introduce yourself by name and state the name of the firm.
- Smile when you answer the telephone.
- When taking messages for colleagues, always use company message pads and ensure that all details are taken down correctly..
- When dealing with telephone messages, return all calls the same day.

2. Main points about how the member of staff's customer service could be improved:

- He should appreciate that all documentation and communications with customers should be right first time, as mistakes give the bad impression that the firm is careless in all its dealings with customers.
- He should have apologized to the customer on behalf of the company about the mistakes, not tried to minimize the importance of the mistakes made.
- He should not have been defensive with the customer about the mistakes made. It is not relevant to the customer whether he or someone else prepared the property details sheet and made the mistakes.
- He should have arranged for the mistakes to be rectified and a new sheet sent out to the customer immediately.
- He should have spoken to the person responsible for the mistakes and made sure that it did not happen again.

Debriefing Activity 2.9

To improve customer communications, Orange would have to improve their instruction manual so that customers find it easy to operate their telephones. They need to provide adequate staffing so that the system they have established to provide customer service actually works and customers can get through to the helpline. They need to rethink the process involving the allocation of security code numbers so that dealerships always allocate a security code and/or that call centre operators can still help customers who do not know their code.

Internal communications need to be improved to ensure that if staff in one department take a message it is always logged and passed on to relevant staff in another department. Staff need to be trained to deal with customer complaints. The member of the customer service team should have apologized on behalf of Orange about the service the customer has received. He should have concentrated on helping her use the telephone, not wasted the customer's time explaining internal staffing problems.

The company should also empower its staff to use reasonable judgement in giving a discount on a bill where a customer has good reason to be unhappy about the product or service they have received.

Debriefing Activity 3.1

You could give each advertisement a reference number which identifies the newspaper or magazine it appears in. When orders are taken you could ask customers to quote the relevant reference number and this would give you the information you require. In this example, you are using marketing research to identify the best media to communicate your message.

Debriefing Activity 3.2

You could do this by leaving in people's rooms a questionnaire which focuses on these areas. You could provide some incentive to reward people for completing the questionnaire – either a free bottle of wine with dinner or entry into a prize draw.

Debriefing Activity 3.3

Although they would probably not refer to what they are doing as primary research and they would be unlikely to consider that they are undertaking in-depth interviews or organizing focus groups, they would in fact be doing this by asking parents of prospective schoolchildren what they want to know when they first visit a school. They would also probably discuss their ideas for a brochure with parents and teachers at the PTA (parent-teacher association) meeting and at a governors' meeting. They may even ask children in the school what they would be interested in reading about in a brochure.

Debriefing Activity 3.4

She could use mystery shoppers to enquire at the branch or by telephone to find out if customer enquiries were dealt with satisfactorily.

Debriefing Activity 3.5

The main focus of communications activity would be to continue to produce leaflets about the homes and distribute these to social workers and district nurses, as these people obviously influence prospective customers.

The display advertisement in the telephone directory would be repeated again next year despite its high cost. In addition, posters would still be produced and displayed in local libraries and any other suitable buildings used by the local community.

Debriefing Activity 4.1

Barrier	Problems caused
Technical noise caused by crackly telephone line.	Mistake by the agency in arranging the duration of the placement.
Social noise caused by Sally's prejudice about Peter's age, gender and appearance. He lacked credibility in her eyes.	This irritated Peter but also stopped Sally working effectively with him.
Psychological noise caused by Peter's anger.	Peter misinterpreted what Sally said to him and this caused conflict.
Contradictory non-verbal communication caused by Peter smiling and saying one thing but thinking something else.	Sally received the wrong message.

Debriefing Activity 4.2

1. Lack of credibility can be a barrier to communication if, for example, a young, inexperienced salesperson lacking in product/market knowledge tries to sell a high-value, specialist, technical product. This barrier to communication could only be overcome if the salesperson had thorough training in both sales technique and the product/market.

    The noise could be reduced if the salesperson had a professional appearance in terms of dress and used a professional demonstration kit to illustrate the product to potential customers. It would also be useful if the salesperson worked for a well-known company and had testimonials from previously satisfied clients. In this way customers would concentrate less on the weak traits of the salesperson and be more aware of the credibility of the product and the manufacturer.

2. Perceptual bias refers to people hearing what they want to hear. By filling in the gaps and making assumptions a significant barrier to the real message can be created. For example, if staff had heard rumours about potential job losses prior to a staff meeting they might 'tune out' from the information being delivered during the meeting and may only select the negative aspects of what was being said.

    The noise could be effectively reduced only if the manager addressed the rumours and allowed staff to ask questions so that he could allay fears and ensure that staff heard the whole message.

3. Information overload is a barrier to communication because if a person is given too much information then the key message is not digested. For example, if a person delivered a talk to their local CIM branch on the effectiveness of an advertising campaign and the speaker provided too many facts and figures, the overall message might be lost in the detail.

    To avoid information overload, the speaker could reduce the amount of detail and emphasize the main points using visual aids, illustration, demonstration and anecdotal examples. In-depth background detail to the campaign could be provided in the form of notes or a handout for those who wanted to read this information in their own time.

4. Contradictory non-verbal signals might be conveyed by a person whose words say one thing whilst their body language says something else. For example, when a customer is complaining about the service in a bank, the cashier dealing with the complaint could be apologizing for the mistake made but at the same time avoiding eye contact and sounding disinterested and bored by speaking in a monotone voice.

    To reduce the noise, the cashier would need to support the words being used by adopting a sympathetic tone, eye contact and positive body language such as nodding to show empathy with the customer's viewpoint.

Debriefing Activity 4.3

Here are some ways of rewriting the sentences:
1. We should attempt to plan ahead to meet future service requirements.
2. The supplies manager has pointed out that the product is difficult to obtain.
3. It is difficult to move as the price of land has gone up.

Debriefing Activity 4.4

1. You could use a poster campaign along the roads where the tolls will be introduced. As with all poster campaigns, you would need to keep the message simple because people need to be able to take in the message as they go past at speed.

2. You could do a demonstration and a short presentation. Your communication style should be persuasive in order to show the benefits of the new product. To communicate the financial data you might use visual communication, such as graphs and tables. Any slides or acetates that you produce may just feature key words that you will explain as part of your presentation.

3. You may write a lengthy, formal report to the Director that deals with the problems and suggests solutions. You may adopt an impersonal tone, using a 'third person' style. For example, 'It appears that the road works on the local motorway network have caused significant delays when our vans depart for the mid-morning delivery run.' As you are writing to your line manager you would not use an authoritative 'tell' style of communication. In your report you would not necessarily avoid longer, more complex sentences or technical terms.

Debriefing Activity 4.5

The buying process	AIDA model of communication	Promotional tool
Need recognition	Gain attention	PR
Information search	Stimulate interest	Advertising and point of sale material in car showroom
Evaluation of alternatives	Create desire	Test drives, sales brochure
Purchase decision	Generate action	Sales force
Post-purchase decision	Create satisfaction	Direct marketing material, follow-up calls to check customer satisfaction, warranty material

Debriefing Activity 5.1

1. 'I'm not sure what we can do about that but if you give me your details I will make sure that someone gets back to you - when would it be convenient for them to contact you?'

2. 'I don't actually handle the payments but if you hold on . . .' *either* 'I will transfer you to x in y department who will help you' or 'I will ask x in y department to come down to speak to you if you could just wait for a few minutes.'

3. 'I don't think we have that in stock but I'll just go and check for you.'

4. 'X is not at their desk at the moment but if you give me your telephone number I will ask them to call you back.'

Debriefing Activity 5.2

MEMORANDUM

To: All Managers

From: Maggie Yorke, Communications Manager

Date: 30 July 20XX

Subject: Weekly team briefings

A number of managers have asked for some guidance on the best way to present themselves in the regular team briefings that have recently been introduced in all departments.

I have observed a number of the meetings and body language is one important area where some simple tips could improve the way messages are put across to teams.

It is important to communicate your verbal message and keep in the back of your mind how the following can either add to or detract from the message you are trying to put across.

Facial expressions

Staff will react more favourably to you if you have a warm, friendly smile instead of looking rather tense or aggressive, which is the message that can be communicated if you have a furrowed brow or pursed lips.

Posture

You may feel more comfortable sitting down with your team round a table rather than standing up in front of them, which creates a more formal atmosphere. If you do sit down, avoid folding your arms as that can appear as if you are creating a barrier. Make sure that you sit upright rather than slouched in the chair as that could communicate that you are too tired or bored to be bothered with the briefing.

Gesture

Many people like to use their hands to express themselves but too much hand waving can be distracting for those listening. Even if you are displeased with the team's performance or recent events, it is better to avoid emotional displays such as banging your fists on the table.

Eye contact

It is very easy to find yourself making eye contact with just one person in the team. However, this may make the person feel uncomfortable as they will feel they are being stared at. Another problem could be that you are tempted to read from your notes and may end up not making eye contact with your team. You should avoid this as it can result in the team not being involved in what you are saying.

I am sure that most of you are happy with your departmental team briefings. However, I do hope that you find these tips helpful so that we can continue to improve our internal communications which are so important in helping to motivate and inform the workforce.

Debriefing Activity 5.3

There are a number of ways in which you can ensure that you are listening effectively in interviews:

- Be patient and let the person express themselves – do not interrupt or complete sentences for the interviewee.

- Use appropriate body language, such as eye contact and nodding, to show interest in what is being said – this will encourage the interviewee to answer your questions fully.

- Ask questions to clarify your understanding of what has been said.

- At intervals sum up what the interviewee has said, to show that you have listened and understood.

Debriefing Activity 5.4

BLUEBIRD HOTELS MEMORANDUM

To: All reception staff

From: George Stakis, Marketing Manager

Date: 9 August 20XX

Subject: Effective telephone use

A recent research survey into the service provided by Bluebird Hotels has revealed a number of areas where we can improve our service. One of these areas is the way customers' telephone calls are dealt with. The following recommendations need to be adopted by reception staff when dealing with calls.

Incoming calls

All calls should be answered by the fifth ring. Too many callers are left waiting for several minutes before their call is picked up.

When calls are answered, it is important that they are dealt with correctly. Staff should clearly state their name and that of the hotel, followed by the question, 'How can I help you?'

Transfer of calls

It is important that reception staff are familiar with the extension numbers for the hotel's various departments and the numbers in guests' rooms, so that calls can be transferred quickly and efficiently.

It is apparent that many calls are being cut off whilst they are being transferred. Therefore it is vital that reception staff ensure that they press the gate (#) button before dialling the extension number they require.

Many suppliers have complained that they are transferred to various departments in the hotel when they are in the middle of speaking to the person on reception. Before transferring calls, please briefly explain to the caller why you need to transfer them and ask for their permission to do so.

Message taking

If the extension number is engaged or not answered, then it is important that an accurate message is taken. Messages should be noted on hotel message pads only. They should state the date and time of the call, name of the caller (company name if it is appropriate) and the telephone number of the caller. Messages for staff should state the purpose of the call. All messages should be put in guest or staff pigeonholes immediately after they have been taken.

Thank you for your co-operation with this matter.

Debriefing Activity 5.5

Presentation plan

How to prepare for and deliver presentations.

Introduction

- Introduce yourself.
- Explain why good presentation delivery is both important and relevant.
- The presentation will cover the following areas: preparation and delivery of presentations.

Main body of presentation

Preparation – stage 1

- Identify the purpose of the presentation (key message and information needed).
- Identify sources of information.
- Identify amount of time available for presentation.
- Identify specific needs of audience:
  - Size of audience;
  - Their experience/prior knowledge;
  - Specific interest in relation to this topic.

Preparation – stage 2

- Organization of information/logical sequence/links.
- Three parts – beginning, middle and end.
- Avoiding information overload.
- Timing.
- Practice.
- Use of cue cards.
- Preparation of visual aids.
- Arrangement of room.

Delivery

- Style must suit audience needs and type of room (formal/informal, participative/lecture style).
- Use of language.
- Use of tone, pitch and pace.
- Use of body language (eye contact, dress, gestures, etc.).
- Use of visual aids.
- Using particiapation effectively to maintain interest.
- Using cases/anecdotes to establish common ground.

Summary

- Sum up main points only – don't introduce new ones.
- Allow time for questions.

Debriefing Activity 6.1

Memorandum

To: Dennis Law

From: George Best

Date: 4 March 200X

Subject: Guidance on leading project management meetings

An important aspect of leading a meeting is to be well organised. This means making sure a room is booked for the meeting and that it is prepared in advance with enough seats, paperwork and refreshments if appropriate. It also means having the correct paperwork and if there is an agenda, following it.

Being responsible for leading a meeting means opening the discussion, setting the objectives of the meeting and then moving on the items you need to discuss.

Another aspect is to make sure that everyone participates, by ensuring that a few do not dominate and some are left feeling they cannot contribute.

To lead the meeting effectively, you need to judge when everyone has contributed, summarize the discussion so that everyone knows what has been decided. For example, who has to do what next as part of progressing the project effectively or that it has been agreed that deliveries of x materials must be increased before y production can go ahead.

One difficult thing to watch is that discussion does not run over and the meeting does not keep to time. Sometimes it is necessary to be quite firm that discussion needs to be hurried along and a decision or a point made.

Finally, you should ensure you clearly inform the people attending when the meeting is closing and after the meeting make sure that a record of the meeting, usually action minutes, are distributed to eveyone who attended.

Debriefing Activity 6.2

The role of meetings

- Decision making/Problem solving
- Dissemination of information
- Motivating staff
- Two-way discussion
- Building relationships

Different types of meetings

- Informal meetings – these occur daily in the work place. Employees getting together on ad hoc basis to discuss progress on work, share out work, agree plans, gather information or generate ideas.
- Formal meetings – likely to feature a chairperson, formal agenda and minutes from the last meeting. These meetings may require a quorum and have a formal voting procedure. These meetings may be at board level where strategic decisions are discussed.

Leading meetings

It is the responsibility of the person leading the meeting to do the following:

- Ensure there is an accurate record of the meeting.
- Effectively control and manage the meeting ensuring that participants listen and give each other a chance to contribute.
- Ensure there is adequate discussion of each item and that the meeting runs on time.
- Bring a conclusion to discussion, clarifying points made, taking a vote and summarising the decision.
- Delegate responsibility as actions arise.

Meetings documentation

- Notice of meeting – gives notice of when and where a meeting will take place.
- Agenda – a list of what will be discussed, sometimes has formal proposals.
- Chairperson's agenda – the agenda plus background notes to help run the meeting.
- Minutes – a note of what was discussed and decisions taken.
- Discussion papers – papers put forward for to participants for consultation and discussion.

Debriefing Activity 6.3

MEMORANDUM

To: All Managers

From: Ann Candidate

Date: 11 August 200X

Subject: Checklist outlining five stages of the interview process

1. Preparation. This includes preparing the content of the interview in terms of the informaiton that needs to be given to candidates and the questions that need to be adked. In addition some thought needs to be given to the logistics in terms of the desk and chair arrangements, paper-work that is needed and identifying the staff who will conduct the interviews.

2. Opening. Interviewers must be prepared to set the tone and the atmosphere of the interview with a friendly greeting and an outline of the structure of the interview.

3. Conducting. This refers to the main body of the interview when the interviewer will be asking questions, listening to answers and making any relevant notes.

4. Closure. It is appropriate for interviewers to make it clear when the interview is about to end, perhaps by saying, for example, 'And now a final question...' or perhaps asking the intervieww if they have any questions before the interview is completed.

5. Follow-up. The interviewer needs to collate the information obtained during the interview and decide on the follow-up action. This could be an appointment letter or one informing the candidate that they were not successful on this occasion.

The benefits of using open questions are that they encourage two-way communication. An open question allows interviewees to express themselves. Open questions tend to begin with words like 'how', 'what', 'when' and 'why'. By using probing questions you can find out about the reasons whya person has said something or help them to justify their answer. For example, 'Why do you feel that you would be suitable for this job?' could be the open question you initially ask and then you could probe deeper into the answer by asking 'How have you recently demonstrated the research skills that you have just mentioned?'

Debriefing Activity 6.4

1. Negotiation is designed to achieve agreement that is mutually acceptable to both parties.

2. To be an effective negotiator, I would need to carefully control my body language in order to appear and act confidently, take client feedback positively and not to create communication barriers. For instance, I would demonstrate confident body language by using eye contact and adopting an appropriate posture. I would be sitting upright but also slightly leaning forward to show that I was interested and paying attention to what the client was saying. I would not show impatience with any feedback on my firm's performance by tapping my fingers or frowning and would not shuffle nervously from side to side in my seat. I would not fold my arms and would sit with an open posture with my hands on my knees. I would use a calm, professional tone to offset whatever underlying feelings of nervousness or stress I might feel.

Debriefing Activity 7.1

REPORT ON SHOPPING HABITS AND SUPERMARKET ADVERTISING

Report Commissioned By: Managing Director, Robinson's Grocery Chain

Report Written By:Any Candidate

Date: 12 September 200X

1. TERMS OF REFERENCE

This report is an analysis of the information resulting from a survey on shopping habits and supermarket advertising conducted by 'Food Retailer' magazine.

2. METHODOLOGY

A total of 1750 mainly female shoppers selected at random from the electoral register, were interviewed in the north of England. The average age of the respondents was 40 and 78 per cent of those interviewed had children.

3. FINDINGS

3.1 Shopping Habits

The survey showed that most people (60 per cent) do a weekly shop, with 17 per cent shopping twice a week and 11 per cent only shopping once every two weeks. The most popular day for shopping was Friday (40 per cent), with 31 per cent doing grocery shopping on Saturday and 24 per cent on Thursday. The least popular day was Tuesday with only 4 per cent of respondents saying they shopped on that day.

The main reasons for shoppers choosing a particular day to do their shopping was because it was the most convenient time (45 per cent) while 30 per cent said that it was because it fitted in with when they were paid and 26 per cent because it was a good day for special offers.

3.2. Store Preferences

The stores that respondents shopped at most often was Sainsbury (11.2 per cent) and Tesco (10.4 per cent). Robinsons and Fine Fare were sixth in the list with 4.5 per cent of shoppers prefering to shop at these two stores, but 6.9 per cent of respondents shopped most often at the Co-op, 5.7 per cent at Asda and 4.7 per cent at Safeway.

Gateway, Spar and Kwiksave each attracted about 3 – 4 per cent of shoppers but just over 40 per cent of respondents cited 'other' smaller stores and shops to do their grocery shopping.

The most popular reasons for shopping most often at a particular store are convenient location (42 per cent), special offers/low prices (38 per cent), good meat (25 per cent), stock all brands (22 per cent) and friendly assistants (20 per cent).

The most popular reasons for not shopping at other stores were high prices (45 per cent), travel distance (27 per cent) and slow check-outs (22 per cent).

3.3 Advertising

Items that are advertised as special offers are frequently purchased by 35 per cent of shoppers although a similar number (38 per cent) never bought them.

Most respondents obtained special offer coupons from newspapers (40 per cent), 25 per cent used store leaflets but only 15 per cent used leaflet drops.

Most respondents preferred Safeway's advertising (20 per cent), with 16 per cent preferring Fine Fare's and 14 per cent preferred Asda's. However, only 2 per cent preferred Robinsons' advertising.

The reasons cited most for liking advertisements were that 'special offers are easy to find' (42 per cent), or that the advertisements were 'eye catching' (38 per cent), 'had large print' (27 per cent) or were 'easy to find specific brands' (17 per cent) or featured 'a variety of items' (15 per cent).

4. CONCLUSION AND RECOMMENDATIONS

The survey presents Robinsons with some interesting findings. From the shoppers surveyed Robinsons came joint sixth out of the top ten named stores for grocery shopping. However, 40 per cent of respondents shop most at stores other than the top ten, which indicates that many people are shopping at smaller stores.

This probably links in with the most popular reasons for store choice, which are convenient location and special offers/pricing.

This indicates that Robinsons should further investigate the convenience of its stores to where people live (which may mean looking at 'free' bus rides if stores are not convenient for transport or looking at where stores are located in relation to housing estates).

In addition, Robinsons should compare its prices with those of its main competitors and if necessary alter its pricing strategy in order to attract more shoppers.

One reason cited for not using stores was 'slow check-outs' and Robinsons could check the average time check-out staff take to deal with customers and the amount of time shoppers spend queueing to ensure that these factors do not put off potential customers from shopping at Robinsons.

The survey also showed that Friday and Saturday were the most popular shopping days and Robinsons should ensure more staff are on duty on these days.

One important feature of the survey related to advertising. Robinsons' advertising was one of the least preferred from top ten stores named in the survey. Therefore advertising needs to be reviewed with a view to making special offers and specific brands more obvious, using large print and making more visual impact on customers.

Media trends showed that newspapers should be the main medium used for special offer coupons advertising.

Debriefing Activity 7.2

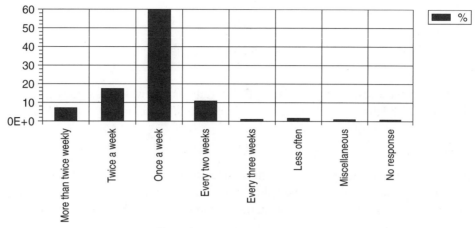

Figure A6.1 Shopping for groceries

Debriefing Activity 7.3

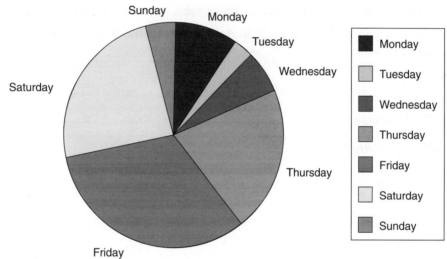

Figure A6.2 Shopping days

Debriefing Activity 7.4

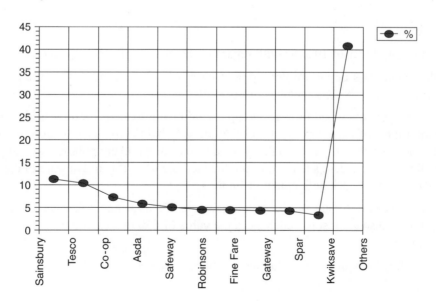

Figure A6.3 Store shopped at for groceries most often

Debriefing Activity 8.1

Healthy Living
17 Haymill Road
Birmingham BH4 2UT

Dear Miss Murray

I notice from our records that your subscription is due for renewal. I thought you would like to know that all current and lapsed members who renew before 30 June qualify for a 25% reduction on their subscription fee to Healthy Living.

This means a 12 month membership for £350!

The next 12 months are looking even better at Healthy Living as we have several new facilities on offer for all our members. We have added two new stretch-and-tone classes to our midweek schedule and have had a new running machine installed in the gym area. We have also extended our opening hours to 10.00 pm.

Renewing your membership could not be easier – just return the tear-off slip below with any amended name and address details to our address with a cheque for £350 before 30 June.

By updating your contact detials you will also be automatically entered into a prize draw. The winner will receive a £50 sports clothes voucher, redeemable at our on-site sports shop.

If for any reason you are not able to rejoin right now, still send in your completed slip, which will be entered into the prize draw.

Yours sincerely

Michael Motivator

Health Studio Manager

Debriefing Activity 8.2

The Lime Tree
Lime Tree Lane
Hightown
Herts

14 June 200X

Mr Beckett
Longley Lane
Northenden
Hightown

Dear Mr Beckett

Thank you for your letter of 10 June with regard to the quality of service you received on 5 June.

I would like to take this opportunity to apologise on behalf of all the staff at the restaurant for the unacceptable behaviour by one member of my staff.

Although I am most concerned to hear about how you were treated, I am pleased that you took the trouble to inform me of what happened. I can assure you that the matter was thoroughly investigated and that the member of staff has been disciplined as part of company policy. It is company policy to monitor performance in a case such as this and the member of staff is fully aware of the consequences if there is any repeat of such an incident in future.

I would be very pleased if you would accept a refund of £50 as a small token for the trouble you have been caused. I am also enclosing vouchers to the value of £50 that can be used at any of our restaurants in the town.

Again I would like to express my apologies and hope to see you at the Lime Tree in the near future.

Yours sincerely

Michael Manager

Debriefing Activity 8.3

MEMORANDUM

To: Sales Managers

From: Meredith Chapman

Date: 19 June 200X

Subject: Internal communication

With the new sales structure in place, it is vital to establish effective communications between the different regions. Although letters are traditionally used at S&G, we need to speed up internal communication because there are several disadvantages in relying on the postal system as the sole means of communication.

Problems with sending letters:

- Letters can be delayed through postal difficulties in certain countries.
- Letters can be quite expensive.
- Letters do not allow for immediate feedback.

It is important for staff to remember that we can opt for a number of different ways to communicate with colleagues in other regions using our existing ICT facilities.

E-mail

Messages go direct to the recipient and can be copied to as many people as required. A hard copy of the message can be printed out if required. It is a quick method of communication and enables our company to protect the security and confidentiality of our internal communication. However, confidential documents should be password protected.

Fax

The fax machine allows immediate communication. Even where there is a time difference and the office you are communicating with is closed, the fax message will be there when staff are next in. It is possible to send hard copies of diagrams and drawings/plans of construction sites quickly and cheaply (for the cost of a telephone call).

Voice mail

This enables the sender's spoken message to be recorded in a digital form by a network computer so the recipient can access the message via a telephone handset at any convenient time. This means that, in spite of the time differences that are experienced in running an international sales operation, colleagues can communicate and express themselves in a way that is not possible with written information.

Debriefing Activity 9.1

1. Calvin Klein fragrances are unisex and aimed at younger people. They are a highly branded product and are usually advertised using photogenic models in creative adverts on television. Consequently local press advertising does not seem to fit in with the image of the product.

2. A small hotel in Wales is unlikely to have the marketing budget to afford television advertising. Also, it would be rather wasteful as it is a mass-market medium. The hotel should specifically target holidaymakers who want to spend their holidays in Wales. They could consider the national press, perhaps a Sunday newspaper, that has a travel section and they should choose an edition when there is editorial coverage about holidays in Wales.

3. Harvey Goldsmith Entertainments are right to use radio as the 'product' fits the medium. They could advertise on national radio, specifically Classic FM, as that station appeals to opera fans. They may even use local radio to tie in with the locations of the concerts.

4. ASH has chosen a good mix of media to target young women. The cinema will be a good choice if they make sure their adverts appear before films that specifically appeal to young women. The magazines aimed at young women also seem an ideal choice for such a campaign.

Debriefing Activity 9.2

The instructions to the printer might be as follows:

- Midchester logo to be inserted where it says 'logo' (see attached compliment slip and pantone references).
- 120 gsm white card with gilt edging.
- Black print.
- Typeface Arial.
- Typesize 12 point.
- Type to be centred as indicated on attached rough layout.
- Print run 250.

Midchester Chamber of Commerce

LOGO

in association with National Westminster Bank

Invite

....

to the e-commerce gala dinner

on

Friday 11th June 20XX

at

The Palace Hotel, Oxford Street, Midchester.

7.00pm for 7.30pm pre-dinner drinks will
be served in the Hexagon bar.

RSVP by 30.5.XX to A. Candidate, Chamber of Commerce.

Debriefing Activity 9.3

To those consumers that The Body Shop products appeal to, its environmentally friendly appeal evokes a feeling of comfort because these consumers see it as an extension of themselves because they either aspire to be or are environmentally friendly in their lifestyle or behaviour.

To those consumers that Benetton products appeal to, its gobal village branding evokes a feeling of warmth and belonging.

Debriefing Activity 9.4

The two main criticisms are that the content is dull and the language is indecipherable.

Somewhere in the text there is possibly a news story but the way it is written makes it difficult to find.

The readers of a local newspaper want to read interesting human-interest stories that relate to the area they live in.

XYZ Farming Ltd is probably a local firm in the area covered by the newspaper, and the writer should make reference to this in the release.

The news story the writer could have developed is that XYZ Farming Ltd has introduced a new product that helps local farmers produce milk that is more popular with consumers and dairies pay higher prices for it.

To add some human interest to the story, the writer could have found a local farmer who actually had sold more milk to the dairies because of this new product. The writer could then have provided him with a suitable quote in the release, stating his delight with the new product. The firm could then have organized a photograph of the farmer, holding a bag of the miracle new product, standing beside one of his cows.

The press release could also have been improved even further if the writer had avoided jargon and used short, punchy sentences. It would also have been a useful tactic to get the name of the product (Granary) into the first few paragraphs of the release, as presumably the objective was to publicize the Granary feed and the fact that XYZ produced it.

Debriefing Activity 9.5

MIDCHESTER CHAMBER OF COMMERCE

PRESS RELEASE

Date of release: 14 June 20XX

Internet dinner launches e-commerce conference

A gala dinner to launch the first e-commerce conference ever held in Midchester took place last night.

Celebrity guest speaker at the event, Bill Gates, said: 'It's great to see all the best minds involved in the Internet business gathered in one place.

'This event certainly puts Midchester on the map as the place if you want to be involved in any aspect of e-commerce'.

Over 200 people attended the dinner and Andy Potts, the Chairman of the Chamber of Commerce, said: 'It's an unprecedented success and there's already talk about holding another dinner next year.

'It's a great opportunity for business people at the forefront of technology to get together to network and enjoy themselves at the same time. It will probably result in the region attracting lots more inward investment from this area of business.'

The dinner launched a two-day e-commerce conference, which will be held this week at the town hall and will be attended by business people from all over the world. It will feature a series of lectures and a number of workshops, some of which will be held online with other Internet businesses in the United States and Japan.

Tickets are still available at £100 per person from the Midchester Chamber of Commerce.

For further information about the dinner or conference, please contact Sally Moss at Midchester Chamber of Commerce, Market Street, Midchester. 0161 234 7890. Fax 0161 245 8923. E-mail s.moss@ madeupnamenet.co.uk

(b) The objective in sending this press release was to promote the chamber of commerce and to publicize the conference. It could even be issued to attract inward investment from e-commerce businesses.

(c) The press release could be sent to the local newspaper and also to specialist Internet magazines.

Debriefing Activity 9.7

Specimen answer: The Society for the Prevention of Accidents

To: Ruth Arnold, Marketing Officer

From: Davina Darcy, Chief Executive

Date: 7 May 20XX

Subject: Brief for marketing campaign

Project details

Marketing campaign 8, summer 1999, highlighting health and safety issues in the workplace.

Background information

Government statistics show a rise of 25 per cent in the last two years in workplace accidents. A recent *Law Gazette* article has revealed a dramatic rise in employer negligence cases where damages have had to be awarded and in some cases the head of the company has been given a jail sentence.

The SPA has a large database of companies that have requested information on accident prevention, have attended one of our training courses or have been added to our list through our own research into accidents.

Objectives

- To send out 3000 posters illustrating workplace health and safety hazards.
- To generate 1000 requests from personnel managers in industry for leaflets about accident prevention. This information to be added to our database.
- To generate 1000 requests from managers in the construction industry for leaflets about accident prevention. This information to be added to our database.

Target audience

- Companies on SPA's database.
- Personnel managers in industry.
- Managers in the construction industry.

Message to be conveyed

- Government statistics show a 25 per cent rise in workplace accidents over the last two years.
- Accidents can result in employers paying substantial damages and they can be held criminally negligent.
- More accidents than ever before are happening in the construction industry.

Media

- Posters illustrating health and safety issues in the workplace to be sent to all the companies held on SPA's database. Each poster to be sent with a covering letter addressed to health and safety officers highlighting the penalties and pointing out methods of prevention. A copy of the letter should be provided so that the health and safety officer can give it to the company's Managing Director.
- Advertising and PR campaign in *People Management* with a direct response mechanism for personnel managers to request more information about accident prevention.
- Advertising and PR campaign in *Construction News* with a direct response mechanism for senior managers to request more information about accident prevention.

Timescale

Campaign should run from the beginning of September to the end of October 20XX.

Budget

A total budget of £8000 is available.

Debriefing Activity 10.1

You should have been able to:

- Check the Frequently Asked Questions section.
- Get access to past papers and examiner reports.
- Update your details, register for exams.
- Voice your view in the voting area.

Debriefing Activity 10.2

The Internet is being used in the following ways:

- To provide information to customers and prospects as another promotional activity.
- To provide information and other services to add value to the customer offering.
- To create a two-way communication flow.
- To capture customer information and for research purposes.
- To sell goods and services.
- To improve internal communication.
- To improve business relationships with suppliers and distributors, etc.

Debriefing Activity 10.3

ICT developments have changed the way people communicate as follows:

- E-mail has become a major means of internal and external communication and large documents can be sent as attachments quickly, which reduces time and cost on paper distribution.

- Fax machines are still used where recipients of messages do not use e-mail and are useful for sending visual information where offices do not have access to scanners.

- Mobile telephone use means staff on the move can keep in touch with colleagues and customers.

- Laptop technology means sales staff have remote access to information when out in the field with clients.

- Laptop computers ensure sales staff can give quality presentations to clients.

- Videoconferencing means excess travel to meetings is reduced but that staff working at different sites can communicate almost face-to-face without too much advance notice.

- Databases are used to track customer purchases and to mailmerge documents when sending out mailshots to different groups of customers.

- An EDI system means that when outlets in the network use up materials, re-stocking requests are automatically received which reduces paper and telephone calls.

- An intranet can be set up for managers to access information on previous projects and client requirements easily and quickly.

- Internet research means that information can be found out more quickly and easily.

The Law courts are a good example of an organization using ICT to improve the way it operates. Computer screens can be used to present evidence electronically. So photographs, maps, witness statements, video stills and Internet pages will all appear on screens in front of judges, prosecution lawyers and witnesses, jury members and defendants.

The technology will speed up the process of communicating information during court sessions. In addition, a digital audio system with microphones is being used to reduce the need for witnesses to speak loudly, recording equipment will speed up the production of court transcripts and e-mail requests will be used to speed up requests for plea and directions hearings.